Into a Raging

TONY WEAVER WITH ANDREW INGRAM

Into a
RAGING
SEA

Great South African Rescues

Jonathan Ball Publishers
Johannesburg and Cape Town

Published in South Africa in 2016 by
JONATHAN BALL PUBLISHERS
A division of Media24 (Pty) Ltd
PO Box 33977
Jeppestown
2043

ISBN 978-1-86842-728-4
ebook ISBN 978-1-86842-729-1

*Every effort has been made to trace the copyright holders and to obtain
their permission for the use of copyright material. The publishers apologise
for any errors or omissions and would be grateful to be notified of any
corrections that should be incorporated in future editions of this book.*

Twitter: www.twitter.com/JonathanBallPub
Facebook: www.facebook.com/JonathanBallPublishers
Blog: http://jonathanball.bookslive.co.za/

Design and typesetting by Johan Koortzen
Printed and bound by CTP Printers, Cape Town
Set in 11.5 on 14pt Adobe Garamond Pro

Contents

Foreword

Dr Cleeve Robertson
CEO, National Sea Rescue Institute (NSRI)

I WAS PRIVILEGED TO GROW up in the coastal villages of Camps Bay and Bakoven and to come home every day from school to an ocean of opportunity. The sea was an integral part of our lives, and members of the local community depended on it for both recreational and economic reasons. It gave life, literally and figuratively, to so many people.

We were taught early on to pay great respect to the ocean and its many moods, learning that it was always the boss, and could change its mind within minutes. Our symbiosis with this three-dimensional monster wasn't without harsh lessons, and every day we were reminded that just as the sea gave life, it took it away, indiscriminately – no emotion, just raw power.

Technology was immature in those heady days when, as kids, we fashioned canoes out of corrugated iron, wood and bitumen. Commercial vessels and small craft were made of wood, radios were hard to come by and unreliable, outboards failed often, safety equipment was extremely basic and the training of most people who ventured offshore was elementary at best.

This was a recipe for emergencies at sea. In 1966, these factors came together when 17 fisherfolk lost their lives in a storm off the Southern Cape coast. It is perhaps surprising that, with our reputation as the Cape of Storms, no maritime rescue service existed at the time, and that there was no capacity to render assistance beyond local boats and passing ships.

In the wake of this tragedy, the power of one was demonstrated by a lady called Patti Price, who, having experienced the benefits of Britain's Royal National Lifeboat Institution (RNLI), lobbied for the creation of such a service in South Africa. Within a short period the South African Inshore Sea Rescue Service (SAISRS) was born; the name was later changed to the National Sea Rescue Institute (NSRI).

I have a childhood memory of the burly men and excited boys who carried a plywood ski-boat from the boat shed at Bakoven, affixed an old Johnson outboard to the transom and set off through the kelp-lined channel past Bakoven Rock to go and rescue vessels or people in distress. It was a hard and primitive operation made safer only by the character and passion of the volunteer crew.

The service evolved progressively, sometimes with great difficulty, but always forward. In December 1986, I was an unexpected beneficiary of the NSRI's services when I ran aground in dense fog at Shelly Beach on Robben Island during the long haul of the Rothmans Week. The rescue crew shall remain nameless to protect the CEO's reputation, but my respect for the ocean, and for the volunteers who go out selflessly to rescue people they don't know, and who may never know them, was affirmed.

Today's NSRI relies on a complement of a thousand volunteers, and its rescue boats and facilities are living testimony to the spirit of 50 years of NSRI volunteers who often rose from their beds or desks to venture onto a cruel sea to save the lives of so many South Africans who would otherwise have suffered a terrible death by drowning.

This book is a tribute to those NSRI volunteers and some small record of their brave professional mission to save lives in South African waters.

Go with the honour that only respect for the sea and humanity can inspire.

Introduction

Tony Weaver

SOME OF MY EARLIEST MEMORIES from childhood centre on the sea. Our playground as children was the False Bay coast and beyond to Cape Hangklip and Hermanus. The eastern side of False Bay, from Gordon's Bay to Rooi Els, is dotted with crosses that mark the spots where fishermen have been swept off the rocks and drowned. It is a coast that is notorious for freak waves that seem to come from nowhere.

Fishing for yellowtail off Whale Rock and Blaauwkrans, my father and his fishing mates, such as Major Dougie van Riet, Nico Myburgh and others, would keep a beady eye on us kids, constantly drumming ocean safety into us. 'Never turn your back on the sea,' they would say. 'Never stand on a wet rock, and always plan your escape.'

We learned that rip currents were our friends when surfing, and we would ride them like a conveyor belt out to the back line. But they were the enemy of the holiday-makers who flocked to our beaches each summer. We came to understand exactly how the tides operated, and the phases of the moon, and how to read the weather by tapping the barometer. We dived for rock lobster, perlemoen and alikreukel, wearing rugby jerseys for protection against the rocks; wetsuits only came much later.

And we always treated the sea with deep respect. It is a wonderful friend, but a powerful and terrifying foe when its mood changes.

So I was delighted when the NSRI asked me if I would be interested in working on a book to mark the 50th anniversary of its founding. It is an organisation that is close to my heart.

We decided to gather together a collection of stories, vignettes really, that would give a glimpse into the world of Sea Rescue, as the NSRI is commonly known. Many of these stories had already been told in *For Those In Peril*, the lavishly illustrated book that Andrew Ingram and Henri du Plessis put together for the 40th anniversary, so we decided not to repeat any of those. I then began researching what I thought would make for a good collection of short stories – snapshots of rescue life. Source materials included the unpublished history of the NSRI written by the former CEO, Lieutenant Commander Alan Hollman RN (Retd), covering the years 1966 to 1991, minutes of meetings, scrapbooks and 41 years of *Sea Rescue* magazines.

We narrowed the list of stories down to around 40 or so, and then began gathering material. What finally ended up in the book is not in any way meant to be a history of Sea Rescue, and inevitably there are many stories that have not been told. Some of the stories I wanted to tell couldn't be accurately verified because people had died, emigrated or simply forgotten the details.

It was also logistically impossible to visit every station in the country to listen to their stories, so we had to select chapters based on what was achievable and affordable. My apologies to those stations and stories that were left out.

And we wanted to make the stories as wide-ranging as possible, so in these pages are not just sea rescues, but also fires, floods, a shark encounter, an air disaster, a mystery that has never been solved, and the invaluable memories of some of the founders of the NSRI 50 years ago.

My thanks to all who gave of their time and memories in helping to make this book happen, and special words of thanks to my co-conspirator and former colleague at the *Cape Times*, Andrew Ingram (who is a damn fine writer and photographer), Meriel Bartlett (who was an invaluable sounding board and guiding hand throughout), NSRI CEO Dr Cleeve Robertson, all the authors who donated their chapters free of charge, and the crew at Jonathan Ball – Jeremy Boraine, Ceri Prenter and editor Alfred LeMaitre.

And the biggest thank you of all goes to the Sea Rescue volunteers: you are all heroes.

1 In the beginning

Andrew Ingram and Tony Weaver

THE OVERBERG AND SOUTHERN CAPE coast, stretching from the eastern tip of False Bay at Cape Hangklip all the way to Mossel Bay and Knysna, is home to some of South Africa's richest fishing grounds. It is also one of the most dangerous stretches of coastline in the world.

These days, fishermen and other ocean users can use the internet to call up an array of weather websites and apps that can tell them what the swell and wind will be doing a week in advance – WindGURU, Yr.no, South African Weather Service, Wavescape, the list goes on. The information is remarkably accurate, as super-computers the world over process data from weather stations and satellites and use complex algorithms to pinpoint almost to the minute when the weather is likely to turn nasty, or when the swell is going to pitch from a benign and gentle ripple to an out-of-control monster.

It wasn't like that in the old days. First thing every morning, ocean users would tap their barometers to see if the needle was rising or falling. Down here on the southern tip of Africa, a rising barometer meant that a high-pressure system and south to southeasterly winds were on the way. A falling barometer meant that westerly to northwesterly cold-front conditions were approaching, and a rapidly falling barometer meant that a storm front was approaching with rain, big winds and, most likely, big swells.

Experienced older hands could read a lot more into that slight movement of the needle. For surfers, a falling barometer and a cold front meant bigger, more powerful waves. For fishermen, the wind direction made all the difference in terms of bringing warmer water inshore, and with it shoals of sought-after gamefish such as yellowtail and katonkel (king mackerel or couta).

In 1966, Gerhard Dreyer was a professional fisherman working out of Still Bay: 'I was there for a good few years. We had small boats, *skuitjies*; they were not big boats, they were all open boats with inboard diesel engines, and that's how we caught our fish. My boat was called *Bakvissie*.'

It had not been a good year. 'The sea can get very rough off Still Bay, and that year, 1966, in January, one night a boat came in, and about 50 or 60 metres from the harbour it capsized. Six men drowned and three came out alive. That was late at night.

'The fishing was very bad that year for January, February, March. My men were crying. Then one morning, it was 12 April 1966, we went out at three or four o'clock in the morning to the Jongensklip side. We anchored off Jongensklip, and that day at last the fish were really, really biting. As fast as you could pull your line in, you caught them.'

Gerhard ran the boat back to Still Bay to offload their catch, and, with conditions still fine, they headed back out again.

'Later, at about four or five o'clock, old Willem Beuker said to me, "There's a wind dog coming." I didn't know what he meant, then he said, "There is a terrible storm on the way." So I said we must go home, but my crew talked me out of it. That was the mistake I made. They said they had had a very difficult time, and that we must turn around and carry on catching.

'And I listened to them.'

Gerhard took the boat back to the place where they had cleaned up the fish that morning, and earlier in the afternoon, and anchored off Jongensklip, away from three other local boats, *Charmaine*, *Seabird* and *Taljaard*.

'I wasn't wearing a watch, but I would guess that at about nine in the evening, the current changed direction. The bow was facing more or less west, and then the current turned due east so that the sea was now coming constantly from the side of the boat.

'And then came the wind, and terrifying waves, and I said, "Pull up the anchor!", and we headed out into the deep sea, and I said to the men, "Throw everything in the boat overboard, throw everything off and pump water." They got angry with me, they didn't want to throw the fish overboard. I said to them, "Listen to me!"

'And so they threw everything overboard, everything, the fish, the lines, everything, until it was just us on the boat. That's what saved us.'

It was still eight hours until dawn.

The swell was terrifying, running at up to 15 m, and it was estimated that the wind was gusting at up to 130 km/h. The little fishing boat was tossed about and it was only superb seamanship on Gerhard's part that kept the crew alive.

'It was just up one mountain of a wave, then down the mountain – big, big seas. And so it carried on and on until I guess it was about two or two-thirty in the morning. It had calmed just a little bit and I turned the boat around and we came back with those big seas running behind us, and we pumped water on that boat. The men pumped all the time, and then when we turned, with the sea behind us, it went a little bit better.

'And we headed for home. We only had lanterns on the boats and then someone said, "There's a lantern." Dawn was breaking and we saw this lantern. And we got to where we had seen the lantern, and there were just planks and fish and jerseys and stuff drifting.

'Then we saw one man in a lifebuoy, and I circled around him three times to get him in the boat, and eventually we got him in the boat, and it was a fisherman called John Arries.

'There had been three other boats out, *Charmaine*, *Seabird* and *Taljaard*, and each of them had six men on them, 18 men altogether. And I picked up the only survivor, Arries.

'Seventeen men drowned that night.'

* * *

The news of the Still Bay tragedy made headlines, especially in the western Cape newspapers. It hit home especially hard for Patti Price, a teacher and swimming instructor who had herself been rescued from the English Channel by the Royal National Lifeboat Institution (RNLI).

Lieutenant Commander Alan Hollman RN (Retd), who joined the NSRI as Operations Officer in 1969, and who became CEO in March 1983, authored an informal, unpublished history of the organisation up until 1991.

He wrote that the story of Patti Price 'goes back to early 1943 when South Africa was still a member of the British Commonwealth and there was a Southern African branch of the Royal National Lifeboat Institution of Great Britain. This was a fundraising organisation and raised the huge sum, in those days, of £36000 to build three large lifeboats to replace some of those lost in the war. These were 42-footers and were named *Southern Africa*, *Deneys Reitz* and *Field Marshal and Mrs Smuts* and served the RNLI for over 20 years.

'Prominent among this fundraising committee and workers had been a small, dynamic woman named Miss Patti Price. She was deeply shocked by the (1966) deaths of the fishermen in Still Bay and found it unacceptable that South Africans should have donated so much to an overseas lifeboat service, yet men should have died in this tragedy for want of a lifeboat to go to their aid. Miss Price, herself, in her early life was rescued by a lifeboat from a wrecked ship in the English Channel.

'Accordingly she wrote in the strongest terms to the press and also to the then president of the Society of Master Mariners of South Africa, Captain John Payn, and said that something must be done about it. As a result, the Master Mariners, at their annual congress in August 1966 in Cape Town, made a resolution to set up the South African Inshore Sea Rescue Service and so the NSRI was launched.

'The essence of the new service would be that its crew members would all be volunteers receiving no payment or allowances, and so it has remained to this day.'

Hollman wrote that 'the next step was for the Master Mariners to invite a number of prominent men in the shipping and fishing industries and yachting and power boating to form an action committee. These gentlemen met for the first time in Cape Town in late 1966 and elected as their chairman Mr PJ O'Sullivan of the SA Fish Canners. Pat O'Sullivan remained in the chair for the next 20 years, and in 1989 was decorated by the State President for this outstanding voluntary service to South Africa.

'The Honorary Secretary was Captain Douglas Milward, who later served on the Port Elizabeth committee. The Honorary Treasurer was Mr GV Myburgh, an accountant and Springbok sailor, who later succeeded Mr O'Sullivan as Chairman of the Institute.

'Foremost amongst their aims was to raise money for the new service and to appoint an Honorary Chief Administrative Officer to organise the seagoing side of the operation. Their fortunate choice fell upon Captain RH (Bob) Deacon, a young master mariner and instructor at the Merchant Navy Academy "General Botha" and a fine seaman. Bob had a Mate's Certificate of Competency in sail, one of several South Africans to achieve this distinction, others being Captain WJ (Billy) Damerell, later a director of the NSRI, and Captain P Nankin, who as Captain Superintendent of the Merchant Navy Academy gave invaluable assistance to the NSRI for many years.

'Late in 1966, the NSRI's first rescue boat arrived from England. It had been donated by the Society of Master Mariners and was a 15-foot six inches inflatable built by the RFD company, and powered by a 40-horsepower Evinrude outboard engine. This was the same type of craft used by the RNLI for inshore rescue work in the UK, and so was of proven capability.

'It should be said that from the very first the RNLI, which was founded in 1823 and is the oldest lifeboat service in the Western world (and only preceded by the Chinese in some much earlier dynasty), has been a very good friend to the NSRI. In those early formative days, the RNLI sent the NSRI copies of all its rules and regulations and fundraising organisation, and on countless occasions subsequently has responded to the Institute's requests for advice on operational and administrative matters.

'But back to *IRB 1*, or *Snoopy* as it came to be affectionately known. This little boat was manned by Bob Deacon as coxswain and Mr Ray Lant as crew. Mr Lant was a power boat racing man and by profession a diesel engineer employed by the Cummins Diesel Company, whose engines the NSRI came to use in some of the big lifeboats as they entered the fleet.'

Snoopy was kept in a municipal boathouse in Three Anchor Bay, but was also loaded onto the roof of a VW Kombi if it was needed further afield. It was first launched on a rescue on 14 January 1967, to search for a missing person who was actually safely ashore.

The second rescue turned out to be very dramatic.

'On 27 March 1967, the motor launch *Lucky Jill* caught fire in Table Bay with six people on board. *IRB 1* was quickly launched and sped to the scene where the casualty was well ablaze and sinking. Knowing that there were only seconds to spare, Bob Deacon drove the rescue boat up onto the hull so that the crew could scramble aboard. He then backed up, and was barely clear when the *Lucky Jill* blew up and sank. This was a spectacular start to the NRSI's service record, with six lives saved. This little boat went on to save seven lives before being withdrawn from service in 1967 being ill-suited to the steep chop in Table Bay ...

'Sadly, both Bob Deacon and Ray Lant died of illnesses at a relatively young age, but not before each had made a major contribution to the NSRI.'

Hollman says that 'the use of the date 29 May (1967) for a great many years as the NSRI's anniversary is shrouded in mystery. Confusion also arose from a formal change of name from SAISRS to NSRI on 12 June 1967. The change was made because of the operating restrictions implicit in the word "Inshore" and the saving of two words in texts and two letters on craft.'

Be that as it may, on 12 June 1967, the South African Inshore Sea Rescue Service was formally, and legally, renamed the National Sea Rescue Institute.

2 The Originals

Tony Weaver

IT'S A STORMY CAPE TOWN Saturday afternoon, with a five-metre swell running. Outside, the surf is crashing, threatening to extinguish the braai fires burning in two half-drums on the slipway. Andrew Ingram and I are sitting in the ops room at Station 2, Bakoven, chatting to 'the Originals', the first NSRI crew members after Bob Deacon and Ray Lant. They are Mitch Brown, Don Nicholls, Pieter Pienaar, Trevor Wilkins and Bob Selman. Later, at Witsand, we chat to Allan Cramb, another of the Originals.

All these veterans had slightly different memories of exactly how the NSRI was started, but all agreed it involved wine, specifically Lieberstein and Tassenberg drunk from a '*ses man kan*' (six-man can) – a gallon bottle (4.5 litres) with a glass ring on the neck so you could sling it onto your shoulder to make pouring easier.

Don Nicholls starts off the reminiscing: 'We were a bunch of guys who used to play darts at the Clifton Hotel, and we were approached by Fred Lighton, who in turn had been approached by Bob Deacon, suggesting we start a rescue service at Bakoven.'

Mitch Brown chips in: 'In 1967, we were aware of a rescue set-up being run from Three Anchor Bay by a very good seaman, Bob Deacon, and a character, Ray Lant, who rode a star-spangled Harley-Davidson, and they had obtained the services of a 16-ft rubber duck with one outboard on the back. Before Bob and Ray started up, there was no sea rescue in real terms.

'In 1959, a Mrs Pearson had left a bequest to start one, and Bob and Albie Mathews began trying to establish a financial set-up that would work. They approached the Sea Point and Camps Bay Round Tables and Lions to fund it. A friend of ours, Fred Lighton, was a member of Round Table, and he said, "I know where we can get some guys to make up a crew." We all used to hang out at the bar of the Clifton Hotel.

'It wasn't really something that was on our horizon; we were fishing from Three Anchor Bay, and fishing up and down the coast here. We were at that time spending a lot of time at Bakoven, we had a couple of glass-fibre dinghies here for fishing; it was the place we came to with our kids on summer weekends.

'When Fred approached us, we said, "What the hell, let's do it." We thought that this would be fun, like "Hey boys, we get a boat to play with" – better than the thing we had, which was a five-horsepower engine and a 12-ft glass-fibre dinghy. It all ended up in a gathering at Fred Lighton's house in Clifton. That was what really got the station going.'

Allan Cramb, who was Bakoven Station Commander for 12 years, and later NSRI Technical Manager and then Operations Director, was too young to hang out at the Clifton Hotel – he was just 15 at the time. But he remembers a follow-up meeting at which the NSRI was launched:

'I had a misspent youth on Bakoven Beach. In early 1967, I was 15 and there was a meeting at the old Camps Bay Hotel, where the Sonnekus Flats are now. Jimmy and Bob Deacon were there, Albie Mathews, Mitch Brown, Don Nicholls, Ray Lant, Ivan Klerck, a bunch of others. And that's where it was decided to establish the NSRI.

'My dad didn't really want me to join; he was very cautious. My first-ever call-out was in the September school holidays that year. I'd just turned 16. The crew had arrived, we tied the engines on, and when the boat got back, my father saw what a great thing this was and said, "OK, I'll sign the papers," because I wasn't 18 yet.'

Mitch remembers the first boat they had: 'We knew a guy, Tony

Munna, who used to build state-of-the-art marine-ply boats, and he offered to help. That was in September 1967, and the 16-ft Munna was named *Excalibur*. Another guy who owned the old green boat shed here at Beta Beach said we could use it.'

Allan recalls that 'Three Anchor Bay had the first boat, but they had no home. They were Rescue 3, because of Three Anchor Bay. Their first boat was a little rubber duck, *Snoopy*, that was kept on the top of a Volkswagen Kombi. Bakoven was next – although there's always a big argument about this; they got their first boat, a 16-ft Munna, that eventually ended up in Mossel Bay.

'That was kept in that first boat shed when you get down to the bottom of the Bakoven stairs on the left-hand side of the path. That meeting at the Camps Bay Hotel was to decide where to build the first base, and they looked at Camps Bay, they looked at the White House, which is now the Twelve Apostles Hotel, but we felt it was too remote and desolate there in those days.

'We then borrowed that boat shed at the bottom of the stairs and the rest is history; that became South Africa's first rescue base.'

Mitch says that launches were something of a logistical nightmare: 'The shed was pretty small, and we couldn't get the boat in with the engines attached, and there wasn't room for the fuel, so we kept the fuel up the hill, in Peter Pullen's outside toilet. We'd pull the boat out stern first, run down with two 40-hp engines, then run down with the fuel. We would bolt the engines on, and then away we would go.'

Trevor Wilkins remembers that they had no slipway, and used logs as rollers: 'By then the adrenaline's up and running – a launch took us about 15 minutes. Then of course we had to start the engines.

'This station [Bakoven] is very together; there is a matrix that kept it together through the early years when there was no real head office. In the early days, we had to launch the boat over the sewerage outfall pipe, until we finally got the go-ahead from the City Engineer to build the slipway over the pipe, which made it considerably quicker. We built the boats, we built the shed, we did all the work ourselves.

There were rocks in the way, we got a pneumatic drill, drilled holes, put expansion powder in the holes, cracked the rocks.'

Don Nicholls holds up his hand: 'And I lost a finger on the launch winch.'

Mitch says that, in the early days, 'we had a lot of say in the boats when they needed replacing; the station actually built a boat, the *Ace Craft*. In the really early days of Sea Rescue, we didn't have any administrative back-up or functions; when we ran out of money, we financed it ourselves. And one of the big, big disappointments we had was that we thought we could fish off the boats, but that was strictly verboten.

'When we launched *Excalibur*, which was christened by Wendy Klerck, the wife of Station Commander Ivan Klerck, the mayor, Gerry Ferry, who was a hell of a character, gave this speech that had us completely puzzled. About a quarter of the way through we realised he had pulled the wrong speech out of his pocket – it was one written for the opening of a crèche!'

Communications were a major issue, both on land and at sea. Pieter Pienaar described their first radios as being military-issue, 'the size of a big rucksack, with big whippy antennae. They didn't work most of the time, they were utterly useless, and the microphones used to shock you.'

There were, of course, no such things as satellite navigation GPS units, cellphones and the like. Mitch says navigation was done pretty much by line of sight, which got a lot more tricky during night operations: 'We used to go out blind, no navigational aids, just a compass. But we all grew up on this coast, so we would look at the street lights and work out where we were from that. We initially put a pole on a rock out here with a blue light on top, but it didn't last very long, one big sea and it was gone, that was that.

'And we got a lot more responsible, because you get a really deep sense of satisfaction in performing a good rescue and knowing that you have actually saved somebody from a really scary situation.'

Pieter remembers that their very first operation happened almost straightaway. 'We had our very first rescue in our first week of operation: we were called out at 17.50, Dudley Turner's yacht got lost. Out we went, but we couldn't get back in, so we had to dock at Granger Bay.'

And then came their first really big rescue. Mitch takes up the story: 'There was this French oil tanker, the *Sivella*, that ran aground at Mouille Point on 4 February 1968. We were all at a party up the road. Out we went in our 16-ft boat to rescue this 81 566-ton tanker! We spent the night out there covered in oil, wearing drysuits; there were no wetsuits then.'

Trevor recalls that 'we were wearing old army-issue kapok life jackets, and the kapok just absorbed the oil, so if we had gone overboard we would have sunk straight to the bottom'.

And all the while, they were pretty much making it all up as they went along. There was no training manual. They were the pioneers; they wrote the training manuals.

Mitch says that 'those early days were a huge learning curve for us. We would rush out at high speed to where the casualty was thought to be. But we soon learned to slow right down, to plan. We learned that people who were blown out to sea on lilos were seldom where we thought they would be, and we learned to plot where they were likely to be.

'We learned to smell the air for diesel when searching for a missing boat. It wasn't top-down, we worked together, coxswains didn't bark orders.

'A lot of the early rescues were crayfish poachers, Hobie Cats – Hobies were very popular then – little fishing chukkies, the boats that ran on paraffin engines breaking down, and some sizeable vessels like the *Sivella*.'

In his unpublished memoir, Lieutenant Commander Alan Hollman recounts that 'from the earlier days in Cape Town, the NSRI had at concession rates the services of Medicall (later Telecall), a highly efficient emergency telephone service so that all the duty port staff had to do was telephone Medicall and tell them to call out a particular rescue boat and crew.

'In those days, the NSRI could not afford to provide its duty crew with pagers, so that for the week a crew member was on duty, he was required to remain close to a telephone, and this severely restricted his private life.'

Pieter Pienaar remembers that 'if you were on a standby crew, the Port Captain's office and station commanders needed to know exactly where you were going to be and there had to be a telephone there. So if you wanted to go to the movies, you had to leave the movie house's number and let the manager know you were there. Halfway through the movie this slide would suddenly pop up saying "Pieter Pienaar report for duty".'

Hollman wrote that 'if he left his home to go to a friend's home or to the local cinema or supermarket, he had to telephone the Medicall Control Room and give the telephone number of the place he was going to, and on return home reverse the process. He also had to remain within 10 minutes' driving time of his rescue station, observing all traffic regulations and speeds.'

Perhaps the record for a call-out at that time was held by Paddy Pryde, of what was then the Paarden Eiland station. 'Paddy was at his desk on the 13th floor of what was then the Sanlam Building on the Foreshore when he was called out by Medicall. From the time of receiving the call, informing his superior along the passage, descending to ground level, reaching his car and driving to SAS *Unitie*, where the rescue boat was being temporarily kept on moorings, being joined by the other members of the "office hours" crew, rowing out to the rescue boat in a dinghy, slipping moorings and reaching the end of the breakwater, was an incredible 14 minutes.

'It took only a few more minutes to reach the casualty, a man on his own in a small dinghy off Sea Point with engine failure, so that they were greatly pleased with themselves and their fast response. They were therefore understandably cross when the man asked, "What kept you?"'

One of the challenges for the first volunteer crews was establishing ways of cooperating with other rescue volunteers, such as the

Mountain Club of South Africa, and with official agencies such as the police, ambulance services, fire brigade and the like.

Trevor Wilkins says that one of their first multi-agency technical rescues was that of a young girl who was reported missing by her boyfriend off the Sentinel, Hout Bay, on 7 November 1974. The couple had walked around the base of the Sentinel to go and look at the seals, and then got cut off by the incoming tide. They started climbing up the Sentinel, when she fell and they lost contact, and he scrambled out, barefoot, to call for help.

'By then we had handheld radios. We got briefed by the SA Police, set up communications with a command post at Hout Bay police station and a UHF and VHF relay station on Chapman's Peak Drive, but we didn't know where the hell the girl was, so we played music so that she could hear us and keep her spirits up. The rescue started at 6 pm and carried on until midday the next day.'

The March 1975 edition of *NSRI News Review* records that 'these teams were having a tough time in the dark but were greatly aided by the [rescue boat] *Hubert Davies* anchoring close in and firing illuminating flares and shining her two powerful spotlights on the cliffs. However, perhaps the best service the rescue boat rendered was to give reassurance to the young girl who saw the lights and flares and knew that help was on the way. Unfortunately, she could not be found that night, though the climbers got within yards of her without knowing it, and the search had to be postponed until first light.'

The next morning, Trevor says, 'Captain Theodore Huddlestone from Court Helicopters flew in with a small chopper but it couldn't handle the wind. So he went back to base and came back in a Sikorsky. I hung below the chopper – there was no winch back then – and we found the girl on the rocks in a white dress. The Mountain Club came in and we sent a doctor down and got her out. We all just cried when she came over the top. She told us she had heard the noise and the music and knew she was going to be rescued, and that was what kept her going.

'The Mayor of Bellville was so moved by this that he donated a

VW Kombi to us, and we used to use it, with the boat strapped on the roof, to get to rescue scenes faster. It was out of this mobile rescue idea that Dr Alan McMahon got the idea for Metro [Medical Emergency Transport and Rescue Organisation].'

As the *News Review* reported at the time, 'this was an excellent piece of cooperation between the police, the Mountain Club, Court Helicopters and NSRI and had a happy conclusion. NSRI soon after received a heart-warming note of thanks from the girl, who said she was recovering well from her injuries.'

I ask the Originals what their most memorable rescues have been, seeing as they have been at it for a long time.

Pieter Pienaar recalls how 'one Sunday morning we were out on a training session and we went out Hout Bay way. There was a big wind blowing and past Sandy Bay a lilo was blown out to sea and a young woman who was staying with Ben Dekker in his cave swam out after the lilo. We spotted her, got the lilo, and she climbed on board the boat. She was stark naked and very calmly asked for a lift back to shore. Needless to say, all the guys wanted to do their practice sessions off Sandy Bay after that.'

Allan Cramb says that 'my strangest rescue ever was possibly my best rescue ever. It was in the late 1980s; I was working in Paarden Eiland. It was a magnificent morning, a perfect Cape day at about 11 am, 12 noon. My pager went off and I got the message that there was a ski-boat overturned off Llandudno.

'I phoned the Port Captain and said, "I don't really understand this, conditions are perfect. When I left Bakoven this morning, the sea was glassy." And he said, "Well that's the report we got, it was phoned in by a Llandudno resident."'

So Allan went to the station, assembled the crew and launched, and they motored around to Llandudno. The report they had was that the casualty boat was near the wreck of the *Romelia*, a derelict tanker that had run aground and been wrecked when it lost its tow in July 1977. Alongside the wreck was a yellow ski-boat, upside down, with twin outboard motors and 'everything that opens and shuts'.

'Two guys from Goodwood were on the hull. They said they had built the boat themselves, and didn't quite know what had happened. So we helped them turn the boat over. We said, "Can we do anything else to help?", and they sheepishly said, "Well, you could take those girls back to Sandy Bay."

'We looked up, and there were three naked women on the *Romelia*. They had been at Sandy Bay, swam out to the *Romelia*, then these guys rocked up and started chatting them up. They offered them a lift back to the beach, and all three girls climbed down onto the gunwales at the same time and they flipped the boat.

'The wind was coming up, so we loaded the girls on one by one, and it was strange, somehow we couldn't find a blanket or a towel for them to cover up with, and the wind was coming up so I had to gun the throttles to go a bit faster, so they had to hang on with both hands. That was my best rescue ever.'

Trevor Wilkins tells the last story: 'We were called out one day to Hout Bay, just off the Sentinel. There was this yacht in trouble, sails flapping, but otherwise all seemed okay. We got there, and there appeared to be nobody on board. So we climbed on board and we found the crew below decks, the owner and his lady, and the only thing that separated them was a thin layer of sweat.

'It was an embarrassing moment, especially as the lady wasn't his wife.'

That's the Originals.

3 Sea rescues of yesteryear

Over the past 50 years, many illustrious South Africans have, in one way or another, donated their time and expertise to the NSRI. One of them was the renowned writer Jose Burman, who authored 31 books, among them Great Shipwrecks off the Coast of Southern Africa *(C Struik, 1967),* Strange Shipwrecks of the Southern Seas *(C Struik, 1968) and* The Bay of Storms: Table Bay, *1503–1860 (Human & Rousseau, 1976).*

This chapter was originally published in the very first edition of the NSRI magazine, Sea Rescue, *Volume 1, Number 1 (March 1982).*

SHIPWRECK IS THE EVER-PRESENT FEAR in the minds of mariners, a fear that has all too often been fulfilled. Nor did it matter how close to the shore a ship was wrecked, for without some means of getting ashore through the boiling waves there was small hope of survival.

The coast of South Africa has witnessed some very brave, and some very novel rescues.

Perhaps the best-known is the wreck of the *De Jonge Thomas* in 1773, though the wreck is not as well known as that of the rescuer, Wolraad Woltemade. It was at the height of a northwest storm on 1 June 1773.

Captain Barend Lameren was at the helm of his ship, *De Jonge Thomas*, when it broke its moorings and began to drag anchor with 191 men, women and children on board. Just after midnight Capt. Lameren ordered the ship's cannon to be fired as a distress signal.

The piteous cries of those aboard the wreck were ignored and the

East India Company's servants ashore set about the task of salvaging the wreckage which was now drifting onto the beach. At this juncture Wolraad Woltemade, a 65-year-old retired German dairyman, who had brought food and wine for his son, Corporal Christian Ludwig Woltemade, took matters into his own hands.

Mounting his horse, Vonk (Spark), Woltemade rode into the sea and swam the horse out through the surf. As they approached the wreck he turned the horse and called for two men to jump into the sea and grasp the horse's tail. After a moment's hesitation two men threw themselves into the water and swam to Woltemade, who urged the horse forward and dragged them ashore.

He repeated the ride again and again until he had saved 14 men. The horse was by now staggering with exhaustion but when the equally exhausted and hypothermic Woltemade dismounted to rest, such a pitiful cry went up that he remounted and rode back into the surf. As the labouring animal neared the ship half a dozen men jumped into the water and grasped the horse, overwhelming it. It was all over in a moment – horse, rider and sailors disappeared beneath the waves.

Woltemade's body was found the next day. Vonk's body was never retrieved. Of the 191 men, women and children on board, 53 survived, and of these 53, 14 were saved by Woltemade and Vonk.

Despite the undoubted bravery of Woltemade there were voices raised in criticism of him, asking why he had not taken a rope out to the ship, whereby the entire crew, and not just 14 men, might have been saved, and this criticism has never been answered satisfactorily.

The problem of getting a rope out to a wreck had already been solved very bravely and very effectively on 5 May 1692, when a storm caught the outward-bound and return fleets, both in Table Bay. The sea rose to incredible heights and soon waves were breaking over the mastheads of some of the 10 anchored Indiamen. Three ships dragged their anchors; of them one, the English Indiaman *Orange*, broke up with the loss of nearly all hands; another, the Dutch Indiaman *Goede Hoop*, was so near the shore that the crew were rescued.

The unfortunate men aboard the third ship, the Dutch *Hoogergeest*, were beyond the breakers and out of reach. No boat could live in that sea, but Jochem Willemsz, quartermaster of one of the other anchored ships, offered to swim out and take a line to the *Hoogergeest*.

The wind was still blowing a full gale, the seas were mountainous, and the temperature icy, with periodic squalls of hail sweeping across the bay. Willemsz struggled gamely outwards, lost to sight from shore every time a breaker hid him. Time and again the men paying out the line thought he had disappeared for good but each time he would reappear, high on the crest of a wave, each time a little nearer to the wreck. One last burst of energy and the brave quartermaster reached the *Hoogergeest*, to be drawn aboard by eager hands.

Soon a stronger cable had been pulled out to the wreck and attached to a raft which was launched from the *Hoogergeest*. With another line tied to the ship, the raft made a series of journeys to the beach, saving everyone from the rapidly disintegrating vessel. Among the last to come ashore was Jochem Willemsz.

His feat was no less brave than that of Woltemade but Willemsz survived – which is probably why everyone knows of Woltemade, and hardly anyone has heard of Jochem Willemsz.

A more novel method of rescue was used when the ship *De Visch* was wrecked off Green Point on 16 May 1740. A boat was lowered from the ship and attempted to carry a line ashore. It was swamped but the three men in the boat were so close to the beach by that time that they were pulled out by those ashore, together with their line.

In a rescue the establishment of a line between ship and shore does not end the matter, for the vital problem of how to travel along the line still remains. At the worst men have sometimes swung themselves hand over hand or have edged their way along the rope, using feet as well as hands. This is not only an extremely strenuous undertaking, fitted for strong men, but is very hazardous, for the line is often under water. The answer therefore is a suitable container that can be drawn backwards and forwards along the line. The Captain of *De Visch* solved this problem, ingeniously using one of the huge copper cauldrons in which the men's food was cooked. This was hung over the cable by its iron rungs and two men climbed inside it and were drawn to the shore. The empty cauldron was then pulled back to the wreck and the manoeuvre repeated.

Between 100 and 150 men had come ashore before there occurred the incident by which the wreck is chiefly remembered:

The Bottelier [steward] got into the cauldron accompanied by his assistant [the Bottelier's mate] and by a little boy. The Bottelier had money on board and he had crammed his pockets with ducatoons thereby materially increasing his weight. The load was too heavy; one of the iron rungs broke off the cauldron and its three occupants were thrown into the sea. The rope was at once slackened so that they could keep themselves above water by means of it. The Bottelier's mate and the little boy were, in fact, saved in this way, but the Bottelier, weighed down by the gold in his pockets, sank like a stone and was drowned – his wealth was his undoing.

The second cauldron was then produced and replaced the broken one, and the rescue went on successfully. Only the Bottelier paid the price of his greed.

Another instance of a brave rescue of another kind took place in Table Bay on 19 May 1793, when the *Sterrenschans* ran aground during a storm. The vessel lay half-filled with water, only the poop rising clear of the waves. On it were crowded the crew, and those with keen eyesight could see the Captain's wife clinging to the vessel's side. The Captain's wife was a local girl named Jacoba Swanefelder, who had been aboard her husband's ship only for a cruise to Simon's Bay. Her father offered a large reward to anyone who would rescue his daughter, but nobody was willing to risk the heavy seas.

A young Frenchman, Louis Grandpré, has left an account of what followed:

Just then appeared the captain of a whaler who, the evening before, had been surprised by the storm and unable to return to his vessel. The relations of the young lady told their story to him and appealed for his help. I regret I cannot record the name of the brave man – an American.

His boat was on the beach, but the crew was near at hand. Assembling them he launched the skiff and braved the danger of the waves. The lightness of his puny craft was its salvation and it reached the wrecked ship – all the spectators cheering wildly. The greatest difficulty, however, lay ahead; he must board the craft and then transfer the inexperienced lady to his small boat, tossing on the waves in a horrifying manner, at one moment high on the crest of a wave, the next speeding down into the trough.

The sea smote mercilessly against the ship, and the rocks which were visible now and again at her stern, prevented the ship from coming alongside, and it was only at the stern this could have been done. We saw him risk his life 20 times, but his persistence, the courage of the young woman, and the presence of mind of her husband eventually triumphed over the elements' rage.

The American manoeuvred himself within hailing distance and he and the Captain agreed on a plan. Struggling against the sea he succeeded in holding his boat within reach of the stern of the ship. In the meanwhile a sailor had set up a pulley at the far end of the brigantine on a yardarm jutting out some feet beyond the poop. Through this he passed a line, thin enough to be cut with a single stroke by a knife, but strong enough to bear the weight of a person. The Captain tied the rope into what is called a running bowline.

We saw him fasten it around his wife; he then embraced her and with the crew hauling on the other end of the line, lowered her over the side until she was suspended a couple of feet above the water. She remained in this position for a quarter of an hour, the waves reaching her and drenching her from head to foot, whilst the skiff battled against the waves until he reached her. It is a well-known fact that no boats are lighter or faster than those used in whaling, where it is necessary to avoid the sudden turns of the wounded monsters.

The American then, standing in the stern of his boat, manoeuvred so well between succeeding waves that, coming alongside the young woman, with his knife in his right hand, he was able to grasp her in his left arm and simultaneously cut the rope above his head. They both collapsed into the bottom of the boat, but he quickly rose again and continued steering with his large oar. In half an hour, amid cheers, he brought her to the shore.'

To climax this heroic account in true romantic fashion, one should be able to record that the ship sank with all hands, the only survivor being the young lady thus gallantly rescued. In actual fact the wind died down that afternoon, and despite a heavy sea still running, the Captain and crew of the *Sterrenschans* were all rescued that evening by boat.

A model example of a rescue was that of the *Abercrombie Robinson*, a British troopship that went aground in Table Bay on 28 September 1842. The ship was carrying 521 soldiers and 84 women and children – a situation with even graver potential than the wreck of the *Birkenhead* ten years later.

The men behaved with model discipline and the Captain proved a tower of strength, cool, calm and giving crisp and sensible orders. The first attempts to get a line ashore, either by floating a cask or firing a gun, proved ineffective. Eventually a line was brought ashore by a boat from the ship.

The sea was high with squalls of wind and rain, when the first surfboat was hauled out to the wreck. Women and children were immediately placed in the boat and it headed back to the shore. By 8.30 that morning all the women and a large number of the soldiers were ashore, the men behaving as if on parade.

That there was still tremendous danger of a disaster was proved at ten o'clock, while the rescue of the soldiers was still proceeding. The *Waterloo*, a convict ship which was anchored not far from the *Abercrombie Robinson*, lost her last anchor and went aground. Immediately the ship began breaking up. Aboard the *Waterloo* were 219 convicts, 18 women and children, and the crew.

Those on the beach could do nothing. There was no means of firing a line aboard the wreck, no life buoys, no ropes fastened to casks, not even enough rope, for the whole rescue had been concentrated on the *Abercrombie Robinson*. By noon nothing was left of the *Waterloo* save her keel. Some 190 souls had perished in full view of the crowded beach.

The triumph of the complete rescue of the *Abercrombie Robinson*'s complement of over 600 was overshadowed by the dreadful disaster of the *Waterloo*.

One good effect of the wrecks was the decision that a lifeboat must be provided. On the very next morning a public meeting was held, and within an hour the equivalent of R208 was raised to build a lifeboat, the first forerunner of the NSRI.

4 Rescue of the 1 800

This classic rescue yarn was told by Jose Burman in Sea Rescue *Volume 1, Number 4 (December 1982). This is quite possibly the most lives ever saved by one individual in the history of sea rescue. It is an extraordinary story.*

THE OVERRUNNING AND CAPTURE OF the South African 5th Brigade at Sidi Rezegh, in Libya, on 23 November 1941 was one of the severest blows South Africa suffered during the Second World War. What tempered the sense of loss and anxiety was the thought that most of the men in the brigade were prisoners and alive.

It was only much later that people at home realised how close South Africa came to losing the entire brigade permanently – not through enemy action, but due to the efficiency of the Royal Navy. The prisoners taken by Rommel during the confused fighting that last week of November were moved westward and assembled at Benghazi. Then, when Rommel's attack collapsed and the British were again on the advance, the Germans decided to ship their prisoners across the Mediterranean rather than risk them falling into Allied hands.

The vessel chosen for this task was the *San Sebastian*, formerly the Dutch merchantman *Jason*, a nondescript grey ship of possibly 16 000 tons, then lying in Benghazi harbour. (Editor's note: most contemporary sources refer to this ship as being the MV *Sebastiano Veniero* but Burman used the name *San Sebastian* in the original article, and we have retained this usage.)

On the afternoon of 8 December some 2 200 prisoners (the bulk of them South African) were marched down to the harbour. It was a bitter moment for them, as they had been living in hopes of being rescued by the British advance. It was dusk when they reached the harbour and the sight of the wrecked ships and battered buildings did something to restore their spirits.

The men were crowded into the holds of the *San Sebastian*, packed like sardines with hardly room to move. A tin of Italian bully beef and two biscuits were issued to each man. Most of them began eating at once – let tomorrow look after itself. Spirits revived – the Navy will rescue us!

The *San Sebastian* sailed that night, its captain anxious to make the most of the hours of darkness. Down in the crowded holds dysentery was rife and men were queueing to get at the single half-drum latrine, which was all that was supplied to each hold of approximately 500 men. Seasickness did not improve matters, as the ship tossed and rolled.

Dawn found the ship well across the Mediterranean, heading towards Crete. Now the prisoners were allowed on deck, a few at a time, for sanitary purposes, as the drums in the hold were full. Suddenly, there was a burst of shouting on the deck, and the holds were battened down. Excitement quickened the men's pulses – was it the Navy coming to the rescue? But no, the last man down the hatch had the true story – a British plane had flown overhead.

Speculation mixed with trepidation – would they be bombed by their own planes?

The moment passed and the hatch covers were lifted – the latrine queue started again. Just before three o'clock in the afternoon there was a blinding flash in the holds and uproar on deck. Most of the prisoners were not sure what had taken place, but somebody shouted that they had hit a mine.

For a moment there was pandemonium as men fought to reach the ladders. Then calmness was restored; discipline told, as men took it in turns to climb on deck.

The scene was frightening. The ship had been torpedoed by a British submarine and was heavily damaged well down by the bows. Some eight kilometres away could be seen the rough, forbidding coastline of Greece. Overhead flew two German planes spiralling round the scene, while an Italian corvette was circling the *San Sebastian* at speed dropping depth charges as fast as they could be prepared, without any apparent pattern.

There were only four lifeboats and a few rafts on the vessel. The lifeboats had all been launched; one wallowed half-full of water, two had capsized, and the fourth, carrying the captain and his officers, was making good progress towards the distant shore.

Thus abandoned, some of the men panicked. A few threw themselves into the water and attempted to swim to the circling corvette, which ignored them, leaving the men to drown in the cold water; others threw rafts overboard and swam out to them, forgetting that they were well offshore, without paddles, and that their chances of survival would be slim.

The escort corvette was carrying a senior prisoner-of-war, Brigadier James Hargest. When he reached the deck, after hearing the explosion, he was appalled at what he saw. Immediately he ran up to the bridge and urged the commander to stop dropping depth charges. The commander did this, and the corvette then turned away and headed for base.

In the meanwhile, a German engineer officer had taken charge of the *San Sebastian* and restarted the ship's engines. Down by the bows as she was, it was obvious that the ship could not be run in the normal manner, so he put the engines into reverse and slowly began backing towards the coast. At the same time he ordered the prisoners to go to the stern of the ship and so try to counterbalance the stricken bows.

As it became apparent that the ship was not in immediate danger of sinking, the panic died down. Gradually, they got under way in reverse; but the ship made very slow progress, for the weight of the water forward was so great that with every swell the screw (ship's propeller) would be lifted out of the sea and race ineffectually in the air. To make matters worse, on one such occasion the screw fouled one of the rafts, and the men aboard it were cut to pieces.

While the *San Sebastian* made its painful way towards the coast, the medical men were counting the cost of the torpedo. One hold had borne the brunt of the explosion, and it was filled with dead, dismembered bodies and men hideously damaged and in danger of drowning, as the sea flooded through the hole torn in the bows of the ship.

The stairs had collapsed and it took a while before ropes could be found and lowered; then began the job of moving the injured. A British lance corporal, with the MM (Military Medal) ribbon on his breast, was doing Herculean work carrying injured men, with a number of South Africans helping him. Many of the injured were naked, and quite unable to understand how they had lost their clothes. The medical supplies were woefully inadequate and the medical men worked under the greatest difficulties, using cabins, saloons and passages as operating theatres and wards.

Squalls of rain made things more miserable. Someone began singing 'Tipperary' and soon the chorus was taken up and swelled in volume.

The coast of Greece was nearer now. All eyes were turned to the forbidding coastline where sheer masses of rock towered out of the sea, with waves lashing savagely against them. They could see one break in the rocky cliffs – a small cove. Could they reach it?

A sickening jar, then another, as the ship struck the rocks.

The shore was still a long way off; the waves battered the reeling ship unmercifully, while the cries of the wounded could be heard above the shriek of the wind. The ship lifted – they were over the first bar of rocks!

More grinding, more jolting, more jarring sounds; but they were nearer the shore and broadside to the little cove. The surroundings had the mysticism of a Lord Byron poem – the mossy walls of a medieval castle looked down on the scene. But there the similarity ended, for the *San Sebastian* was hard aground and busy tearing herself to pieces.

With every swell the ship lifted, then shivered as the sharp-toothed rocks ground her keel. Every now and then came the sound of rending metal as sections were gouged loose, or buckled under the strain. The surf was breaking right over the wreck and water was leaking into the corridors. It was a matter of time before she was torn apart.

Tantalisingly near lay the land – a few hundred metres away – but it might as well have been 10 km, for the sea between ship and shore was filled with broken waves that dashed in fury on sharp rocks, while the howling wind carried the foam onto the shore.

A volunteer tried to take a line ashore, was overwhelmed, and lost in the surf. Lance Corporal Bernard Friedlander of the Third Transvaal Scottish had been busy helping move the wounded until the ship struck. The first thing that met his eyes as he came on deck was an arm, attached to a shoulder, swaying back and forth in a gap in the deck plating.

Bernard was always a powerful swimmer (I recollect him giving me 100 yards start and beating me in 500), but he liked cold water as little as I do. The idea of a swim in the wintry sea was, to say the least, unattractive; but there was a job to be done – a line had to go ashore without delay. Bernard Friedlander volunteered to take that line.

Stripping to his vest and pants, he was given a cork jacket, and the rope. A couple of seconds' hesitation, and then he jumped overboard.

The intense cold of the water was the first shock. As he surfaced he was almost swamped by the broken waves that filled the cove, but he struck out strongly for the shore. Numbed by the fierce cold and buffeted by the heavy seas, Friedlander was thankful that the ship formed a lee protecting him from the worst of the wind and the heavy surf.

As the waterlogged line fed out, so it hampered him increasingly – he was pulling a dead weight that was yet a live enemy in the grip of the waves. Soon he passed the point of 'no return' – if he weakened now they could not pull him back to the ship alive. He gritted his chattering teeth and forged ahead.

Friedlander had been battling the heavy seas for nearly 90 minutes, and he was beginning to weaken, to flounder under the weight of the line, when he sensed the rocks ahead. One last burst and he was clawing desperately at the wet rock, trying to lift himself higher before the next wave sucked him back out to sea. Then he was lying above the water level, coughing and spewing, while strong hands pulled him higher.

He looked up and saw a young Greek who bent down and untied the rope from Bernard's waist. Between them they dragged the heavier line ashore and made it fast, and then the rescue began as man after man passed down the lifeline to the safety of the rocks.

Nearly 1 800 men came off the wreck (the death toll being 430), and most of them owed their lives to the brave deed of the young South African.

As for Bernard Friedlander, he was arrested by two Italian soldiers with machine guns as soon as he left the rocks. He spent an interesting war, partly in prisoner-of-war camps, and partly as an escaped prisoner living with an Italian family in a village, before being recaptured as he tried to cross the German lines, and sent to Germany.

The *San Sebastian* remained stranded at Methoni, near the southern tip of the Peloponnese, and on 15 December 1941, the British T-class submarine HMS *Torbay* hit her with another torpedo, destroying her.

A German officer witnessed Friedlander's heroism and recommended the lance corporal for a UK bravery award. He returned to South Africa in time to receive the George Medal (for bravery in saving life) from King George VI at a special parade at Voortrekkerhoogte on 31 May 1947 – and how many medals were better deserved?

5 The boy on the beach

Andrew Ingram

LIKE SO MANY CHILDREN WHO grow up close to the sea, Howard Godfrey found its pull irresistible. As a child, he was taken out on the water in his uncle's 30-ft cabin cruiser, *Matie*, and, through necessity, learned how to navigate a boat safely. 'They would take me out almost every Sunday,' he remembers. 'Every Sunday I got seasick. Their remedy was a mix of sardine oil and a tot of brandy,' he says with a laugh. 'But it didn't scare me off.'

Often the men would take the cabin cruiser, with Howard, who was aged 11 at the time, to Clifton. By 10 am, in the shelter of the bay, the first gin-and-tonics would be poured. By late afternoon the only person capable of getting the boat back to Royal Cape Yacht Club was the tenacious youngster. He was simply the only sober crew member.

Howard went to Sea Point High School, but studies held no interest for the high-energy teenager. Listening to the teacher bored him, and he would drift off, looking out of the classroom window, dreaming of boats and being out on the water. Often, the daydream was shattered by a bellow from the teacher and a sharp smack to the side of his head. 'I was always in trouble,' laughs Howard. 'At school and at home.' In desperation his mother would tell him to go down to Three Anchor Bay and watch the boats. Little did she know how happy this made him. And how it would mould his adult life.

Howard closes his eyes and leans back in his chair, remembering the event, on 1 July 1966, that altered the course of his life.

'It was a terrible night. A northwest gale was blowing; it was raining and freezing cold – one of those real Cape Town storms. We were returning home from the Alhambra [a popular theatre and cinema in Cape Town at the time],' says Howard.

Chartleigh House, the block of flats that the Godfreys lived in, is a mere two blocks from the present NSRI head office in Glengariff Road. In those days their sea-facing flat had a clear view of Table Bay, including Three Anchor Bay and the Green Point lighthouse.

'I saw a ship very, very close in off Rocklands and Three Anchor Bay, and a short while later we heard the terrible sound of metal crashing on rocks.'

The 8 000-ton passenger/cargo ship *SA Seafarer* had run aground off Green Point Light, and the 12 passengers and 63 crew were in a desperate situation. The wreck was 50 m from the shore, in front of the lighthouse, and was being punished by a terrible sea. The lighthouse keeper fixed his beam on her, illuminating the massive waves smashing into the ship and shooting more than 30 m into the air. For the young Howard Godfrey, now standing with his father in the driving rain and gale-force wind watching the drama unfolding, this was the moment when he realised that rescue was his calling.

During the night, several attempts were made to rescue the ship-wrecked crew and passengers with rocket lifesaving equipment, but in vain. The ship was taking too much of a beating, the wind too strong for the rocket lines. And then word came that Alouette helicopters of the SAAF's 22 Squadron would attempt a rescue at first light. Howard and his dad spent the entire night watching the drama.

'We watched her break in half forward of midships, and at first light we were amazed to see what was the first helicopter rescue evacuation of crew and passengers, including a baby. Having seen a real ship drama and the rescue, I was intrigued. I bunked school for a few days to watch what happened.'

Three Anchor Bay beach became Howard's local hangout. It was just a few hundred metres from where the *Seafarer* had run aground. He loved watching the fishing boats launching, and he helped out when he was allowed. Everyone knew the kid who was always on the beach offering to help carry kit and launch boats.

In 1967, the South African Inshore Sea Rescue Service's first rescue boat was manned by two Capetonians, Captain Bob Deacon and Ray Lant. Their boat, donated by the Society of Master Mariners, was a small inflatable named *Snoopy*, driven by a 40-hp Evinrude outboard engine with rubber fuel tanks. Initially the first two Sea Rescue volunteers used their VW Kombi as their rescue base, but soon they were given one of the garages on the beach.

Howard knew Ray Lant, who was the commodore of the Oceana Power Boat Club (OPBC). In those days, the OPBC had one of the boat sheds on Three Anchor Bay beach. 'One Saturday afternoon, just after the station opened, friends of mine, the Van Embden family, launched their 16-ft fibreglass boat, *Lucky Jill*,' Howard recalls. He was upset not to have been invited along for the ride and went to sit down in front of the rescue shed.

'About half an hour later the *Lucky Jill* was on fire, and I helped Bob and Ray to launch *Snoopy*. They raced off and rescued the family of six in two sorties.' The *Lucky Jill* wasn't so lucky and burned out.

Soon the SAISRS underwent a name change and became the National Sea Rescue Institute (NSRI), which, importantly for the time, was much easier to use in Afrikaans. With both the Oceana Power Boat Club and the new Sea Rescue boat being based at Three Anchor Bay beach, Howard was in his element.

The Sea Rescue volunteers were locals and fishermen, all of whom knew the boy who seemed to live on the beach. One Saturday, as luck would have it, Howard was hanging out with the Sea Rescue guys on the beach when they got a call about a swimmer in difficulty off Rocklands, a short distance from Three Anchor Bay.

'I helped them launch and, as we pushed out, I jumped into the bow of *Snoopy*.'

In the excitement of going out on the rescue, they let the boy stay. It was a false alarm, but Howard was 14 and he had been on his first call-out.

'*Snoopy* was the first Sea Rescue boat, and, as she was operating from Three Anchor Bay, they chose the radio call sign Rescue 3. If one had to be correct it should have been Rescue 1,' explains Howard.

At that stage it was planned to open a number of rescue bases around the Cape Peninsula. Three boats were ordered under the NSRI flag. The first was going to be stationed at Bakoven, the second would be stationed in Table Bay Harbour, on the Paarden Eiland side, and the third would replace *Snoopy* at Three Anchor Bay. Two of the new boats were 16-ft wooden Tony Munna designs and the third, destined for Table Bay, was an 18-ft Munna.

'The first boat that came from the Tony Munna boatyard was 16-01 (16 referring to the boat length and 01 referring to the first in her class), call sign Rescue 2, and went to Bakoven; 16-02 replaced *Snoopy* and took the Three Anchor Bay call sign Rescue 3; and the third boat, the 18-footer, 18-01, was given the call sign Rescue 1,' says Howard, explaining a rather complicated bit of Sea Rescue history.

Howard would do anything for the Three Anchor Bay Sea Rescue crew. When they asked him to paint the underside of the brand-new rescue boat, he jumped at the chance. He was given some bright yellow paint containing a special hardener, and the crew went off to the Bay Beach Hotel. The paint job took Howard three hours. As he was finishing he noticed that thousands of small black kelp flies had been attracted by the wet paint. They had settled on the surface and became trapped, their feet glued to the paint. Howard was mortified. He rushed off to the bar and had to tell the crew that the rescue boat they all admired so much now had a black hull. 'When they flipped the boat and pulled it across the beach the flies were scraped off. And I wasn't in so much trouble,' grins Howard.

From just two volunteers initially, the NSRI quickly grew at its Table Bay, Three Anchor Bay and Bakoven rescue bases. Having got to know the crew well, Howard was allowed to go out for the odd ride. Just before his 16th birthday he submitted his paperwork to officially join the Station 3 crew. In January 1971 he went on his first call-out – illegally, as in those days crew members had to be 18 to go on an operation.

'It was my proudest moment, as I was invited to crew on Rescue 3 for the *Kazimah*, an oil tanker aground on the western tip of Robben Island.'

For the next 15 years the Rescue 3 base was the Three Anchor Bay garage. In winter storms the crew sometimes had to evacuate as seas broke up into the garages, sometimes smashing the doors and destroying anything left inside. In the mid-1980s, they moved to a safer launching spot in the harbour. They operated for around five years from Granger Bay, before it was decided to build a new rescue base at the East Pier, seaward of the Victoria Basin.

The Cape Town harbour breakwater had suffered serious damage during a vicious winter storm during the late 1980s and the port authorities planned to rebuild it using specially designed 20-ton *dolosse* (shaped concrete blocks used to strengthen harbour walls). Armed with six-packs of Castle Lager, Howard managed to persuade the delivery drivers to drop some of the huge concrete blocks off in a position that would protect the Sea Rescue launching ramp at the East Pier.

Unfortunately for Howard, this happened in direct line of sight of the Port Captain, who got on the telephone and demanded to speak to Howard at once. 'I apologised profusely,' grins Howard. But the *dolosse* that they needed to protect the Sea Rescue boat launch were in place. And there was no way that they were going to be moved.

'While operating from this steel rescue base, which housed Station 3's third boat, an eight-metre Renato Levi design, sponsored by I&J and called *I&J Rescuer*, we operated successfully from the East Pier.'

In November 1988, word got out that the Victoria Basin, together with much of the working harbour, would be redeveloped by visionary David Jack. Howard, who by now had travelled extensively for his work in the clothing business, always finding time to visit other rescue stations, was keen to be part of what was to become the Victoria & Alfred (V&A) Waterfront.

'One afternoon I rode my bicycle to introduce myself, on behalf of the NSRI, to David Jack. I explained the NSRI to him and showed him photographs of an RNLI boathouse in Lymington [UK], which had a glass side wall, allowing visitors to see the rescue equipment inside. He loved the idea. The spot that I asked to build our new base on was the exact spot that in the early 1900s was a sea rescue base manned by railway workers.'

David Jack announced early on that the NSRI station at the East Pier would be moved to the heart of the V&A Waterfront, next to Quay 4. He took Howard at his word that the NSRI would build a state-of-the-art glass-walled rescue base that would allow visitors to see the floodlit rescue boat inside. A 20-year lease was signed for the rescue base and adjoining memorabilia shop at the bargain-basement price of R500 a year.

Again Howard found himself in a rather awkward position when he took the design for the new rescue base to the NSRI board meeting. 'I was asked by the then Chairman of the Board, Captain Bluet, where the funding was coming from.'

'My heart dropped.

'The building was 60 per cent complete, so I told a white lie saying that I was concluding the sponsorship, and left the meeting feeling under extreme pressure.

'At that time the NSRI funding was in dire straits. Early the next morning I was at Central Boating to ask David Abromowitz for help. He called the Chairman of I&J, and by 9 am David and I were sitting in his office with the model and he had agreed to sponsor the cost of building the I&J Sea Rescue base!'

Howard then went out and got another 50 sponsors involved to help kit out what was to be the flagship station of the NSRI, in the hope of increasing funding through the station's high-profile position.

By 1991, the 'silent service', as some knew the NSRI, was no more. After a pledge week run by Radio 5 that raised a good few million rands, Sea Rescue was back on its feet. 'NSRI had to become more businesslike in attracting sponsors,' Howard reflects today.

Howard was by then busy with his own business, and he had to juggle spending time with his young family, training the 45 volunteers at the rescue base and, of course, responding to emergencies.

It was around this time, during one of the Cape's fierce storms, that Station 3, Table Bay, was called out to assist the Hout Bay rescue boat with the yacht *Pambrien*. It was 7 June 1997, and a young professional delivery skipper had sailed the 39-ft *Pambrien* out of Simon's Town and around Cape Point in weather that was fast deteriorating. Rain was sheeting down, the wind was pushing 50 knots from the northwest and a four-metre swell was building.

By 9.15 pm the wind was force 10 and the swells were in the region of eight metres. *Pambrien* was under a storm jib but, even with her motor assisting, the crew were making no headway. All four crew members were seasick and, with the boat only seven nautical miles off Cape Point with an engine that kept overheating, things were looking desperate.

Pambrien called for help.

The Hout Bay rescue boat, *Spirit of Rotary*, was launched at 9.55 pm, and was alongside the yacht at 10.44 pm. By midnight, in conditions that were beyond appalling, Hout Bay called for backup from the Table Bay Sea Rescue station. At 12.50 am Howard guided the 40-ft *Spirit of Safmarine II* out of Cape Town harbour into one of the worst seas that he had ever helmed a boat in.

Heading out into the relative safety of deep water, the rescue crew fought their way towards Hout Bay. The terrible conditions became unbearable as engine fumes were blown into the cabin and the entire rescue crew became seasick.

The *Pambrien* rescue was a 14-hour struggle in which the towline constantly parted in the pitch darkness. Sleeting rain and biting cold made the conditions beyond what any volunteer could be expected to endure.

But the one thing that stands out in Howard's memory is not the sea conditions, the battle with the towline or the exhaustion; it was the desperate struggle to get a rescue swimmer onto the yacht. This task demanded extreme seamanship – and a stroke of luck, without which things might have turned out differently.

'Seeing the weather by daylight was scary. The seas were breaking at 25 ft in all directions,' says Howard. 'I had two rescue swimmers aboard. Rescue 8 [NSRI Hout Bay] and ourselves arrived alongside *Pambrien* and we decided to send a swimmer to *Pambrien* in very tricky conditions to help set up the tow.'

'Vanessa Davidson was chosen, but her attempt was unsuccessful. There was no way that she would reach the yacht.'

The rescue boat needed to turn to pick Vanessa up and to try again. But Howard, up on the rescue boat's flybridge fighting the wheel, had lost sight of Vanessa.

In those huge seas and filthy conditions, the realisation that they had lost Vanessa slowly sank in. Howard managed to get the bow around and, working out where Vanessa should be, he opened the throttles to climb another huge swell.

'In my heart of hearts I was panicking,' Howard remembers. 'I was unable to see her.'

Vanessa remembers the ordeal as clearly as if it happened yesterday: 'I saw them coming towards me. I could see Howard swinging the wheel and I knew that there were three options. They would go to port, they would go to starboard … or they would go over me.

'At the last second the rescue boat veered to port and I was pulled on board on their starboard side.

'It was close. Very close.'

The second attempt was made by rescue swimmer Andrew Mayes, who managed to get aboard the yacht. Battling the huge seas, Andrew managed to rig a bridle (attached to the towline) on *Pambrien*. The towline broke more than once, but Andrew's bridle held, allowing the yacht to be towed extremely slowly to safety. Four hours later, they reached Hout Bay harbour.

The seas were so rough that it was decided that the *Spirit of Safmarine II* should not risk the trip back to Cape Town, and so it was moored in Hout Bay and the crew were sent home to sleep.

Howard recalls: 'The scary part of this rescue for me, as the coxswain, was that, even though we successfully recovered Vanessa ... it was sheer luck.

'We came off that swell and the rescue boat crashed down four feet from Vanessa. It could have landed on her. That was my final wake-up call. I felt that I had used all my luck up. After the *Pambrien* call, I stood down from active crew.'

Today Howard is a retired businessman who has been a volunteer with Sea Rescue for 46 years – as a junior crewman, coxswain, Station Commander and board member. Now, in Sea Rescue's 50th year, he is still a volunteer. His time on the water is for pleasure and his volunteering for Sea Rescue is as Chair of the Awards Committee and as an Honorary Life Governor.

6 A rough night on Robben Island

Andrew Ingram and Tony Weaver

IF THERE'S ONE THING SEASONED journalists know, it is that if you want the real story behind dramatic sea rescues, you need to look beyond the press releases. The NSRI, like other rescue organisations, such as Wilderness Search and Rescue, has a reputation for being exceedingly modest and playing down the drama and the heroics behind their operations. As one senior NSRI employee puts it: 'We issue the vanilla version.'

On many occasions, a fairly bland account of a rescue will be released, but when you phone one of your friends or contacts who was on the rescue, their response will be 'It was an epic.' Then you know that there is one helluva story behind the story. And in the case of the story that follows, we are lucky enough to have three different accounts of the high drama on that wild and stormy August night.

August 2013 had been a rough month. Cold front after cold front lashed the Cape Peninsula. More heavy weather was predicted for the week starting Sunday 11 August. The City of Cape Town issued two severe weather warnings and flood alerts in the week. Snow had fallen on Table Mountain, the Boland mountains had a thick snow layer, and even the Northern Cape had had unusual snowfalls.

It was exactly the kind of weather that prompts news editors to assign a reporter to spend the day doing a 'weather wrap'; the round of phone calls go out to Disaster Management, farming contacts in the Boland, police contacts in outlying villages and, of course, the NSRI.

On Tuesday 13 August, the early shifts on the Cape Town newspapers already knew that a dramatic sea rescue had taken place that morning. The NSRI press release was out by 7 am, and it was a classic, worth quoting in full:

At 00h04 on Tuesday the 13th of August NSRI Table Bay, Melkbos-strand and Bakoven duty crews were activated by the Transnet National Ports Authority following a Mayday distress call from the 19.6-m Hout Bay fishing trawler *Claremont* with 12 crew on board reporting to be running aground on the southwestern side of Robben Island.

Pat van Eyssen, NSRI Table Bay station commander, said: 'It appears that the vessel lost motor power and they were drifting ashore in storm seas with five- to six-metre breaking swells.

'Our Table Bay, Melkbosstrand and Bakoven volunteers launched our sea rescue boats *Spirit of Vodacom*, *Rotary Endeavour*, *Spirit of the Vines* and *Rotarian Schipper* and responded to Robben Island.

'NSRI Hout Bay and the WC Government Health EMS were placed on high alert. Telkom Maritime Radio Services provided VHF radio communications for the rescue operation. NSRI rescue vehicles responded to Signal Hill to assist with communications and a WC Government Health EMS JOC [Joint Operations Command] vehicle was dispatched to assist on Signal Hill.

'While responding to the scene, the skipper and owner, Marcelino da Silva, 49, from Table View, confirmed that his 11 crew members, all from Hout Bay, had moved to the back of the vessel, only four had time to retrieve and don their life jackets and he reported that he remained in the wheelhouse while their vessel had waves breaking over the vessel and that they were already in amongst the rocks and the vessel was being battered against rocks and was breaking up.

'On arrival on-scene, efforts to get the crew off from the sea side, with our NSRI rigid inflatable rescue craft darting in between wave sets under the illumination of white illuminating flares proved fruitless as waves of between five- to six-metre sets rolled in, forcing our rigid inflatable rescue craft to abandon the efforts each time to avoid being capsized or rammed into rocks.

'By this stage it was clear that the crew aboard the casualty vessel were understandably panicking and showing a willingness to take their chances if they abandoned their ship but NSRI controllers, using calm and reassuring voice tones, consoled them over the VHF radios to stay on the relative, although precarious, safety of their ship, particularly since only four crew members were wearing life jackets. They were still at that stage a few hundred metres offshore and their vessel was gradually being swept between and over rocks and breaking up as waves crashed over her as she was forced closer to the island.

'The Red Cross AMS Skymed 1 helicopter was placed on alert by Metro Control but they could only fly at first light and MRCC [Maritime Rescue Coordination Centre] activated the SA Air Force 22 Squadron Oryx helicopters with NSRI Station 29 helicopter rescue unit, but they would only become airborne in two hours.

'The situation intensified when it became clear that the vessel was hard aground on rocks and listing to a 40-degree angle, and casualty crew had no further choice and they began to abandon ship under their captain's instruction.

'NSRI rescue crews raced into Murray Bay Harbour and summoned the Robben Island security who mustered their staff, and with an ambulance (that is kept on the island), a minibus and two bakkies the NSRI crews were driven by the Robben Island security to the side of the island where the casualty crew were abandoning their ship.

'The Transnet National Ports Authority activated a pilot boat to transport additional NSRI rescue crew, Metro rescue paramedics and rescue and medical equipment, including lighting, to the island from the V&A Waterfront.

'WC Government Health EMS ambulances and response para-medics were activated to respond to NSRI Table Bay rescue base to stand by.

'At first only one of the casualty crew managed to get to shore and NSRI rescue swimmers waded, swam and jumped from rock to rock, in between crashing waves to reach the ship where four casualty crew members were found perched on a rock below their listing vessel. They were helped ashore (NSRI rescue swimmers swam them, and helped them over rocks to reach the shore) while wave sets continued to crash over the vessel and over the rescue effort.

'In relays all 11 casualty crew were helped ashore by the eight NSRI rescue swimmers who had gone around to the land side. Only the skipper remained at his wheelhouse and he reported to require assistance as he was exhausted and he had succumbed to hypothermia. NSRI rescue swimmers were able to retrieve him from the casualty vessel and he too was brought to shore.

'By 04h17 all 12 crew members of *Claremont* were accounted for and ashore on Robben Island. They were transported by Robben Island vehicles to Robben Island's Murray Bay harbour and treatment for hypothermia and shock was commenced.

'They were taken aboard *Spirit of Vodacom* and transported to our sea rescue base at the V&A Waterfront. All 12 men were handed into the care of the Metro ambulance paramedics. They have been transported to Groote Schuur and New Somerset hospitals. All are in stable conditions, for treatment for hypothermia, and two also for treatment for back injuries.

'All are men aged between 18 and 52.

'The rescue operation was completed at 05h17 today.

'SAMSA [South African Maritime Safety Authority] will investigate any possible environmental impact and any chances of a salvage of the vessel, which remains hard aground on Robben Island.'

Pretty dramatic, insofar as NSRI press releases go – but that was the 'vanilla version'.

Some of the real drama began to emerge later in the day when veteran former *Cape Argus* reporter Murray Williams wrote up the story for the next day's edition of the newspaper. He quoted NSRI spokesperson Craig Lambinon: 'They did unbelievably well, it was a mammoth effort – swimming, wading and hopping from rock to rock, in foul weather, pouring rain, with huge waves breaking over them – for more than an hour and a half. All our rescue crews are trained to the highest standards of the NSRI – and, frankly, when you're out there in action there is zero distinction between old and young, men and women … It's a bunch of volunteers giving their all to save lives.'

The *Cape Argus* report also quoted NSRI Bakoven (Station 2) volunteer Coralie McDonald, who said of the harrowing rescue: 'You wouldn't be human if you didn't have fear, but it keeps you alert.' Rescue swimmer Ernesta Swanepoel described the huge swells as being 'like a washing machine'.

And then Andrew Ingram, who was on the dock to photograph the crew being brought ashore, got his teeth into the story for *Sea Rescue* magazine:

Mark Thompson was the duty coxswain at the Bakoven Sea Rescue station. He remembers switching the light out just after 10.30 on Monday night, 12 August 2013, and although the sea was big the predicted front had not yet arrived.

Two hours later he was dragged from his sleep. The rain was lashing his bedroom windows and a gale-force northwesterly wind was battering Cape Town. It took Mark a few seconds to work out what had woken him, and looking at his cellphone, he saw the SMS … 'NSRI Rescue 2 Bakoven, contact Port Control.'

He turned to his wife, Barbara, now also awake, and said, 'I can't believe that this is a Sea Rescue call.' Now wide awake, Mark called the Sea Rescue emergency line to be told that there was a fishing boat running aground on Robben Island.

Spirit of Safmarine, the big Table Bay rescue boat, was launching, and their Station Commander, Pat van Eyssen, had asked for Bakoven and Melkbosstrand rigid inflatable boats [RIBs] to assist.

'Call out the crew,' Mark told the Port Captain as he grabbed his

Sea Rescue bag. Driving along Beach Road, the huge surf smashing into the coast was barely visible through the driving rain.

Across Cape Town NSRI volunteers were being dragged from their sleep as the emergency SMSes went out. 'NSRI Melkbosstrand … Call-out. Report to the base' … 'NSRI Bakoven … Call-out. Report to the base.'

It was just after midnight.

Melkbosstrand coxswain Kobus Meyer had been asleep for just over ten minutes when the call woke him, and he followed the same procedure as Mark. Arriving at his rescue station, he went straight up to the balcony and, with the aid of the beach floodlights, studied the sea. 'It was raining and the wind was howling but fortunately in Melkbos we have good lights,' said Kobus.

After choosing two of his most experienced crew, *Spirit of the Vines* was launched, and, while still in the safety of the bay, behind the kelp banks, Kobus made radio contact with his base, and then turned the bow of the rescue boat out towards the darkness as he opened the throttles. They jumped the first wave easily, but the second wave was too close. If he accelerated into it the wave might flip the 6.5-m RIB, so Kobus pulled back on the throttles, as he had done so often in training exercise.

'It wasn't a huge wave. Perhaps three metres,' said Kobus. 'It broke just in front of the boat and the white water hit us. It flooded the boat and we lost the electrics. And one of our engines.

'We're taught that if you have one motor, you don't turn around. It is too dangerous. You get out (beyond the back line) and sort it out on the outside. Unfortunately, with the boat now heavy and slow, we were in the dumping zone for too long.'

The next wave hit the rescue boat with force. It shattered the windscreen and the front console hatch that protected the electrical system. 'We lost radios. GPS. Everything. We lost the second motor as well. Sitting in the wave line, we were dead in the water.'

The crew had trained for just such an emergency. Their anchor was thrown out to turn the nose into the waves and then, luckily, they managed to get one engine going. The anchor was pulled and the damaged rescue boat limped out to safety behind the wave line where the crew could try and restore power and get the second engine going.

At Bakoven, a crew of four volunteers had launched *Rotarian Schipper*, and in driving rain, with very little visibility, the rescue boat nosed out of the narrow channel from Bakoven beach. It was low tide, so the channel was fairly protected. As it got deeper, Mark pressed the throttles down and the rescue boat jumped forward. 'We didn't have any idea what was waiting for us when we got out there. I knew that the sea was big, but didn't know how big,' said Mark.

There was no moon. One hundred per cent cloud cover. A howling wind and driving rain. It was pitch dark. 'There was zero visibility,' said Mark.

'We started picking up massive swells that hit us on our port side.'

Because helming in such conditions took all of Mark's concentration and skill, he asked Ernesta Swanepoel, standing behind him, to call the incoming waves. All she could see was the white of the wave feathering just before it slammed into them.

'Big one to port,' she would shout.

If there was time Mark would swing the bow of the little 6.5-m RIB into it, but a couple of times the waves would be on them already. 'At times they were smacking the boat so hard that it spun us through 90 degrees. We would have to reorientate ourselves and get back onto course.

'Some were so big that they just broke into the rescue boat.

'Conditions were extremely bad. Coupled with the zero visibility it was very, very difficult for us to navigate our way to Robben Island. The safety of the boat and the crew was in my mind the whole time. But we were picking up the radio traffic from the *Claremont*. The skipper was calling desperately for help. That is pretty much what kept us going. Hearing how much trouble he was in was a galvanising factor in getting us there.

'Unless we took a wave that capsized the boat we were going to keep going so that we could help.

'His calls for help were getting more and more panicky as we got closer ... initially they were aground, then hard aground and then the boat was breaking up ...

'At one stage he said, "I am an old man. I don't want to die." That was the end for me. There was no way we were going back,' said Mark.

As *Rotarian Schipper* was fighting her way through the wild seas from Bakoven, sometimes as slowly as four knots, the crew of *Spirit of the Vines* had got the boat's second engine going.

In the lee of Robben Island, they had made good speed to the southwest corner, where the big Table Bay rescue boat had its spotlights trained in the direction that *Claremont* was aground.

'We couldn't see the vessel. Even with illumination flares. All we could see was the little flashing lights on their life jackets,' said Table Bay station commander Pat van Eyssen.

The two smaller RIBs tried to get close to the *Claremont*. They darted in towards the stricken trawler, their path illuminated by flares, but, each time, with three- to four-metre breaking waves, they had to retreat. Fast.

It was simply too dangerous.

A decision was made to try and get to the crew by land. The Bakoven and Melkbos rescue boats, each with a rescue swimmer from *Spirit of Vodacom*, made their way to Robben Island's Murray Bay harbour. There they found the Island's security people, and, taking a very long swimmer's line, the NSRI team organised a lift to where the trawler was.

Kim Germishuys, one of the rescue swimmers from *Spirit of Vodacom*, takes up the story: '*Claremont* was perched up on the furtherest ridge of rock from the island,' said Kim.

'There were four guys who had managed to get through the first gully and climb onto a rock before we arrived. They had a rope from the *Claremont* to the rock. But then they were stuck.'

Kim held the line from the *Claremont* while Mark tied the NSRI swimmer's line to it. Once the team had the lines connected, Kobus moved under the bow of the *Claremont*. There was a lot of movement on the bow. But Kobus was focused. His job was to coach the *Claremont* crew to jump off the bow and then swim each man halfway across the gully where Kim met him and swam the crewman to the rock where he was passed down the line of rescuers.

'You didn't dare let go of the line,' said Kim. 'I was really scared. It's the point that you realise how bad it can actually get that the fear kicks in. I was scared that the boat would be picked up by a wave and be dumped on us in the gully. I was scared that we would be ripped off the line by a wave … I was scared for everyone's safety.'

'You appreciate your training. You appreciate your skills. This is what you train for.'

The worst part was getting the captain off. He did not want to jump. Kim went right underneath the bow to where Kobus was to help, and shouted, 'Look me in the eye. We are going to do this. We are going to get across.'

'Kobus was behind him. We had him sandwiched between us and that's when I injured my back. A massive swell came through, picked us up, and the backwash ripped me off the line. Luckily I was holding his hand. I pulled him onto my chest just before my back hit the rock.'

And then it was all over.

The NSRI volunteers had pulled off a remarkable rescue of 12 men in extremely dangerous conditions. 'It only sank in when we were back on the island waiting for a lift to our boats,' said Kim.

At a quarter to five in the morning, almost five hours after the call-out came, the three rescue boats entered Cape Town harbour.

The rescue crews were ecstatic. Watching the 12 *Claremont* crew being helped ashore in the V&A Waterfront, Bakoven coxswain Mark Thompson summed it up: 'It was quite an emotional thing, this whole operation. We have been training to do this for so long.

'It's the best thing that I have ever done in Sea Rescue. That is for sure.'

The 11 crew members, all from Hout Bay, were: Salie October, 49; Conroy Adams, 27; JP Arendse, 25; Johnson Buya, 42; Ryan

Thomasa, 36; Bonani Galela, 34; Reagan Thomas, 36; Lungisani Mangeli, 28; Xolisa Mbangi, 35; Fundile Nzame, 31; and Sakhumzi Mazule, 25.

For the *Claremont* rescue, the Directors' Thanks was awarded to:

- **Melkbosstrand, *Spirit of the Vines* crew:** Kobus Meyer, Ryan Minnaar, Quinton Luck
- **Bakoven, *Rotarian Schipper* crew:** Mark Thompson, Luke van Riet, Coralie McDonald, Ernesta Swanepoel
- **Table Bay, *Spirit of Vodacom* crew:** Rudi Fisch, Patrick van Eyssen, Gordon Botha, Giles Daubney, Lourens de Villiers, Pieter Engelbrecht, Gerhard Esterhuizen, Kim Germishuys, Tome Mendes.

7 Aground in Clifton

Andrew Ingram

SOMETIMES WHEN SEA RESCUE GETS an emergency call, the details are precise, and the rescue crews know exactly what they are responding to. At other times, it is not quite as clear. This was the case when Paula Leech, then Station Commander at the Table Bay rescue base (Station 3), was dragged from a deep sleep just after 5 am on Saturday 12 May 2012.

The caller told her that there was a container vessel sailing into Clifton. Paula thanked him and, not really believing what she had heard, called Cape Town Port Control.

'I spoke to Amy Adams, who was the senior vessel traffic controller, and she said that she couldn't see anything on their vessel identification systems – but she had just had the same call.'

By 5.14 am a Camps Bay security company was en route to Clifton to confirm the sighting. The message came back that there was a ship off Clifton, but that it was leaving, and that visibility was very low because of thick mist.

'At 05h20 the same caller was back on the line confirming that the ship was leaving Clifton. Then again at 06h05 to say that it was back in the bay. And it wasn't a container ship but a large fishing vessel,' said Paula.

She decided to go and look for herself.

'The mist was very thick. Pea soup,' remembers Paula.

Standing on the road above Clifton's First Beach, Paula heard the unmistakable growl of big diesel engines, and then, through the thick mist, she saw a vessel's mast lights. They were way too close to the beach. The vessel was aground.

'I called Amy and asked her to activate the duty crews,' said Paula. It was 6.22 when the SMS went out ... 'Station 2 Bakoven. Call-out. Report to the base. Station 3 Table Bay. Call-out. Report to the base.'

The Bakoven crew were already on the way to their base for an early-morning exercise, and so when the emergency call came it took them only a few minutes to launch their rescue boat.

'Thank goodness for GPS,' said Bakoven duty coxswain and Station Commander, Bruce Davidson. 'The mist was very thick. Visibility was around 10 m. Without our chart plotter, navigation would have been a nightmare.'

For safety in the thick mist, Bruce and the Bakoven crew went well out to sea, around South Paw, and then they edged slowly towards Clifton's Fourth Beach, creeping along the beach looking, and listening, for the grounded ship. At the reef between First and Second Beach they found it, stern sticking out into the bay. It was well aground.

'As the rescue boat glided close to the vessel's stern we could read her name: the *Eihatsu Maru*, a 50-m Japanese-registered long-liner. The fishermen started shouting and lowering a massive towline – it must have been 70 or 80 mm in diameter,' laughed Bruce.

Using hand signals, the rescue boat crew declined the line and told the crew to stay where they were. There was no way that the little six-metre rescue boat was going to tow this vessel off the beach. The two Table Bay rescue boats were on the way and they would then work out how to rescue the crew.

Patrick van Eyssen was coxswain of the 12-m *Spirit of Vodacom* and Giles Daubney was at the helm of the 5.5-m *Rotary Endeavour.*

'The mist was very, very thick,' remembers Pat. 'Giles tucked in behind me and we navigated to Clifton by instruments. We couldn't see a thing.'

The snoek were running that day. As the two Sea Rescue boats made their way past Granger Bay, snoek boats that had launched at Oceana Power Boat Club came racing past, seemingly unworried about the complete lack of visibility, in their haste to reach the fishing grounds.

Spirit of Vodacom turned into Clifton and held off while the smaller rescue boat moved in closer. Communication with the crew of the *Eihatsu Maru* was impossible. They were all Taiwanese nationals and none of them could speak English.

Two Sea Rescue crew, carrying a VHF radio and a cellphone, were put aboard the long-liner. Just before 9 am, as gaps started to appear in the mist, a Taiwanese interpreter was found. Passing the cellphone between the captain and the rescue crew, a three-way conversation was set up. At last they could explain that the South African Maritime Safety Authority (SAMSA) had given permission for non-essential crew to be evacuated from the grounded vessel and that a tug would be dispatched.

At 9.10 the first of the crew were taken off the *Eihatsu Maru*, and by 9.39 all 19 crew who were to be evacuated were safely on board the rescue boats. The captain, eight of his crew and the ship's dog, a Border collie cross named Alley, were left on board to assist with the salvage.

At 10.00, as the Sea Rescue boats were leaving the scene, the mist started to roll back. A crowd was gathering on the beach. And Clifton First Beach residents, owners of what are some of the most expensive apartments in Africa, stood at their windows looking at the stranded ship.

Over the next days the *Smit Amandla*, a powerful salvage tug, held a line on the stranded trawler. The salvage crew set up a bladder on the beach and pumped off the fuel from the *Eihatsu Maru*. Twice, as the *Smit Amandla* increased the pressure on the towline, it parted, shooting spray high into the air. The crowd, who would gather just before high tides in case the long-liner was pulled free, would gasp and then slowly drift away, knowing that nothing would happen until the next high tide.

On Friday 18 May, just after 3.30 pm, the line from the *Smit*

Amandla was tight. From where I was standing, on Kloof Road, high above the scene, I could see that the tug was pulling hard, swinging slowly from port to starboard by a few degrees. Suddenly the man standing next to me shouted, 'She's moving!'

Lining up the *Eihatsu Maru*'s mast with a bungalow behind it, I saw that he was right. Almost imperceptibly, inch by inch, the tug was pulling the stranded long-liner off. Suddenly it was free. A cheer went up and, looking rather undignified, the *Eihatsu Maru* was pulled stern-first through breaking surf.

As if on cue, a rainbow appeared, arching over the First Beach apartments and pointing to where the *Eihatsu Maru* had been hard aground. The Clifton residents had their pristine view back again.

8 The yo-yo man

Andrew Ingram

It had been a long Monday at work for 35-year-old IT specialist Sean Serfontein. His wife, Karen, was asleep and he was relaxing in front of the TV when the SMS snapped him back to reality: 'Code red: all crew report to the base.'

The adrenaline started pumping instantly. He glanced at his watch. It was 10.30 pm on the night of 2 November 2009.

'Normally on the way to the base, I'd see others responding; this time there was nobody, so I called the duty controller. He told me that a ship was sinking 78 km offshore and that a helicopter would pick me up,' Sean said.

Durban's Portnet pilot helicopter, contracted by Acher Aviation, had been preparing to take a pilot out to a ship when the Mayday call was intercepted. It was from the *Acechador*, a 37-m Spanish-registered trawler with 17 crew on board. The engine room had flooded, the trawler was in grave danger of sinking, and the crew was abandoning ship.

The rescue coordinators worked fast.

The ships *Grand Orion*, *Pacific Scorpio* and SAS *Protea* were close to the trawler and were asked to make haste to the scene. In the meantime, the port helicopter was asked to pick Sean up at the Durban Sea Rescue base (Station 5).

'I was still struggling into my wetsuit when I heard the helicopter. It was about three minutes after I got to the station that I ran out and saw the hook being lowered for me,' says Sean.

As he was pulled into the hovering Agusta 109, Sean recognised engineer Andrew Cochrane and, pulling on his headset, found that the pilot was his old school friend Rob van Wyk, and the copilot Marinus 'Dup' du Preez.

With the doors shut, the nose of the aircraft dropped, and Rob turned out to sea. The wind was from the southeast at about 20 knots and the swell was running at two to three metres, well within the operating range of the powerful twin-engined helicopter. Perhaps best of all, though, there was enough moonlight to give the pilots a clear horizon.

Beads of sweat ran down Sean's back as he spent the 25-minute flight doing final checks on his gear, and ensuring that the small portable radio was securely strapped to his chest.

It was a relief when the helicopter's searchlights snapped on, illuminating the stricken trawler, as the helicopter crew tried to get their first view of what was in store for them.

Rob van Wyk takes up the story: 'Our biggest problem was that all the sailors had climbed off onto life rafts on the starboard side of the vessel and they had tied themselves together, but the wind and swell were pushing them into the vessel. So, we didn't have a visible reference, and you need that when you're trying to do a chopper rescue.' (For a helicopter pilot to lose spatial orientation due to loss of visible reference is a huge danger. To keep the machine flying safely, he or she needs to be able to look at something close by to judge distance, height and orientation.)

'I needed to get Sean into the water, upwind of the vessel. So we lowered him in and he swam over to them and commandeered one of their rubber ducks. Then he took three guys at a time and brought them to the opposite side where I could actually look at the ship. Then Andrew, our hoist operator, picked them up from about 50 m.

'It wasn't really that difficult; it was cloudy and we had a little bit of drizzle towards the end of the rescue, but the moon provided us with a horizon, which gave me the reference I needed. The positioning of two other vessels, the car carrier *Grand Orion* on our left, and the bulk carrier *Pacific Scorpio* on our right-hand side, also helped.

'The *Acechador* had no lights, but the searchlights on the helicopter lit up the area, so generally we had good visibility. Our biggest problem was the 20-knot wind and the fact that the vessel was lying across the swell – and there was a 2.5- to 3-metre swell running at the time.

'I think Sean had the most difficult job. In the aircraft, it was a controlled, very sterile environment, if I can put it that way. Everybody worked well together, everybody knew what they were supposed to do.'

An incredible 54 hoists were performed that night. 'There was some seriously good flying from Rob and Dup,' says Sean. Eleven of the crewmen were first taken to the *Grand Orion*. The navy survey vessel SAS *Protea* then arrived and three more fishermen were winched into the helicopter and onto the deck of the *Protea*, and those aboard the *Grand Orion* were moved to the *Protea*. The helicopter returned to Durban to refuel, before picking up the remaining fishermen.

Sean got home at around 4.30 in the morning, waking Karen as he opened the bedroom door and turned off his alarm. 'It was almost light, so it wasn't worth putting my head down.'

A couple of hours later, he was sitting at the breakfast table with Karen and their two children, Mitchell, 5, and Amy, 2. They listened, fascinated, as their dad told them how he had flown far out to sea in a helicopter to rescue 17 men whose ship was sinking.

As their dad was driving them to school, the SAS *Protea* was sailing into Durban harbour with the 17 shaken sailors, and a specialist salvage company, Subtech, was preparing to try and save the *Acechador*.

Paul Bevis, a former Station Commander at Station 5 and now spokesman for Subtech, said that 'a full dive team, consisting of six members – a dive supervisor, two divers, two men to tender the divers and a medic – sailed on our tug, the *Reier*, at 11h30. We arrived on scene at 15h00 and put two divers into the trawler and started pumping.'

Realising that the three pumps were holding their own, the *Reier* took up a towline and started the slow pull back to Durban.

And then began the long process of trying to save the equipment that had spent so much time in sea water. Paul says, 'You can't just pump the engine room dry; the machinery will be destroyed. So we pump down to machinery level, then pump fresh water in, repeating this until only fresh water is left. Special chemicals are added, and then the engine room is pumped dry.'

It was an epic rescue, involving one of the highest number of helicopter hoists performed by a rescue team at night. Saving the *Acechador* depended on well-trained, dedicated specialists going well beyond the call of duty, something that all of them see as being completely normal.

For his role in the rescue, Sean was awarded the NSRI's Directors' Thanks. The citation reads as follows:

November 26, 2009: The Directors of the National Sea Rescue Institute accord their thanks to Sean Serfontein, a rescue swimmer on Station 5, Durban, for his actions on the night of 2nd/3rd November 2009 when he was part of the helicopter team activated to respond to the Mayday call from the fishing trawler *Acechador*, taking water 42 nautical miles off Durban.

When the Transnet National Ports Authority helicopter ZS-RRB arrived on scene, 15 of the casualty's crew were safely aboard 4 life rafts and another two were in a small motorised rubber duck. There was a 15 knot SW breeze and a 3 metre swell, in cloudy conditions. The only form of lighting illuminating the various craft was occasional moonlight. Two large vessels which had responded to the distress call were standing off some 2 nm.

Sean was lowered into the sea near the rubber duck, climbed in, started the outboard motor and, with the assistance of the two *Acechador* crew already on board, proceeded to one of the life rafts. Then began the process of transferring the trawler's crew, three at a time, into the rubber duck, from where Sean assisted them one by one into the helicopter winch strop and they were lifted into the aircraft. From there the sailors were transferred three at a time to the *Grand Orion*, the nearest support vessel. This process was repeated until the final three of the *Acechador's* crew remained in the rubber duck, at which point Sean motored the craft alongside the SAS *Protea* which was now on scene and he and the other occupants boarded her.

ZS-RRB then proceeded to transfer the 14 rescued sailors now aboard the *Grand Orion*, onto the SAS *Protea*. Sean Serfontein controlled the *Protea's* helideck and hoisting area throughout this process. In all, the rescue took four hours and the helicopter made 54 personnel lifts. The whole operation was most professionally executed. All the *Acechador's* crew were recovered without a scratch and they and Sean were transported back to Durban by the SAS *Protea*.

Sean Serfontein that night displayed professional skill, steadfastness and fortitude. His decision-making was excellent. Sean's actions were a credit to the National Sea Rescue Institute. We are proud to be able to recognise his achievement with this vote of thanks.

9 *The sea was full of holes*

Tony Weaver

'JUST A NORMAL BLOODY WORK day.' That's how Ian Gray, Station Commander of the NSRI's Port Elizabeth base (Station 6), describes Tuesday 22 October 1996. But that day would turn out to be anything but normal.

Gray recalls: 'Then, early in the morning, Colin Alexander, who was the Station Commander at the time, called me to say that this wooden trawler, the *Dassenberg*, with 22 crew on board, was sitting off Seaview, about 20 nautical miles south of PE. Conditions had come up very suddenly, and they had sprung a leak in the bow area and they were worried they were going down.'

There was a six-metre swell running, and it was building all the time. It would eventually peak at around ten metres, with the wind blasting at 94 km/h and gusting up to 120 km/h. In their panic, the crew of the *Dassenberg* had launched both the vessel's life rafts but failed to tie them down, and the gale had simply plucked them up and they disappeared.

'Colin and I usually flipped a coin to see who would skipper, but I had a bout of really bad gastro, so I stayed ashore as operation coordinator, and Colin took the *St Croix* out at about 7 am.'

Built in 1976 by Thesens in Knysna, the *St Croix* was a ten-metre Renato Levi-designed craft powered by two Detroit Diesel two-stroke engines.

The crew set off from Station 6, next to the Algoa Bay Yacht Club in Port Elizabeth harbour. 'Running across Algoa Bay was fine; the *St Croix* kept to about two miles off Cape Recife. Conditions were still okay, well within the boat's capabilities. Meanwhile, I contacted the Air Force; they only had Alouettes in PE. I drove over to near the Minetti Hotel [now the Seaview Hotel], and set up communications with the *Dassenberg's* skipper, Shaun Paarman. He said they had to get off; they had lost their life rafts. He said, 'I'm going to beach it.'

'But that area is just a mess of jumbled-up reefs, rocks and pinnacles. I told him there is no way they would survive a beaching. So we tried to fly a salvage pump out to him, but the boat was pitching and yawing so badly there was just no ways the Air Force chopper could drop it.'

The storm was intensifying, and then reports started coming in of chaos and multiple casualties down the coast off St Francis. Two chokka boats, the *Loligo 4*, with 19 crew on board, and *Opkyk*, with 14 crew, as well as a ski-boat with ten crew, had flipped as they ran for shelter in the mouth of the Kromme River. The wind was howling at 90 km/h, and Ian decided to rather deploy the Air Force helicopter there. Then a trawlerman on a fourth boat had a heart attack and had to be lifted off.

Ultimately, the NSRI crew from St Francis Bay and the Air Force rescued 30 people off St Francis that day, but 13 fishermen drowned.

Amid the chaos, Colin and his crew were being battered as they rounded Cape Recife. The NSRI crew entered a zone where anything could happen. They were confronted by a maelstrom unlike anything they had seen before: 'The sea was like a washing machine; it was full of giant holes. I have been in seas with bigger waves before, but never in such confused seas,' said Colin.

On land, Ian Gray continued talking to skipper Shaun Paarman. 'When he realised that he was able to maintain his position he calmed down, and soon the *St Croix* came into view, and that made a huge difference to the morale of the *Dassenberg's* crew. Colin had the hazardous task of putting the two boats together in that massive swell; we had a nail-biting view from land. We had all the emergency crews there – the fire department, ambulance, police, the works – all ready to jump into action if needs be.'

Colin recalls: 'My men were incredible. We shouted to the fishermen to jump across, and my men caught them one by one and bundled them below deck. It took us about 20 minutes to get them across. If one of them had fallen into the sea, the waves would have taken them away immediately, the weather was that bad.'

Shaun Paarman and three of his men decided to stay on board the *Dassenberg* to try and save the trawler, and the *St Croix* prepared to run back to port.

And that's when the operation turned even more hazardous.

The *St Croix* was designed to carry a maximum of 30 people – in good weather. Now there were 26 on board in some of the foulest weather and seas any of them had experienced, and it was getting worse.

Ian says: 'They started the trip back, and the boat was heavily weighed down, the sea was on her bow, the well deck was flooding and as they got to the Cape Recife area, things got really, really tough.

'There was a southwesterly ground swell of ten metres running, marching up on them from behind, and an east wind of 90-plus km/h creating these really nasty spikes coming at them from the front. So they had a swell from behind, and these wind-driven spikes from in front. They would crest a wave and literally fall into the trough and then be smacked by a wave from the starboard side. Peaks would just appear from nowhere as the swells interacted. The way they described it to me, it was like Indiana Jones dodging giant spikes that shoot up from nowhere. Among our crew of eight, they suffered cracked ribs, an injured knee, a concussion.'

And that's when Ian got a scary radio call: 'Colin called me and said, "I don't know if we can make it back, I don't know how much more the boat can take."'

Colin later said: 'I didn't think we would sink because of the load, but if we had lost a motor at that point we would have been in deep trouble. We had to head right into the waves. Sometimes there would just be holes in the sea with giant waves coming at us at right angles.

'Our blue flashing light was smashed off the boat. My crew were anchored with safety harnesses to stop them being washed off the boat. We all ended up very tired, stiff and sore. The waves would knock us down, and for a few moments you wouldn't know where you were. Then you would look up and there would be nothing in front of you.

'*St Croix*'s hull was badly bashed a few kilometres from Seaview, and I thought her engines had been knocked out, but somehow she held together. In my 19 years of sea rescue, I've never seen as wild a sea. We were descending into troughs so deep that the swells above us were higher than our tallest radio mast. We were hitting the bottom trough so hard that I later had no feeling at all in my lower body.'

Back on shore, Ian was desperately worried. 'I got hold of the Port Captain, and said "You have got to send help, a tug," and he said "Conditions are too bad; we can't go out." This went on for an hour. I cajoled, I argued, and eventually he sent a tug out just as the guys made it back to port at 2.30 pm. They had been out in that crazy, crazy storm for over seven hours.

'They were shattered. They had had no idea whether or not the boat would hold up, and it's a damn good thing they didn't know just how badly it was damaged. There were so many "ifs" in that rescue – if we hadn't had such a brilliant coxswain in Colin, if the boat had been knocked down, if she had lost one or both engines. The *St Croix* wasn't self-righting [designed to right itself after capsizing], there's no reserve buoyancy and only an eight-person life raft – they had 26 on board.

'When the *St Croix* was originally built, the guys at the time thought she wasn't robust enough and sent her back for extra strengthening. Thank heavens they did.

'The engines had shifted, the exhaust brackets had disintegrated, the hull had twisted down the length and there were cracks through the watertight bulkheads. The surveyor said the boat could be repaired, but could never again be used for sea rescue purposes. I joined this station in 1982 and I've been Station Commander since 1998, and, in my experience, that's the closest this station, probably any station in South Africa, has ever come to losing a boat and a crew.'

As a parting shot, I ask Ian to describe the unique geography of Port Elizabeth that added up to make this storm particularly horrible. He ponders the question briefly, then says: 'We get big southwesterly ground swells coming through, and when that happens, the wild side, from Cape Recife south, gets very wild and very nasty. When the easterly blows up a gale, Algoa Bay is horrible. Normally we have one or the other.

'That day we had both.'

10 Drama in Sardinia Bay

Andrew Ingram

THE PORT ELIZABETH TO EAST London Challenge – the PE2EL – is the stuff of legend in the surf ski community. The race, which has been held for the past 40 years, takes paddlers 250 km over four days from Port Elizabeth to East London along one of the most beautiful, but harshest, coastlines in the world.

It was the attraction of this extremely demanding paddle that saw Clinton Hempel, 44, set out from Port Elizabeth's Summerstrand Beach with a group of about 25 other paddlers on a qualifier for the PE2EL race. It was 5.30 am on Saturday 1 November 2014.

'During the briefing we were told that it was rough on the Cape Recife side, so some guys decided to pull out and paddle the river,' said Clinton, who lives in St Francis Bay.

'But I decided to do the sea.'

It was just getting light when the 25 or so paddlers launched through the Summerstrand surf. The sea was fairly rough in Algoa Bay. The wind was nagging at a bumpy chop, but the water was relatively warm, and Clinton, being an experienced paddler, was not concerned by any of this.

Clinton has paddled surf skis since his early teens. He loves the feeling of freedom, the physical challenge and being out on the water experiencing the beauty of nature.

On this paddle, Clinton was on his wife's Fenn ski. Wearing his black paddling shorts, red rash vest and orange personal flotation device (PFD) he hopped onto the ski, got his balance and powered forward. But his timing was out, and seconds later a wave picked the ski up and rolled him off.

'It took a few minutes to sort things out and I had to paddle hard playing catch-up, but soon got back into the second group,' said Clinton.

Once back in the group he could settle down, get into a paddling rhythm and start to enjoy being out in the bay as the sun nosed up into the sky. The first 20 km was a lap in Algoa Bay before the paddlers rounded Cape Recife to paddle to Sardinia Bay, 22 km away.

'I was in a group of three or four paddlers as we went around to the wild side,' said Clinton. 'It was pretty big so we went wide. There was no drama and it was downwind all the way to Sardinia.'

Slowly, as the paddlers moved down the coast, the conditions started to deteriorate. The water temperature had dropped to about 12 °C and the wind picked up. A few swells started to feather and break around the paddlers.

'I lost visual contact with the other guys; in those conditions you have got to concentrate on steering the boat. With hindsight, I should have pulled out. I didn't know that stretch of coast and I went too far out to sea to avoid Cape Recife.'

Clinton did not see any other paddlers for the 20 km on the wild side, and when he got to the 42-km mark he looked to his right but didn't recognise the shore. Convinced that Sardinia Bay was a little further, he paddled on.

'It was probably two kilometres before I realised that I had paddled past Sardinia, so I turned the ski around.

'I paddled for 20 minutes or so but in those conditions it started to go wrong. I got caught in a gnarly spot. There were plenty of rocks and waves on the shore side but I couldn't see where to go in.'

And then Clinton was knocked off the ski. He had been paddling for four hours by now and he was tired. So it took some effort to remount the ski. And he was knocked off again. And again. And again.

'By the fifth time I realised I couldn't get back on. I just didn't have the strength. All I could hope for was to be washed onto the beach.

'I had to stay with the ski. It was the only thing that was going to save me. I knew I was in serious trouble, and I could feel that I was losing consciousness.'

Hypothermia was taking its toll and things that should have been easy to do became impossible.

'In my muddled state, I thought that perhaps the water bottle clipped to the foot straps was throwing the ski off balance, so I tried to unclip it. But I couldn't work the clip.'

His thinking was now seriously impaired, and control of basic movements was impossible. Clinton wrapped his hands through the foot straps, put his chin on the deck and felt himself drifting away.

Port Elizabeth (Station 6) Sea Rescue coxswain Daniel Heimann was at Builders' Warehouse doing some DIY shopping with his three-year-old son, Thomas, when his phone rang. It was Station Commander Ian Gray.

'Daniel. We have a paddler missing at Sardinia Bay. Can you go?'

'My gut told me to get my arse into gear,' said Daniel.

As luck would have it, Daniel's brother lives on the way to Sardinia Bay. He was at home, and agreed to look after Thomas while Daniel responded to the call-out.

'I dropped Thomas off and then floored it,' said Daniel.

The road to Sardinia Bay beach dead-ends at a huge sand dune. Fellow paddlers standing at the top of the dune and scanning the ocean had spotted Clinton clinging to his ski. He was about a mile past the take-out point, being pushed towards a dangerous set of reefs.

When Daniel pulled into the gravel parking lot, low cloud was scudding across the sky, the waves had picked up to just under three metres, the wind was whipping the tops off the waves, and a sea mist reduced visibility.

At the base of the dune, Daniel let down the tyres of the NSRI rescue vehicle for better traction in the sand. He did the same with the trailer tyres of *Boardwalk Rescuer*, the little 4.2-m inflatable rescue boat.

A group of volunteers arrived together in the Port Elizabeth Sea Rescue vehicle just after Daniel. Ian Gray asked Daniel if he would take the tiller and Steven van den Berg if he would crew.

And then things happened fast.

'The first time we couldn't get over the dune,' said Daniel, 'but the second time we were over.'

Steven and Daniel pulled on wetsuits and life jackets as other volunteers got the boat ready. Fuel lines checked. Kill switch checked. As they were preparing, Daniel kept looking at the sea.

'There's a reef just to the west of the launch spot that normally shelters it, but that morning a two-and-a-half-metre swell was breaking on the beach.'

The PE crew were holding the nose of *Boardwalk Rescuer* into the sea, and Steven jumped into the forward crew position. 'We've been together for eight years on the same crew, and we work well together,' said Daniel.

He twisted the throttle open; the rescue boat's nose rose and instantly got up onto the plane. 'I ran to the east, around the rocky outcrop and then swung west. A big swell was bearing down on us, so I floored it and we punched through. We were about 100 m offshore and the sea was all over the place.'

Station Commander Ian Gray was at the top of the dune watching the tiny rescue boat ducking and diving through the waves, smashing straight through some of them. He moved away from the group of paddlers.

'I was very worried about the conditions. It was at the edge of the boat's capability. I thought that I was going to have to call that boat back before they got to him.'

And then Daniel saw the ski.

'It was in the trough between two waves. The ski looked like a cigarette, but in the blink of an eye it was gone again. He had drifted into the break zone.'

Daniel helmed the boat inshore of the surf ski and turned the nose back into the sets as he pulled up next to Clinton.

'He was completely unresponsive. His hands were clamped onto the foot straps, his face was a blank stare.' Clinton's hands were frozen in a vice grip on the straps.

With a swell starting to crest, the rescue boat had to leave the paddler, punch through the set, and then turn to come back to Clinton.

'Steve grabbed him but could not get him into the boat, so I reached across to help. And pulled the kill switch.'

The engine instantly cut.

Working very fast now, Daniel got the kill switch reconnected, pulled the cord and the engine started again.

Another set was bearing down, but Steve couldn't pull the semi-conscious paddler into the boat. In desperation, Daniel grabbed Clinton's leg. Steve held onto his arm and PFD. They had to prise his hands free, and with Clinton hanging against the side of the pontoon Daniel opened the throttle to move the rescue boat away from the impact zone, into a safer area.

'It was absolute hell on the way back,' said Daniel.

'He was frozen stiff and Steve tried to cradle him in the front to protect him as we smashed into wave after wave. We try to be careful with hypothermic patients, but this sea was something else.'

'Emotionally, this is one of the hardest calls that I have done,' said Daniel.

'He kept losing consciousness and we shouted at him, "SIR. DON'T SLEEP. SIR."'

Daniel depressed his handheld radio transmit button. The message was short and to the point. 'Get us an ambulance. Now.'

'Please.'

Clinton spent four days in ICU after his ordeal, but recovered fully. 'Things go wrong very quickly,' he said later. 'By the time that I realised I was in serious trouble it was too late to do anything.

'Never paddle alone on a stretch of coast that you don't know; paddle with flares; and have a cellphone with a tracking app in a waterproof bag. Make sure that your paddle is attached to your ski and that you are

leashed to the ski. Have bright colours on your ski and paddle wearing bright colours.'

- *Daniel Heimann and Steven van den Berg were awarded the NSRI's Gallantry Award, Bronze Class, for risking their lives to rescue Clinton Hempel.*

* * *

The tragic death of Mark Feather
Tony Weaver

JUST TWO WEEKS AFTER THE dramatic rescue of Clinton Hempel, the paddling community was rocked by the tragic death of Mark Feather, a 43-year-old paddler from Rivonia. Mark was one of 133 paddlers taking part in another tough race, the 23-km Pete Marlin Surf-Ski Race from Orient Beach, East London, to Yellow Sands at the Kwelera River mouth on the Wild Coast on Saturday 15 November 2014.

The downwind race started in relatively mild conditions at 7 am, but conditions began deteriorating with the swell picking up to 6.5 metres and the wind to 47 knots (87 km/h), and soon 27 paddlers had pulled out. By 10 am, six paddlers were reported missing, Mark among them.

The NSRI's East London station (Station 7) launched *Lotto Rescuer* and were joined in the search by the Eastern Cape government's EMS rescue helicopter. They found five of the missing paddlers safely ashore.

With the wind picking up in speed to a gale-force 60 knots (111 km/h), a massive search was launched for Mark. Six fixed-wing planes from the local flying club took off and searched the course up towards Kei Mouth, and all ships and fishing vessels in the area were put on the alert.

Prominent KwaZulu-Natal paddler Barry Lewin wrote later that 'I personally chatted to Mark on the Friday about the race and it really hurts to know he has passed … I couldn't actually write a race report, as I can't now recall much of the paddle. The reality of losing a friend is overwhelming.'

He wrote that 'The rescue operation was unparalleled to anything surf ski has ever seen.

'What also blew me away was the support from our paddling fraternity. When the doubles on the Sunday was called off, some 200 people arrived at the NSRI to help with the search … Walking a section of beach myself and seeing so many people doing the same will certainly bind us all closer together as a community, one I am very proud to be a part of.'

The massive search continued on the Sunday morning in an area plotted by the Maritime Rescue Coordination Centre (MRCC). Resources thrown at the operation, besides the Sea Rescue volunteers and the aircraft, included the South African Police Service dive unit and K-9 search and rescue unit, the local 4x4 club, motocross and quad bikes, Surf Lifesaving volunteers, members of the Border Canoe Club, a private helicopter, Buffalo Toyota, the local paddling fraternity and private citizen volunteers from both East London and the Wild Coast.

Early in the morning, just after first light, part of Mark's missing ski was found on the shore at Morgan Bay, and during the day more debris was washed up a bit further north, and the search was concentrated in that area.

Sadly, on the morning of Monday 17 November, Mark's body was found washed ashore by a group of hikers near Trennerys Hotel on the Wild Coast, 40 km north of the race finish.

11 *Mayday off the Wild Coast*

Andrew Ingram

THE FIRST TIME I MET Kyle Castelyn, he was walking off the Sea
Rescue boat *Spirit of Vodacom* at the Table Bay rescue base (Station
3). It was just after 9 am on 20 October 2015. He had a smile from
ear to ear as he walked up to his mother, Linda. She threw her arms
around him and pulled him towards her in a hug. It was an intensely
emotional moment as Jean Sitruk, skipper of the *Llama Lo*, stood on
the rescue boat, tears streaming down his face as he watched mother
and son reunited.

Only a couple of days before this, as the two men struggled for
survival in the yacht's tiny inflatable tender boat, Jean had thought
they would die. 'We were nearer death than life,' he said. 'I hoped to
live for my family. But especially for Kyle.'

Later, I hear the story of their rescue. With the Table Bay rescue base,
and *Spirit of Vodacom* lit up inside it, as a fitting backdrop, the story
that unfolds is one of exceptional seamanship and determination.

Two of the men at the table, one wearing a Sea Rescue South Africa
hat and the other a Sea Rescue beanie, have pronounced French
accents. Hervé Lepage, captain of the 277-m French-registered
container carrier *CMA CGM Rossini*, and the ship's chief engineer,
Lyes Lassel, recount the harrowing story of their search for Sitruk,
65, and Castelyn, 20, after their capsized catamaran was found
50 nautical miles off the Wild Coast.

I look at Kyle, sitting across the table from me. A rake-thin young man with long blond hair and a moustache, he sits ramrod straight in his chair, his brown eyes focused, unblinking, on Captain Lepage.

Jean Sitruk, skipper of the 52-ft catamaran *Llama Lo*, is from Lyon, France, and his crewman Kyle is from Strand, near Cape Town. They were sailing from the Maldives to Cape Town, and were on the last stretch from Durban to Cape Town, where Kyle was to leave the yacht.

Late in the afternoon of Saturday 17 October 2015, they were sailing at 12–13 knots in rough seas with moderate winds off the Wild Coast. The boat was on autopilot and both men were down below when, with a loud bang, the yacht momentarily stopped and then swung hard to port.

Rushing up on to the deck, Kyle saw a whale on their port side. Water was flooding into the hull through a massive 70-cm hole. The boat was going to capsize. With a hole that big there was nothing that the two sailors could do to prevent it.

Kyle went for the life raft, loosening it from its position. He threw it overboard and then dashed below to grab emergency supplies. Crucially, Jean grabbed the Emergency Position Indicating Radio Beacon (EPIRB).

Kyle unhooked the VHF microphone and transmitted the call that every seaman dreads: 'Mayday, Mayday, Mayday, this is the yacht *Llama Lo, Llama Lo, Llama Lo …*'

The catamaran was listing heavily to port as the two men rushed back on deck, only to see that the life raft was floating more than 200 m away. It was not, as Kyle had thought, tethered to the yacht.

Their only chance now was a small, bright yellow inflatable boat, the yacht's tender. Kyle tried to start the tender to go to the life raft but the engine wouldn't kick in. Wearing life jackets, clutching emergency rations, some flares and the yacht's EPIRB, they pushed away from *Llama Lo* and watched as it slowly rolled over.

It was just after 6 pm, and as darkness descended on the Indian Ocean the two men drifted away from the capsized catamaran and switched on their EPIRB.

Sea conditions were deteriorating, and a gale force wind of 50 knots was battering the two men. However, many thousands of kilometres away, the French Maritime Rescue Coordination Centre (MRCC) at Cap Gris-Nez picked up the EPIRB signal on their computers.

Following international protocol, they alerted the South African MRCC to the signal, as it was coming from off our coast, and a huge rescue effort began. Five ships in the area were diverted to the position from which the EPIRB was transmitting to try and find the yacht, and the East London Sea Rescue volunteers, as well as an SAAF Oryx helicopter, were put on standby.

Through the night, Kyle and Jean took turns to paddle the little rubber boat, trying to keep its head into the sea. Huge six- to seven-metre swells, sometimes crumbling at the top, threatened to turn them over. Kyle ignited a handheld flare ... with no luck. They decided to keep the flares for the next day. In the distance, they could see the lights of the ships searching for them, and with some luck they hoped they would be able to fire the flares when the ships were closer.

Then disaster struck.

As the sun rose on a seemingly empty ocean, a massive wave, bigger than the rest, flipped the little boat, dumping Jean and Kyle into the sea. Kyle had tethered his backpack to the dinghy and as soon as they had scrambled on to the upturned hull he pulled it up. Inside was his laptop and, more importantly, enough fresh water to last the men up to six days. But the supplies that weren't tied to the boat, including their flares, were gone.

'I saw my packet of FutureLife cereal floating past and grabbed it so at least we would have that to eat,' said Kyle. After resting on the capsized tender for about two hours another huge wave flipped it again, right side up, and Kyle and Jean scrambled back into the boat.

Out on the horizon they could see ships. The men were exhausted and, resting on the rubber boat, they hoped that the ships were searching for them. By now they had drifted far from *Llama Lo*, and the first ships to arrive at the wreck reported no signs of life. Soon after that the life raft was found. Also empty. By now the NSRI craft

Spirit of Lotto and an Oryx helicopter from the SAAF's 15 Squadron were on their way to the search area.

Sailing southward down the East Coast, nearing the search area, was the massive French container carrier *CMA CGM Rossini*, 277 m of ship. As the sun rose off the horizon, the duty officer called Captain Lepage to the bridge. It was 7.10 am. The Cap Gris-Nez MRCC had alerted the crew to the distress signal from the French yacht. By a strange twist of fate it was the same MRCC where Captain Lepage had done his military service in 1988. On the bridge, he asked for the coordinates of the EPIRB pings and plotted them on his chart. A master mariner with vast experience on super-sized ships, Captain Lepage is also a volunteer with the French sea rescue service, the SNSM, in his hometown of La Rochelle.

'At 12.15 we called Port Elizabeth Radio and told them that we were getting close to the position. They asked me to proceed there,' said Lepage. 'I changed my course.' Watching his chart plotter, he knew that there were already five ships in the area. One had found the capsized catamaran, another the empty life raft. But none had followed the EPIRB position, which was drifting down the coast.

'I contacted my company and the MRCC in Gris-Nez and suggested that we chase the EPIRB,' said Captain Lepage.

At 4.15 pm the *Rossini* glided up alongside the wreck of the catamaran: 'It was close to my starboard bow and we gave a blast on the horn thinking that they might be inside. There was no response. No sign.'

He gave the order to increase power and bent over his chart. The EPIRB pings that he had been given by France were two hours behind. They were in a straight line indicating the drift of the EPIRB – but how could it be that it was not with the life raft?

'I thought immersion suits. They must be wearing immersion suits. And holding the EPIRB,' said Lepage.

'We had six pairs of binoculars on the bridge, so I called six men up and divided the area to search into sectors. Each man must concentrate only on his sector.'

And then came the curve ball.

The French MRCC gave the next EPIRB position way off to the left of where the drift should have been. With darkness approaching, this called for calm thinking and some careful calculations. Captain Lepage gave the order to turn to port, although he believed that the position was wrong; he had worked out that they would have just enough time to check, to make sure, and then, if need be, to loop around and sail back up the drift line that they had been searching.

There was, as he had thought, nothing where the last EPIRB position was thought to be.

Increasing the speed of the massive ship, Lepage looked at his watch. Sunset was too close. Calculating where the correct position of the two-hour-old EPIRB ping should have been and where the drift would have it now, he gave the order to keep the heading down the coast.

'Sir, should we not turn now?' the chief officer asked.

'Not yet,' replied the captain. 'Not yet.'

It was a call that needed to be taken by instinct. The calculations showed a position, and then it came down to a master seaman's hunch, a feeling, which some have in them, and others do not.

At 5.50 pm the captain gave the command.

'Turn to starboard now.'

The *Rossini*'s bow came around and Captain Lepage lined it up on his track in the opposite direction, before the wild goose chase off the drift line.

Conscious of the fast-approaching darkness, he called for an increase of speed. The tension on the bridge was palpable. The crew knew that if they did not find the two yachtsmen before dark their chances of survival would not be good.

'There!'

The call was from the chief engineer, Lyes Lassel, who was scanning the port sector. He had seen a single flash of orange. Binoculars swung on to his quadrant and, clearly now, the men on the bridge spotted two orange specks.

They had seen the horseshoe collars of the life jackets that Kyle and

Jean were wearing. The great ship slowed down and turned towards the spot indicated.

Kyle and Jean had been watching the ship for a couple of hours, slowly paddling towards it. 'And then they gave three blasts on their horn,' said Kyle, 'and then we knew …' His voice trails off and he looks down at the floor.

It was 15 minutes before sunset. Ahead lay one of the biggest challenges ever for the captain and his crew: how to get the huge ship alongside the tiny rubber boat and then get the two men up the wall of steel to safety?

'I used the wind and the currents,' said Captain Lepage.

With consummate skill, he edged the *Rossini* close to the little yacht tender, leaving Kyle and Jean only a few metres to paddle to reach the side of the ship.

Despite his exhaustion, youth was on Kyle's side. He was up the ship's ladder in a flash. But Jean, knowing that Kyle was now safe, simply had no energy, no strength left. He had held on bravely through the 25-hour ordeal, focusing on getting his young crewman to safety. Now exhaustion washed over him. As he started the nine-metre climb up the rope ladder, his hands slipped and he crashed into the sea, losing his life jacket.

The *Rossini's* chief officer, Sadi Resdedant, rushed to help. Dropping a helicopter strop (a padded loop) on a rope and shouting encouragement to the exhausted sailor, he and the crew managed to get the elderly skipper on board.

'I thought that we would lose him,' said Captain Lepage.

The two sailors were given five-star treatment on the huge ship. Hot showers, new clothing and shoes were presented to them. The food was exceptional and soft beds a welcome treat as the ship sailed for Cape Town. At last, three days after their ordeal started, they were taken ashore by the Table Bay Sea Rescue volunteers on the *Spirit of Vodacom* for an emotional reunion with Kyle's parents.

12 One lucky man

While writing and researching this book, I went through scores of operation reports, news stories, interviews and scrapbooks. Every now and then, something would leap out and be so compelling, that I would make a note and say to myself, 'This has to be in the book.' A rescue operation run out of Hout Bay (Station 8) on 2 and 3 February 2016, and written up by coxswain James Beaumont, was one of those. But instead of trying to convert it into journalese, I decided to run the report verbatim with a few minor edits. That's how riveting it is. The name of the yacht and skipper have been left out to spare him some blushes.

ASSISTANCE TO SOLO SKIPPER ABOARD the 26-ft yacht ... suffering mechanical failure approx. 69 nautical miles west of Slangkop Lighthouse. The vessel had also run out of diesel fuel. The mechanical failure of the vessel turned out to be a broken rudder, rendering the boat inoperable in the sea conditions.

Attempts were made to tow the vessel back to Hout Bay, but in the prevailing sea conditions, the tow became too dangerous as the vessel could not keep a fixed course due to the broken rudder. The decision was made to evacuate the skipper of the stricken vessel and abandon the tow. The yacht was released and a shipping hazard was broadcast by Cape Town Radio. The casualty vessel was released at approx. 20.00 hrs.

Location of casualty vessel: 70 miles West of Hout Bay at 34° 19.0'S 16° 58.5'E on the 3 000 m contour.

Crew: Coxswain – James Beaumont (Cat A: >9m, commercial SAMSA certified and endorsed for Class 1 rescue craft); Deputy Coxswain – Sven Gussenhoven; Crew: Spencer Oldham and Karin Tunley.

Casualty vessel: Yacht type – Home-built Dudley Dix Fin Keel Sloop, Length 26 ft, Beam about 6 ft.

Wind conditions: On departure it was blowing about 25 knots southeast. Built up quickly to 30–35 knots south once out of lee of the peninsula. On scene: 30 knots gusting to 45 knots south. On return: 35 knots gusting to 45 knots south/southeast.

Sea state: On departure two-metre swell from SW, prominent wind chop building to three- to four-metre sea, severe wind chop with bad quartering seas (striking at 45 degrees to the vessel's heading) and difficult helming conditions.

On scene: Three- to four-metre sea with bad quartering seas and difficult helming conditions. VERY confused seas. Vessel was completely unstable and moving violently with the sea when stationary.

On return: Horrendous sea state – the worst I have experienced. VERY short confused and quartering sea; four-metre-plus waves breaking over the bow constantly and periodically five-metre-plus right over the top of the boat from the starboard quarter. All crew need to be strapped in and holding on to avoid injury even when not under way.

Visibility: On departure, very good.

On scene: OK.

During attempted tow: Failing light.

On return: Zero – night with no moon and full cloud cover.

Communications: Our communications with Cape Town Radio remained very good on VHF 16 throughout the operation, even at 70 miles out. We had no need to use the HF SSB radio. VHF comms with Station 8 was lost on the repeater at about 15 miles out. We had no comms with the casualty vessel at all until we got broken comms at about 1.5 miles from his position. Cape Town Radio lost all comms with the casualty about two hours before our ETA.

Making way to the casualty: Conditions were rough but with careful helming we were able to average 12 to 14 knots. The continuous exaggerated motion of the boat caused diesel to leak from the fuel tank breathers (later determined to be a crack in the breather) – causing an almost overpowering smell of diesel in the cabin so we had to leave the stern cabin door open and the top hatch open to create an air flow. This let some water into the cabin, but it was our only option. Eventually the hinges on the hatch sheared off and we made running repairs to keep it shut with lashings. Fuel flow was averaging 70 litres per hour (35 per motor).

Locating the casualty: We received two known positions via Cape Town Radio about an hour apart. From this we were able to calculate the drift pattern of the casualty and calculated a position one mile to windward of his predicted position at the time of our predicted ETA, which we updated as we got closer. Once we reached this position, we proceeded in the direction of the drift while radioing the casualty constantly on Channel 16 while we looked for a reading on the RDF and for a blip on the radar. We vectored on to the right course based on the weak RDF signals and eventually got audible comms and a good RDF signal, and a short while later we picked him up on radar. We only got sight of the casualty mast at about 500 m due to the sea state.

On scene: The skipper was found sitting on deck in shorts and a T-shirt with no life jacket and no harness. After correcting all unsafe situations, we established that the yacht had no rudder at all. The vessel was lying with its sails furled, but with a sea anchor (too short) streaming from the bow. We transferred the towline with instructions and (with almost absolute doubt as to the potential success) began the tow.

Some very important points on yachts: This yacht has a fin keel. The keel serves two purposes: first, to act as ballast to increase the righting moment on the yacht ('stiffness'), and, second, to create lift through its foil shape and angle of attack to the water. It basically converts sideways force into forward force.

The effect of this physics means that when the yacht heels over the angle of attack of the keel is changed and it generates lift in the opposite direction to the heel. This is a desirable characteristic and is designed into the yacht. The counterbalance to this lift required to keep the yacht going straight and not just pointing up into the wind and falling over onto the opposite tack is the rudder; this is known as 'weather helm' and if you do not counteract it the yacht just flops over violently from side to side.

It therefore stands to reason that with no rudder you will have no means of counteracting this force. If you were only relying on the wind the yacht will eventually just lose way and flop from side to side.

However, if you are towing, then you are generating forward force and, accordingly, lift, so the vessel will go sideways on one tack until the angle of tow pulls it over onto the other side (violently) and it will repeat the process on the other tack. And so it is that you end up zig-zagging all over the ocean with no way of preventing it. Add to this a violent quartering sea and a healthy crosswind and you have a no-win situation. Nevertheless, we decided to give it a go.

The tow: In our case we started the tow at 2 knots and the yacht was skidding and bouncing all over the show. We then deployed a bunch of lines off the yacht's stern to create a stabilising drag, but the situation was only mildly improved. The skipper on the yacht, at 2 knots, declared 'this is not working'; he was in a dangerous situation and injury was imminent. The light was failing and it was a hopeless situation. Even if we could have towed, we had nowhere near enough fuel to get back if we were towing. It was a sad but obvious decision and I made the decision quickly to drop the tow and transfer the patient before the light failed completely.

The transfer: There are no words to describe the complexity of this manoeuvre in the conditions we were in. We were lucky – I managed to transfer the yacht skipper with no injury to crew, casualty or vessel. Plan B was to swim the casualty across on a line but that would have been another problem altogether.

The return trip: All crew and the casualty were then strapped down as tightly as possible and we began the slow trip back in zero visibility (with all lights off to retain night vision, you could not even see your hand in front of your face) and in unspeakable conditions. It was not possible to speak on the radio or manually navigate on paper (as I always do as a backup) – the boat was bucking like a mechanical bull. Both hands were needed to hold on. Eating, drinking, etc. was not an option; even with the boat not under way, the action was so severe that one could not maintain a footing. Helmets were worn by crew if not on a seat. In these conditions seasickness is inevitable, and two of our crew went down badly and were totally disabled. I even started to feel nauseous (but fortunately not sick), and we were unable to eat or drink, which made the nausea worse.

With careful helming, based on feel, we were able to maintain an average of 8 knots with a fuel burn of about 50 litres an hour. The boat was quartered continuously due to our direction and the boat was knocked over a few times and once right on to her port side to about 60 degrees (fortunately we were all strapped in). At no point did the hull feel incapable or unable to deal with the conditions. Slamming was avoided at all costs, but in such a short sea (very choppy, with a short swell interval) with zero visibility there were one or two slams, but nothing bad. Ventilation and diesel fumes remained a big challenge on the return trip. The motors were operating outside of their design parameters as they are not commercial motors. There were a great many oil pressure warnings and engine shutdowns to clear alarms and check for problems as the boat pitched and rolled. Fine throttle response was critical in the conditions, and the electronic throttles were great, but their position relative to the sitting position of the skipper became ergonomically tricky over the long period.

We were only just within our safety margin of fuel on arrival in Hout Bay.

Arrival at Station 8: This deserves mentioning and admiring. In spite of it being the early hours of the morning, the majority of the active crew of Station 8 were at the base to assist on our return, all with smiles and ready to muck in and do the refuel and extensive clean-up. It was an exemplary display of camaraderie, teamwork and selflessness.

Learnings and observations: I should start by saying that if we were to do it all again tomorrow, as we did it on this call, we would do so without hesitation. We make do with what we have, and this is not an issue, but it would be remiss not to take these opportunities to learn and improve on the tools we use and the way we go about things. These are covered below.

The rescue boat

The hull: While built incredibly solidly and well, the Breede-class boat is just too small to deal with this sort of call. She did well, but the waterline length worked against her in a big way. The sea was tossing her around like a piece of flotsam.

The engines: Power (or more specifically, torque) was more than adequate, but multiple engine alarms due to the motion is sub-optimal and difficult to manage in these conditions.

Towline configuration: Having the towline on the bow is really not ideal on a call like this. Deploying the towline in this configuration is a very time-consuming and arduous task that is not without risks. Comms are impossible and it requires significant physical effort and results in large amounts of rope lying on the deck at certain times. A far better solution would be to deploy the towline from the stern in some way, but this needs careful thought and a good look at what the Royal National Lifeboat Institution (UK) and US Coast Guard are doing.

Steering: The steering gearing is pretty low, and in conditions like this we experienced some times when rapid, aggressive steering was required and this was hard to achieve with the steering on the Breede.

Seating: Simply put, you MUST be strapped in in these conditions and we have only four seats capable of this in the cabin. Helmets are also required but not usually carried (we took spares). The damping (cushioning) on the helm and navigator's seats was really necessary and worked very well.

Ventilation: This is a serious problem, as it is completely inadequate, and needs to be addressed as a priority.

Engine noise: This is also a problem as it becomes extremely uncomfortable after several hours. My ears were ringing for some time after our return. This cannot be a healthy long-term solution. Moreover, you cannot hear engine alarms or bilge alarms (the forward cabin door was closed).

Fuel: The boat does not carry sufficient fuel for this range.

Rations: This should be an easy one. We must have rations available. Our long-haul rations had been 'raided' on the base and were all but depleted, so we effectively had to make another plan but had no time to do it. Some of us (me included) cannot eat high-GI foods (for medical reasons) and we need low-GI sustainable energy, such as nuts. I strongly suggest we enforce the long-haul ration rules and make sure we have a couple of sealed low-GI packs as a rule. As it happened, I had not eaten a scrap for over 30 hours on our return as there was nothing available – doable, but not pleasant!

Seasickness: This is inevitable on a call like this, and I do not allow people on the boat who have taken prophylactics, as it causes drowsiness, etc. This basically excludes people who are prone to seasickness from doing calls like this, which reduces the risk for me, BUT what do we do when the malady strikes at sea? Two crew went down and both have good sea legs. This needs thought as well.

Diesel fumes: This was a big problem. We need to make a plan here. The tanks were 100% full on departure and we rotated all the tanks early to drop the levels uniformly but the fumes prevailed from start to end (later determined to be a leak on the breather pipe).

Night vision: The lighting on the engine instrumentation is far too bright (particularly the fuel gauges). This is probably an easy fix.

Screen wipers: While not too relevant on this call, as the visibility was zero, the wipers are not able to keep up with the spray in these conditions.

Communications: Somewhat incredibly, the comms with Cape Town Radio were remarkable all the way out to 70 miles on VHF. I think we should see this as an anomaly rather than the rule. Needless to say, long-range comms are a necessity if we are to do calls like this. We had HF and I know how to use it, so we would have been OK, but most crews are not that comfortable on HF. A satellite phone would be first prize but would also have been tricky to get a satellite lock and keep it with the boat pitching the way it was.

Crew capability: Crew competence and capability were exemplary. This is testimony to the training and selection process we go through. I am unable to make even one critical observation regarding the performance of the crew. Simply put, it was flawless.

The casualty: The hapless skipper had no idea as to the peril he faced. His only sailing experience is on the Vaal Dam. There is very little chance he would have survived as his radio was only broadcasting up to about a mile at sea level and he had no mast-mounted antenna and he had drifted out of range of Cape Town Radio. His battery was starting to fail and he had no backup. He had no diesel for charging. His vessel was not certified for offshore let alone Category A (ocean-going) – he had no life raft, no HF (high-frequency radio), no EPIRB (Emergency Position Indicating Radio Beacon), he did not even have flares … He was unable to give us a coherent position when we located him on RDF and eventually got comms and only had one, erratic, handheld GPS with failing batteries. I don't know what co-competence he holds, but I doubt it is more than an E. He basically did not know where he was.

In short, he is one lucky man.

Conclusion: Firstly, I must point out that I have been at sea for over 35 years, all over the world, in many different oceans, seas and vessels, either in my professional capacity, as a rescue coxswain or for leisure. Needless to say, I have seen and experienced a great deal of circumstances and situations.

The conditions and circumstances we operated in on this call were without doubt the most challenging I have ever experienced. I have been in worse conditions, but on much bigger vessels, which handle it without too much fuss.

The success of this call is testimony to the professionalism, equipment and training we do as an institution and we all need to be congratulated on that.

Lastly, the way Station 8 and the crew pulled together on this call was nothing short of remarkable.

13 Disaster off Duiker Island

Andrew Ingram

> On 14 October 2012, the Hout Bay-based whale-watching
> charter boat Miroshga *capsized off Duiker Island, with 37*
> *passengers on board, after a pump failed and the boat flooded.*
> *Crewman John Roberts and Welsh tourist Peter Hyett died in*
> *the tragedy.*

IF THERE ARE TWO THINGS that a Sea Rescue volunteer has to be
able to do, they are juggle appointments and manage time. And so
it was that the traditional Sunday morning training session at NSRI
Station 2, Bakoven, had been moved to Saturday afternoon. I was
the duty coxswain that day.

The five of us who were on duty met at the Sea Rescue base, on
Bakoven beach, at 2 pm. It was a pleasant enough afternoon and, as
predicted, the southeaster was starting to work up into a good blow.
Which was what we had hoped for, as our crew had not yet put our
new 6.5-m rescue boat, *Rotarian Schipper*, through its paces in the
notorious Cape wind.

We started off slowly, practising some first aid and working with a
spine board in the shed, and as usual there was the joking and good
laughs that a tight team has.

Bakoven Station Commander Bruce Davidson arrived unex-
pectedly, and a couple of the crew wandered into the boat shed to
fetch their wetsuits as I stood and chatted with him. He pulled a

portable VHF radio out of his bag and said with a smile, 'How's this for a nice birthday present?' Perhaps it is only something that two males could admit to, but it was a beautiful radio …

I noticed him switching it on as he moved towards the shed door, and I turned to my crew and said, 'Okay, let's suit up and get going, PJ needs to be home by 18h00.'

And then Bruce burst back in through the door 'Mayday,' he said. 'Guys, there is a Mayday on 16.'

A Mayday is no joke.

It is an urgent call for help, and it took a second or two for this to sink in. Bruce was being absolutely serious. He had switched his new radio on and the first message that he heard was 'MAYDAY … DUIKER ISLAND … MAYDAY …'

I felt my throat tighten and yelled, 'Suit up, let's go!'

Bruce went into the ops room and the crew, quiet now, started pulling on their gear. We were in automatic mode. This is what we train for. Hours and hours down at the base so that when we need to work fast it just happens, our hands know what to do.

At one stage I found myself passing our inflatable life jackets to rescue swimmer Ernesta Swanepoel: 'Throw them in the boat. We can put them on when we have launched.'

As she pushed them through the boat cradle, there was a sound like an explosion as one of the life jackets inflated. We both recoiled in shock.

The defective item was discarded and another passed across.

Someone was at the winch control. I grabbed the trailer tiller and yelled, 'Clear out front?'

The response came back. 'Clear.'

'Coming down.'

It was a blur. Bruce was yelling, 'Duiker Island … people in the water … boat capsized …'

And then I was in the boat. At the helm. Radio aerial up, engines down. Start port. Start starboard. Life jacket on.

I looked at my crew.

Already in the boat was my second in command, Howard Bell. I couldn't have wished for a better man. On the port side in the water, looking up at me, was Ernesta – as close to fearless as they come. A scuba diver, and a lawyer by profession, she is game for anything. Next to her was PJ Rabie, big and strong with a quick smile and a logical mind – the thinker on our crew. On the starboard side was Luke van Riet – our terrier. Everything Luke does is at double speed. In a tight situation when quick thinking is needed, he is the guy you want to have with you. I remember thinking that it was a great crew to have for what could be a very difficult situation.

I looked up and towards Bakoven Rock. The bow of the rescue boat was lined up so I yelled, 'Okay, let's go!' and slipped the engines into gear.

The three volunteers hauled themselves over the pontoons and into the boat, found their positions and started helping each other put their life jackets on.

I hit the engine tilt button with my right thumb and watched the gauges until they showed that the engines were lowered all the way down. I glanced at Howard: 'Crew okay? Can I go?'

'Ja, go!' came the response.

I pushed the throttles forward hard and the boat leapt onto the plane. We curved around the inside of Bakoven Rock and turned to port, towards Hout Bay. I scanned the sea, taking in the clouds pouring over Table Mountain, the deep swell and powerful wind further out, and the short chop with windblown spray close to the shore. I needed to find the sweet spot, the line that I could run on at full throttle, not too close in to be dangerous and not too far out that the crew would be hammered and physically exhausted before we got on scene.

And then the port engine died. We all felt it. My heart sank. I pulled the throttles back into neutral and needlessly yelled, 'Port engine dead,' as I slid down to check the ignition.

Luke moved to the engines, opened a hatch and yelled 'The bulb is soft!'

Fuel starvation.

How on earth did that happen, I wondered. Ernesta opened the fuel hatch, and we all saw that the port fuel lever was in the wrong position. The lever was pulled across, fuel line opened, the bulb primed and the engine swung into life on the third try.

We had lost at most two minutes. Again our training had paid off.

I focused on the sea, swinging the boat to port to try and get us on top of the wind-driven waves.

'Crew okay?' I asked Howard. He wiped the spray from his face, looked back and confirmed, 'Ja, all okay.'

We took some big hits, smashing into swells with the force of a car crash, once knocking us to the deck.

And then I found the sweet spot. Just before Llandudno.

The wind whipped at our heads as I juggled the engine trim, looking for the perfect position. We were flying at around 30 knots as I turned out of Sandy Bay. Looking up from my instruments I saw a life raft ahead. Perhaps a mile out to sea, but even in those conditions it was clearly a life raft. As we moved out of the protection of Karbonkelberg, the swells deepened and I was forced to pull back on the throttles. We were becoming airborne too often.

It seemed like seconds later that we were alongside. There was one man in the life raft, and I remember clearly thinking, 'That's strange, he's dry.' Then he was in our rescue boat and we were again flying towards Duiker Island. Howard had radioed in to our base that we had one man from the life raft.

And then we were on scene.

I scanned from the left. There was an unmarked rigid inflatable boat (RIB) with about six men in diving suits. There was *Nauticat*, a big, red tour boat that runs out of Hout Bay, and there was the rescue boat from Station 8, Hout Bay, *Albie Matthews*.

It was only then that I saw the upturned catamaran hull with a diver on the stern, trying to hold on to a body in the water. I edged as close as I could and turned to Luke, 'Go, go, go!'

He was already in midair.

Seconds later, Luke had the man at the side of our rescue boat, and then they were in the boat. PJ started CPR.

The boat with the divers aboard came closer, their faces etched with tension, and the guy on the helm yelled at me, 'There are people stuck under there,' pointing to the upturned hull.

I looked at the wash and decided instantly that it would be way too dangerous to send any of our crew under the boat, so instead turned towards the Hout Bay rescue boat.

Lying on their starboard pontoon was a big man, his chest naked. Towards the stern of the boat a couple of the rescue crew were huddled around a small woman. She was very pale and had the thousand-yard stare of someone in severe shock. I looked at the Hout Bay coxswain and shouted, 'I'm going to run for Hout Bay. Can I take her for you?'

He nodded. We pulled alongside and in a flash she was on our boat. I turned the helm for the harbour.

Howard depressed our mic's transmission button: 'Rescue 8 base, this is Rescue 2. We are leaving the scene. We have two casualties aboard and CPR in progress.'

The wind was strong and the swell deep so it was impossible to get the speed that I would have liked. Two of my crew were holding the woman in the stern. She was wrapped in blankets. And Ernesta had just taken over CPR from PJ.

Luke had cut his hand on the propeller of the upturned boat, so he was on the radio.

'Rescue 8 base, this is Rescue 2. ETA four minutes. Are the medics on standby? Over.'

'Rescue 2 from 8 Base. Affirmative. Come alongside at the refuelling jetty.'

And then we were there. It seemed like there were hundreds of people on the quay as we entered the harbour. Medics swarmed onto our rescue boat, Ernesta handed her patient over, and suddenly it was only our crew on the boat again.

'Rescue 8 base, this is Rescue 2, I am heading back. Over.'

'Rescue 2 from 8 Base, affirmative.'

'Let go fore, let go aft.' And I played the throttles swinging the bow around, quickly opening them up, turning out of the harbour towards the Sentinel.

We flew through the gap between Duiker Island and the mainland, carved through the channel and made for the position where we expected to see the hull.

The sea was empty.

'Ask Rescue 8 base where she is,' I told Luke.

The response was quick: 'Drifting towards Die Perd.'

That is one heck of a drift, I thought, as we got back up on the plane. The sea was getting bigger, and then suddenly, between swells, close inshore, one of my crew spotted the tiny 4.2-m *Nedbank Rescuer* from Hout Bay. I turned to meet it, but our talk was cut short by a huge wave racing towards us. Both boats sped forward and then moved out to a safer area. I was told that the upturned catamaran hull was being pushed towards the rocks.

Among the crew on the tiny rescue boat was Riaan Steyn, whom we know as Tank.

Tank is young and very powerful. I had one crew spot open on my boat and asked if I could take Tank. There was a nod and he jumped across. I swung our bow around and we turned back in towards Maori Bay and the rock known as Die Perd.

And there was the hull. It was way too close in for my liking, but those divers' words were echoing through my mind, 'There are people in there …'

'Tank, will you go?' I asked.

His eyes fixed on the boat, he just nodded. We were close enough now, and over the side went Tank. A few strokes later he was pulling himself up between the two hulls. We heard him bang and shout … and then, with complete clarity, a return bang, bang, bang.

Ernesta turned towards me, her face alight. 'They're alive! Did you hear that? Did you hear that?'

I turned away, covered in goose bumps, and yelled to Tank, 'Ask how many are in there.'

'Three,' was the answer.

'Rescue 8 base, this is Rescue 2. We have three survivors trapped in the hull. Please get those divers here as fast as possible. Over.'

I put Luke in the water and he swam to the hull, joining Tank in trying to reassure the people trapped inside that we would get them out.

Carefully we circled the hull, avoiding the rope floating around it. There was no way that we could dive under the hull. It was simply too dangerous. So all we could do was hold the hull, which had now drifted into Maori Bay, and try to prevent it from being pushed onto the rocks.

It was with relief that we then saw our big sister from the Waterfront arriving. *Spirit of Vodacom* is a powerful rescue platform, and at once I asked for her to take over the tow.

It seemed to take an age, but at last the first divers arrived – the Metro dive squad. They assessed the situation and put divers in the water.

Juggling my throttles I held the rescue boat close and then suddenly there was an explosion of bubbles and a diver surfaced, holding on to a woman. We moved in fast. The diver's mask had been knocked off and everybody seemed to be yelling.

'I've hit my head. Take her, take her!' shouted the diver.

Her long hair swirling around her is the last image that I have of her in the water, and then she was in the boat. Two of my crew were with her and the other helped the Metro diver into the boat.

The flood of relief was immense. We had done it. Another person was safe. We turned for Hout Bay, leaving the other rescue boats and the police divers to work out how to get the last two out.

'Rescue 8 Base, this is Rescue 2. We have one patient aboard. ETA 15 minutes.'

As we entered Hout Bay, I turned to my crew and again asked, 'All okay?' Howard looked up and shook his head in the negative.

'She's convulsing. GO, GO!' he shouted.

I clenched my jaw and floored the throttles. There was no way that we were going to lose her now.

No way.

We flew into the harbour and up to the jetty. Again medics swarmed on to the boat and our patient – who now had a name, Bronwyn – was safe.

Howard looked across at me and grinned. It felt good.

Again we headed back out to the huddle of rescue boats around the hull, and one after the other the last two women were brought to safety by police divers.

Suddenly we found ourselves alone with the hull. The other boats had all left with the rescued women. We were asked to stay with the hull. Our adrenaline was gone and the cold started to bite. The sun had set, and I was worried that two of my crew were hypothermic.

Every ten minutes we gave our position, and there was no talking apart from a shout when wind-driven spray drenched us.

And then the radio crackled to life.

'Rescue 2, this is Rescue 2 Base.' The tone was urgent.

'I have another call for you. Two people in the water, boat overturned, Saunders Rocks. Go now.'

There was a brief silence, and then the exhausted crew sprang into action. We covered the five or so nautical miles in record time, only to find that it was a false alarm. An emergency beacon had been lost off a boat, and the misunderstanding took a little while to sort out.

For the Bakoven crew, the call-out was now over. We were finished. Slowly this time, I turned for home and tried to duck when the spray sheeted across the boat.

After what seemed like an eternity, we turned into the Bakoven channel. It was pitch dark and the tide was very low. Slowly I guided the boat over the last few metres and, glancing up, could see silhouettes of people waiting for us.

Suddenly they burst into applause. I turned away, pretending to wipe seawater from my face. It had been a very intense six hours.

14 *Another chance at life*

Rob Mousley

IT WAS 3 DECEMBER 2006. The big SAAF Oryx helicopter hovered over Casper Kruger as he lay semi-conscious on his surf ski. 'It was flying only about two ski-lengths above the water, about 12 m,' he said. 'It flew past about 200 m. Then I saw it turn and I knew I had another chance at life.'

By the time he was found, Casper Kruger had been in the water for nearly seven hours.

Casper had been taking part in the seventh Cape Discovery *Men's Health* Surf Ski Series race from Monwabisi Beach to Gordon's Bay, a distance of just over 19 km. An unseasonable frontal system had arrived in Cape Town, bringing with it a strong northwesterly wind and rain squalls. There was no doubt that conditions would be testing, but Casper had made a conscious decision to take part. Although the wind was strong, he'd done the route before and was confident of his abilities. He had one B-grade time in the series and needed another to be promoted from C grade.

He was prepared, too. His paddle was attached by a leash to his new Robberg Express surf ski. He was wearing a Neoprene top and red windbreaker under his personal flotation device (PFD). He also had a New Balance cap to keep his head warm. His clothing would play a vital role later in the day.

While he was preparing for the paddle, Casper's wife, Sandra, asked him if he was going to take his flare. He tried briefly to take the thick plastic packaging off the flare, then threw it impatiently to one side.

At the briefing, the number of the local NSRI station was given out and some of the paddlers keyed it into their mobile phones, which they would carry with them in protective waterproof bags. But many of the paddlers, including Casper, weren't carrying them.

The start at Monwabisi was deceptive: the beach was sheltered from the wind and the waters of False Bay were flat, except for small swells coming in from the south.

Soon after setting off, however, the paddlers felt the full force of the wind. The waves built rapidly and started to break. Then the wind veered to the north, driving the skis offshore, blowing side-on to the paddlers' course instead of coming from directly behind as they had expected.

About 40 minutes into the race, a breaking wave combined with a strong gust of wind knocked Casper from his ski. He clambered back on, but almost immediately fell off again. And again. And again. He'd get back on the ski, but would lose his balance every time he tried to pick up his paddle.

Very soon, he started to get cold and tired. He decided to rest in the water for a while and then try again.

While he was clinging to his ski he saw the race safety boat go past some 20 m away. The crew didn't see or hear him and the boat soon disappeared. Now he was truly on his own.

After a while, he mounted his ski again, but 'I was already very cold and weak,' he said. 'Everything seemed to be moving in slow motion and my reactions were very slow.' He soon fell off again.

Frustration at his inability to stay on the ski began to be replaced by the realisation that he was in serious danger. His body was shaking with cold, and that became his primary concern – how to minimise the effect of the cold water. He reasoned that he had to get as much of his body out of the water as he could, so, placing his paddle underneath him, he draped his body over the ski. However, it was 'so uncomfortable with the paddle there, that I let it go to drag behind the ski on the leash'.

He realised that he was drifting in the direction of Cape Hangklip, some 40 km to the south, so he started kicking his legs, trying to make progress towards the shore to the east of his position. At first the paddle got in the way as he tried to kick, and after a while he realised that it was gone. The leash must have become detached from it.

By this time he was shivering violently and had lost all feeling in his hands. 'My hands and fingernails went white,' he said, 'and I couldn't tell how secure my grip was on the ski.'

Meanwhile the breaking waves had become much larger. While the rest of the fleet made their way through two-metre waves, the seas were much bigger further out in the bay. 'About every seventh wave, I could hear one coming,' he said, 'and it would break right over me.' Being tumbled by the waves was terrifying. He knew that his only hope was to stay with the ski, and, without any feeling in his hands, he wasn't sure he could hang on to it. He thrust his arms through the foot straps and attempted to tie himself to the ski with his paddle leash. 'I couldn't tie a knot,' he said, 'but I sort of wrapped the leash in a tangle.'

Meanwhile a massive search operation had started.

The first paddler to cross the finish line had alerted the race organisers to the fact that conditions had drastically deteriorated. The organisers had contacted the local NSRI station, at Gordon's Bay (Station 9), to tell them that their help might be needed.

When Casper did not arrive at Gordon's Bay, the NSRI immediately activated rescue craft from Gordon's Bay, Strandfontein and Simon's Town. Simultaneously, the Metro Red Cross AMS and Vodacom Netcare 911 helicopters were scrambled.

After two hours of fruitless searching, the NSRI requested assistance from the SAAF, and this came in the form of an Oryx helicopter. The NSRI and the SAAF cooperate in rescues, in the form of a joint Air Sea Rescue unit (designated Station 29), and the rescue call-outs are considered training for the chopper crews.

Casper saw the searching helicopters several times: 'They were so close I could see the faces of the people inside. I tried to wave but they didn't see me.' He added: 'The sun came out several times, and I wished I had a stainless steel signalling mirror.'

By this time he'd stopped kicking: 'I couldn't kick any more, my hamstrings were cramping.' In fact, his entire body was going into spasm.

By 5.30 pm the rescuers were giving up hope. The two civilian helicopters had reached their fuel limits and had returned to base.

'Eventually,' Casper said, 'I stopped shivering and started blacking out. It was actually quite peaceful. It seemed to be getting darker and I was seeing little stars.'

And that was when he heard the thudding of the Oryx helicopter's rotors and lifted his head to see it flying over him.

The wind had suddenly died, swinging to the south and calming the seas almost magically. The Air Force crew were on the third leg of their search pattern when one of the flight engineers thought he saw something. 'There it … no it isn't … yes it is – he's there.' The all-white ski was difficult to spot among the white crests of the breaking waves.

But there it was, with the semi-conscious Casper draped over it.

Two rescue swimmers, Tony Onwood and Miles Bisset, dropped into the water. 'He was very weak,' one of the swimmers later reported, 'and we got him off the ski very quickly and hoisted him in the rescue basket.' In the helicopter Casper began shaking uncontrollably. 'We see a lot of hypothermia cases,' one of the crew said, 'and I estimate that he had 15, maybe 20 minutes left. It was that close.'

They flew him to Mediclinic Vergelegen in Somerset West. 'They were great,' Casper said. 'They warmed me up and pumped me full of fluids.' He spent Sunday night and most of Monday in the hospital before being released in a painful but otherwise healthy state.

Looking back on his ordeal, he's mostly just thankful. 'An important point is that I made the decision myself to do the race,' he said. He'd looked at the conditions; he took into account the fact that Billy Harker, the race organiser, had himself withdrawn from the race. 'If

I'd known the wind was gusting like that, I'd probably not have done it. But that's the risk you take in racing.'

Bruce Bodmer, in charge in the NSRI component of the SAAF/ NSRI Air Sea Rescue unit, said afterwards, 'Casper owes his life to two things: number one, he stayed with his craft, which made it easier to find him; and number two, he kept his torso out of the water, which delayed the onset of hypothermia.

'But it was lucky that this took place in the warmer waters of False Bay,' he added. 'On the Atlantic side you've got an hour, maybe two hours at most.'

Bodmer also praised the race organisers. 'A big factor was that their admin was right,' he said. 'They knew exactly who was missing and when.' A key figure among the organisers was Billy Harker, who went on to raise over R3 million for the NSRI through the surf-ski community following this rescue.

As Casper said, no one forced him to do the race. He considered his options and made his own decision to go ahead. We all make similar choices and sometimes we get it wrong. Surf ski is a sport that includes extreme conditions, and that element of danger is often what makes it worthwhile. But there are things we can do to minimise the risks and to help rescuers find us.

Minimising the risks

If Casper had had a signalling device he could have contacted the race safety boat and would have been out of the water and safe within minutes.

Shortly after he got into trouble, the rescue boat passed within 20 m of his position. The helicopters passed over him several times later in the day. They could not see him.

The best option is to carry a mobile phone.

Everyone has a mobile phone. Waterproof bags are available from almost every kayak shop. They're not difficult to get, and not difficult to use. Memorise the national emergency number: 112.

Used properly, pencil flares are highly effective. But popping them off four kilometres out to sea when no one is looking is not using them properly. Keep some of them for when you can see your rescuers. Remember, THEY CAN'T SEE YOU. But they will see a flare.

Smoke flares are also highly effective, but you generally only have one smoke flare; you get six pencil flares.

Call for help early – while you still can.

Casper said that he was amazed (and frightened by) how quickly he lost feeling in his hands. Within 30 minutes of being in the water his hands were so cold he could not have used a cellphone or flares even if he'd had them. The lesson here is to recognise early that you're in trouble and call for help immediately while you still can.

The next best option is marine VHF radio. Why next best? Government legislation makes it difficult and expensive to own a radio. But radio is the easiest thing to use and allows you to talk directly to the boats and helicopters that are searching for you. Buy a waterproof marine VHF like the Icom IC-M71 or M32.

Whistles are very effective. Their high pitch means the sound carries for a surprising distance and is audible above engine noise. Remember that searchers will be cruising at low power (i.e. quiet) settings with all senses alert. Whistles work: I have personal experience of this.

The flight crew on the Oryx helicopter said Casper's surf ski 'looked like the crest of a wave on the water'. If you're going to be paddling offshore, paint the tips of your ski a visible colour. Neon orange is highly visible. Consider painting your paddle blades neon orange. From personal experience I know that orange blades are highly visible from a long distance.

Absolute must-have equipment

Consider Casper's equipment. He may not have had a means of signalling, but he did have the basics.

Appropriate clothing: Casper emphasised that he had been wearing a warm cap. 'Apparently some 80 per cent of your body heat is lost through your head,' he said. (His cap was blown off by the helicopter's downdraught as he was winched up.)

Paddle leash: his leash helped him stay with his ski.

Some paddlers disdain paddle leashes. Mike Schwan was one of many to fall off his ski that Sunday, and as he did so he lost his grip on his paddle – which was leashed to his ski. The ski was instantly blown out of his reach. 'I absolutely shat myself!' was his comment. But the paddle acted as a sea anchor and slowed the ski down sufficiently for Mike to be able to swim after it and catch it.

Casper couldn't get back on his ski. Several others, including at least one elite-grade paddler also battled to get back on their skis. Practise getting on your ski, and be aware that getting on bum-first can be an easier, albeit slower method than face-first. Practise both ways of doing it.

Don't stop paddling

The surf ski community was shocked by this episode. But we shouldn't let Casper's horrible experience put us off the sport. Paddling in big seas and strong winds can be exhilarating. However, we can learn from Casper's experience and reduce the risks to ourselves, our families and the people who are called in to look for us.

Finally, warm words of thanks and praise are due to the NSRI and the SAAF search and rescue team, who saved Casper in the nick of time.

Postscript

In 2015 the Marmion Marsh trophy was presented to Billy Harker for raising an incredible R3.5 million over ten years, through the surf-ski community. The citation read as follows:

In 2006, following a long search by air and sea units in foul weather conditions, in fading light, the NSRI eventually found and saved the life of surf skier Casper Kruger. Race organiser Billy Harker approached the NSRI about starting a surf ski paddlers' fundraising project. The concept was simple: a R25 per month debit-order campaign marketed into the surf-ski community and ring-fenced to fund Sea Rescue boats around the country. The funds raised have been used to build 4 rescue boats to date. *Spirit of Surfski 1* in Gordon's Bay, *Spirit of Surfski 2* in Simon's Town, *Spirit of Surfski 3* in Durban and *Spirit of Surfski 4* is currently in production and will serve at Port Elizabeth.

15 Close call on a Miller's run

David Black

THURSDAY 13 DECEMBER 2012 WAS the day the sea almost claimed me.

Summer in the Cape is when downwind surf ski paddling comes alive. The notorious prevailing southeasterly wind blasts the coastline, sometimes relentlessly, serving up ideal downwind paddling conditions.

The competitive surf ski paddling season culminates in the Cape Town Downwind races in the middle of December, followed by the Cape Point Challenge, a gruelling 50-km race around Cape Point from Scarborough beach to Fish Hoek beach. The potential for great paddling conditions, combined with these exciting races, draws many national and international paddlers to the Cape each December.

It was nine days before the Cape Point Challenge. I had been training for my second Challenge over the preceding months, set to be my first in a single ski. My intention was not to race competitively but rather to finish. The southeaster had been tearing through the Cape the whole week, and paddlers had been doing rounds of the well-known Miller's Run, a thrilling 11- to 12-km beeline from Bakoven Rock, 500 m off the Miller's Point Ski Boat Club, to Fish Hoek beach in the north.

Conditions were wild by that Thursday afternoon. A 3.5-m ground-swell was running and the southeaster was howling at 40 to 50 knots (75 to 92 km/h). While I considered myself, at 26, to be a relatively experienced paddler, with six years of river and sea paddling under my belt, these conditions were different, and I arrived at the Miller's

Point slipway with a good dose of nervous anticipation. But with what I considered to be sufficient safety precautions – a quality life jacket, a paddle leash and a ski leash in the form of tie-downs, and a mobile phone – I was ready.

I was part of a large group of about 30 paddlers that left the Miller's Point slipway shortly after 5.30 pm. We rounded Bakoven Rock at about 5.45 with the customary 'See you in Fish Hoek.'

On a downwind run, even a slight swell can make it easy to lose sight of fellow paddlers between troughs. I struggled to find my groove at the beginning, unsettled by the conditions, but I soon worked my way onto some exciting runs, heading in a north-northwesterly direction towards Fish Hoek.

But then disaster struck.

I was just over a kilometre offshore of Murdock Valley, on the southern end of Simon's Town, when a big swell broke off my aft quarter, crashing over my ski from the back right. I fell out of the ski as the wave passed, and my instinctive reaction was to quickly remount. But with alarm I realised that the seams of my ski had split; the ski was semi-submerged, and nowhere near 'paddleable'. This was at about 6 pm.

I was far from shore, in a 3.5-m swell and strong southeasterly wind – not ideal conditions in which to tread water. I could have chosen to swim; as a capable swimmer, there's a chance I would have made it. But, treading in conditions like this, it's tough to get a good fix on your exact distance from land. I could have been one, two or maybe even three kilometres offshore. With a mobile phone in hand, the obvious decision was to stay with the ski, remain as visible as possible, and call for help.

I didn't have the number for the NSRI Simon's Town (Station 10) on my phone, and my first call to the NSRI Table Bay (Station 3) was met with an engaged tone. I quickly redialled, connecting with the Table Bay station, who in turn put me in touch with Simon's Town. I explained my situation, but, again, while treading water in conditions like this, it is difficult not only to determine your distance offshore, but also to judge your orientation to the closest stretch of coastline. I gave my estimated location as one, maybe two kilometres offshore, in a line perpendicular to Boulders Beach. This proved vital in the rescue process.

At this stage, I was still quite calm and methodical. I was in constant contact with an amazing liaison officer from the Simon's Town station, Yvette du Preez, and I hoped that one of the NSRI boats would reach me in at least the next 20 minutes.

However, even with two NSRI boats in the search – the 5.5-m RIB (rigid inflatable boat), *Eddie Beaumont II*, and their deep-sea vessel, *Spirit of Safmarine III* – I grossly underestimated the difficulties of a search in big seas, and how even a minor error in presumed location might hamper the process.

As time lengthened, my calls became more urgent and frequent. Added to this, I had a cheap phone that kept switching off of its own accord.

Stuart Buchanan, the coxswain on *Spirit of Safmarine III*, said later that 'it was the worst sea I have experienced as a coxswain in charge of a rescue. The southeaster was blowing at what must have been a force 8 gale. The swells were three to four metres and the sea was full of holes. There was white water all around us, and the boat was constantly being sprayed as we negotiated the swells.'

After roughly half an hour of treading in 12 °C water, at about 6.30 pm, due to the action of the wind and swell, my surf ski tore in half, and the front half forward of the foot-well quickly drifted away. I was left tied to just the back half of the ski, which served little purpose other than visibility. I was now roughly one kilometre offshore, and drifting at a rate of nearly two kilometres per hour. I still wasn't fully aware of the effects of the cold, but desperation was creeping in, and my phone calls and conversations became even more urgent.

I found out later that Yvette du Preez was on the road above Boulders in the one spot where there was reasonable cellphone reception, and was relaying information from me to the Station

Commander, Darren Zimmerman, via handheld radio.

(Yvette later told *Sea Rescue* magazine: 'I had to stay confident. I could hear he was anxious but I had to keep calm. The sea was rough with huge holes and we had no visuals whatsoever from land. I asked David to look towards the land and tell me if he could see our red flashing lights, but he couldn't. *Spirit of Safmarine III* had its siren on, but he couldn't hear that either. Then I heard there was a visual on David, but it turned out to be the broken-off part of his ski. My heart sank.')

At about 6.40, I caught sight of the *Spirit of Safmarine III* roughly 400 m to the south of me, tracking from east to west. Much to my dismay, my shouts and screams did nothing to attract the boat's attention. But in that wind and swell, this was hardly surprising. Ten minutes later, the bottom edge of the sun began to dip behind the Simon's Town mountains, and I knew that, under the shadow of the mountain, my chances of being found would rapidly diminish.

I wasn't yet resigned to my fate, but panic was setting in. I still didn't 'feel' cold, but I was shaking badly, a sure sign of severe hypothermia. I began screaming into the wind, pleading to be rescued, a call only for myself and a desperate way of dealing with the hopelessness of the situation. Yvette had lost cellphone signal and I was on my own.

A minute or two later I turned downwind. Amazingly, I saw the NSRI rescue boat, *Spirit of Safmarine III*, a mere 40 m away. They had spotted me, and one of the crew had already lowered the boat hook. I was helped aboard, together with my paddle and the remaining half of my ski, and quickly wrapped in thick blankets. As I realised my ordeal was over, I felt an intense surge of relief and gratitude towards the NSRI Simon's Town station crew.

The *Spirit of Safmarine III* rescued me at 6.51, 1.5 km offshore of the Simon's Town golf course, after having drifted 1.6 km to the northwest in just 51 minutes. My body temperature was down to 32 °C, just 2 °C above the temperature below which the body's vital organs begin to shut down. I had been rescued with very, very little time to spare.

One of the major factors in my good fortune was the role played by Derek Goldman, owner of Paddlers' Kayak Shop in Simon's Town. Derek's house is on the hill above the town, and he happened to be on his deck testing some new lenses for his telescope when he spotted the two NSRI boats heading out. He immediately called Darren Zimmerman, and was briefed that the NSRI was looking for a paddler doing a Miller's Run – a route well-known to him.

Derek stayed glued to his telescope, acting as a spotter for the rescue crews. It took a full 20 minutes before he managed to find me through his spotting telescope, after which he then coordinated the NSRI rescue boats towards me. Thanks to my incorrectly estimated location, the NSRI boats were searching approximately two kilometres away from where I was. Without Derek's efforts, there's every chance that the NSRI boats would not have found me, especially as the light was fading and the swell was big.

That Thursday, 13 December 2012, I owed my life to an incredible combination of good fortune. First, there was my decision to paddle with a mobile phone. Second, there was the serendipity of Derek Goldman being out on his deck with his spotting telescope and his knowledge of the Miller's Run. Third, there was the incredible and unwavering dedication of the Simon's Town station crew, both those at sea and shore-based. Without these together, I simply would not be alive today. For all of this, it is difficult to express the extent of my gratitude.

I learned many things from this experience: most importantly, choose to paddle in conditions that are within your ability; paddle in a 'buddy system' with others of a similar level; make yourself visible by wearing brightly coloured clothing; flares are essential; and your exact GPS location will go a long way to reducing search times.

That I am very fortunate to still be here goes without saying. Thank you, everyone.

16 Talking Heads

Tony Weaver

KNYSNA IS ONE OF THOSE places that breed stories and storytellers. Think of Dalene Matthee, Hjalmar Thesen and a host of other writers.

And so it is that after one and a half hours of listening to sea rescue stories, my hand starts to seize up with writer's cramp and I am forced to down pen.

We'd arranged to meet with 'a couple of the guys' from Station 12 at the NSRI's *Alex Blaikie* Museum on Thesen Island, on the Knysna Lagoon waterfront, just after lunch on a balmy Sunday afternoon. But when 'a couple of the guys' turned out to be eight men with an extraordinary combined 203 years of sea rescue experience – including four Station Commanders – we needed to find somewhere bigger to sit.

No problem. We pop into the busy waterfront restaurant, Sirocco, where the NSRI men are greeted like royalty, and are ushered to a closed-off upstairs area, which we have to ourselves.

Sitting around the table are the current Station Commander, Jerome Simonis; the station doctor, Dr Berend Maarsingh; former Station Commander and current training facilitator at NSRI headquarters, Graeme Harding; former deputy Station Commanders Chris van Staden and Mike Jacobs; former Station Commander and current Operational Board Member, Mike Elliot; former Station Commander Rein Hofmeyr; and senior crew member George Parkes.

And the stories start flowing, many of them featuring the eight-metre Renato Levi rescue boat, the *Alex Blaikie*. Built in 1976 at the old Thesen's boatyard in Knysna and powered for most of its life by twin 225-hp Mariner outboard engines, it was decommissioned in 2008 after 32 years' service.

Inevitably, the treacherous mouth of the Knysna Lagoon, the Heads, features prominently in the stories. The Heads are relatively narrow, at just 229.5 m wide, and shallow, with a spring high tide maximum depth of 12 m, and an average low tide depth of 4.59 m. The Knysna Lagoon, with a surface area of 18 sq km, rises and falls by up to two metres twice a day, and when a big swell is running, the Heads get very, very treacherous.

Mike Elliot kicks off with the story of 'Flippie and Dippie'.

'It was around 1996, it was a bloody cold and very miserable winter's evening, a classic "dark and stormy night", and we couldn't go out to sea for our training session, so we decided we'd have an exercise up the lagoon. We had a radio technician who'd joined us and we thought this was an ideal opportunity for him to sort out our radios. So we took the two bigger boats up the lagoon, the five-metre *Jaytee* and the *Alex Blaikie*.

'But unbeknown to us, a crewman and his sidekick came down late – Mike Jacobs gives everyone a nickname, and he called them "Flippie" and "Dippie" – and they thought we had gone out to sea. They decided they were going to come out to sea to join us. They took this little boat, the *Olga*.

'We're up the lagoon and we see flares, and get reports from shore of flares out there. There was pandemonium. We were just dressed in civvies, no wetsuits, so we put our life jackets on, dropped the radio technician off, and had a very rough passage through the Heads.

'We hit a wave and lost Rein Hofmeyr overboard, he was washed off. Rein very, very nearly drowned that day.'

Rein chips in: 'I really, really thought I was dead that day. When I came up after being knocked overboard and a parachute flare was fired, I couldn't believe the *Blaikie* was still upright, I was convinced she would be upside down and all the guys were in the water.'

Mike Jacobs says that when he heard the shout of "man overboard,

Rein's overboard", 'it might sound weird, but I was glad it was Rein. I knew that Rein was very, very competent in the water, although he had brand-new boots on that he didn't want to take off.

'I said to Georgie [Parkes], I'm going to close my eyes so I don't lose night vision, then you switch that spotlight on and start shouting. We spotted Rein, and it was between sets of waves and I said, "We've got to pick him up *now*, we're not going to have a second chance." And we got him on board, and headed for the outside. The *Blaikie* was limping along because she had lost a motor when she was hit by a massive wave, and then we saw the flare going off again, and I said, "Sorry, Rein, I'm going to have to put you back on the *Blaikie* and go get those guys." So we transferred him, headed out and loaded up Flippie and Dippie and the *Olga*.'

Chris van Staden says that, as a measure of how big and dangerous the Heads are, 'when that wave broke on the cabin on the front of the *Blaikie*, it snapped the one support between the windows in half, from that day on it had two stainless steel flat bars bolted there. That aft deck was up to the gunwales in water, and only one engine was running.'

Mike Jacobs says that 'that night was very frightening, it was a comedy of errors right from the beginning, when Flippie and Dippie went around the corner and saw lights out to sea – which was a trawler – they thought it was the rescue boats, so they tried to join us, but we were up the lagoon. Our language wasn't very kind when we found Flippie and Dippie. It was absolutely horrific conditions. They were suspended for six months.'

The yarns start flowing thick and fast.

One of them was a story from the apartheid years, when the authorities were paranoid about anything Russian. It was in the early 1990s, and a Russian trawler sent out a Mayday that there were three medical emergencies on board. The message came over the radio that the captain was very sick, and that two crewmen had malaria.

Mike Jacobs recalls: 'We loaded up the *Alex Blaikie* with a big oxygen bottle, we had saline drips on board and our medic, Berend, came with us, and as we approached this massive, deep-sea trawler which had a tarpaulin across its aft deck covering something up, these two SA Navy strike craft came flying in across the horizon at high speed. And they want to know what is under that tarp on the aft deck of the trawler.

'Berend Maarsingh told them, "Look, we've got a medical emergency, I'm doing what I have to do here, when I'm finished you can have the ship, I don't want it." I went on board with the paramedic. There was this huge rusty hole in the deck, so if you mis-stepped, you were going to fall a long way.'

George Parkes was also on board, and Berend asked him to use the ship's radio to contact Mike Jacobs. 'So I walk into the radio room, and bang, they slammed the door in my face, there was kit in that room like you won't believe, more than just normal radios, some very specialised stuff.

'One of the guys says, "You want to speak, go to bridge." So I go to the bridge, and I'm trying to establish comms with the *Alex Blaikie* and there's Commander Bryan Donkin from the strike craft SAS *Jan Smuts* interrupting me and trying to find out what I can see, and I tell him "We have a medical emergency, I'll sort you out later."

'Eventually we got help from the crew, and we managed to get the casualties off. The captain was in severe shock; he was in a very bad way. Mike Jacobs was at the helm, and Berend said to him, "We are going to lose this guy, he's going to die on us, put foot, give gas."'

Berend went with the ambulance to the hospital and into casualty. 'But we couldn't get a medical history out of the captain, we couldn't find the problem because he had no English. Then one of the nurses said she knew an old lady up in [the suburb of] Concordia, and she fetched her, and in walked this coloured lady speaking fluent Russian. She used to work for a Russian family who lived up at the Crags.'

Mike Jacobs remembers that the navy escorted the ship to Mossel Bay, and the two crewmen rejoined the ship there after being treated for malaria. 'But the captain flew back to Russia and he died ten days later; he had had a semi-bleeding ulcer.'

And the object of the navy's suspicion under the tarpaulin? George Parkes sneaked a peek: 'There were just two rusty old Lada Niva 4x4s.'

With all NSRI stations, there are the inevitable false alarms, and with a busy station like Knysna, these are a regular occurrence. But one of those false alarms stood out for Mike Elliot.

'All the craft going in and out of the Heads need to check in and out. But this one guy couldn't get through to report, so he phoned his daughter, and in Afrikaans asked her to report that they have '*Vier aan boord, suid van die Koppe*' (four on board, south of the Heads). And she phoned us in tears, and says her dad had reported '*Vuur aan boord, suid van die Koppe*' (fire on board, south of the Heads).

'It was major, we began searching. Silvermine [Marine Rescue Coordination Centre] plotted where they could be and it was exactly where we had been searching, but nothing. We searched for six hours, and the conditions were rough. It was bad out there, and at about 6 pm we decided, no, this is getting dangerous, so we stood down for the night. In the meantime, the daughter and the rest of the family were at the base, very distraught when we said we couldn't continue in these conditions. There was a howling southeaster; it was vicious out there.

'And then we had comms from another boat, who said, "No, these guys are quite happy out there, they are fishing 20 miles out to sea." And eventually the story came out that it was *four*, and not *fire*, on board.'

Mike recalls that, back in the early 2000s, there were as many as 60 boats operating out of Knysna with commercial hake licences, and they would go up to 20 miles out to sea.

'These guys were subsistence fishermen mostly, and when there was a good run, they would make good money, and then there would be a week or two where the conditions were bad because of rough seas, or very thick fog, and they would start getting anxious because there was no cash, no food on the table. And you would have 60 boats hanging around just inside the Heads.

'They would sit there, anxious to go out, and one or two of the skippers who really know the Heads well would make a gap for it and go through, and the guys who didn't know the Heads that well would follow them and, bang, they've capsized. It was terrible, really tragic; at one stage we had four bodies in the boat shed, and two years running we had five, six dead a year. It was horrific, the one year we lost 12 fishermen.'

Chris van Staden tells the story of a particularly challenging rescue in September 2002.

'A boat called *Haka Hana* went down and we saved 13 guys, with huge breaking swells in the Heads. We had two rescue boats coming through the Heads completely overloaded. It was getting dark, and the coxswains said, "We have to come in now, it is getting too dangerous; once it gets dark you're not going to make it." There were five of us on the *Blaikie*, three on the five-metre boat, *Jaytee*, plus the 13 casualties.'

Rein Hofmeyr says the last two fishermen on the *Haka Hana* almost didn't make it: 'They were hanging on; we persuaded them to jump, and as they jumped, the boat went down and we grabbed them mid-jump. Nothing ever came up of that boat.'

And here's the irony of Sea Rescue operations.

Chris van Staden laughs and says that 'by a miracle and very good seamanship, we saved 13 guys under horrendous conditions, and not a word was said. There was no report in the paper, no publicity, no one asked us for the story.

'And the next week, we pull a whale off a sandbank, and the whole community comes down, they keep the whale cool by throwing water, they've got water pumps there, and they're keeping the whale wet.

'We organise a specialised strop to put around its tail, this beautiful towline, and we're powering up the boat, plenty of power on the *Blaikie* with its two 225-hp engines. And I couldn't see what was happening and I suddenly saw we were running backwards, and I said, "Guys, what's happening?" and the whale had lifted its tail and dragged us straight backwards.

'We started all over again, and eventually we got the whale moving, and I said to the guys: "Watch the whale very, very closely, because if it starts to swim, we've got to get rid of that tow very, very quickly or we are in deep shit." That side of it all worked, because the whale came off, and she started to swim towards what looked like the direction of the Heads, we dropped the tow and managed to pull our towline in, and suddenly the whale hooks a right to starboard to go up the lagoon instead of a left to port to go through the Heads.

'So the two smaller boats were now trying to herd it back and turn it around, and eventually we shepherded the whale out through the Heads, and two days later, some guys flying around spotted the whale and said it was swimming beautifully.

'And man, the publicity was unbelievable. I was interviewed on 702 Talk Radio, on TV, it was all over the major newspapers. We've never had it like that before.'

That year, 2002, was a rough one. Chris remembers that in May a boat called *Sea Sonnet II* went down in the Heads with six men on board.

'We searched the Heads in horrendous conditions for over an hour trying to find them. We ended up in trouble twice; we were in breaking sea with all that debris in the water, and at one stage I had a blanket wrapped around my propellers – that's when it all comes down to very good training and keeping calm and cool. I said to the guys, "We've got no power," and one guy looked over the back and said, "There's something wrapped in the props."

'And there was no going wild; it's a cliché but it happens – everything seemed to be in slow motion. We lifted the motors, got the blanket out and as soon as they told me "clear" it was motors down again, and we only just managed to get out of there alive.

'Eventually, a few months later, we did an exercise on the Western Head and we found a small amount of debris. She went down in the middle of the Heads, and not a single body was ever found and nothing else of that boat ever came up. That's the power of the Heads.'

Then there are the days when not even the toughest crews can get through the Heads. One of those days was Monday 1 September 2008.

Chris van Staden was the duty coxswain, and the current Station Commander, Jerome Simonis, was one of his crew. The station had just received a new boat, an 8.5-m rigid inflatable boat (RIB) christened *Colorpress Rescuer*. Chris said it was one of the foulest days they had seen in a while: 'The sea was breaking two miles out that day, there was a huge swell running – five, six metres. That was silly season.'

Jerome says that the sea was so wild that 'in one of the photographs, all you can see of the boat is the aerial sticking out of the white water.'

The sea was so churned up that the surface foam was a metre deep.

The crew had been called out after a panicked call from friends of 20-year-old American exchange student, Terrance De'Shawn Davis, who had been washed off the rocks at Kranshoek, near Harkerville, on the way to Plettenberg Bay. He and four other exchange students from Georgetown University, in Washington, DC, who were studying at the University of Cape Town, had hiked down to the beachfront.

Chris van Staden recalls: 'There were four of us on *Colorpress* and we launched through the Heads, and all four of us ended up flat on the deck three waves in a row. That's how big the sea was; it was massive. I managed to get the boat in behind Black Rocks on the western side, where normally you've got a bit of a chance of sheltering.

'But it was just too big, there was no way through, so we turned around.

'And we got back into calmer water, and I turned the boat around to look at the Heads again and I'll never forget it. Jerome looked at me and said, "You will not believe how relieved I was when you turned this boat around." Because if we had tried to take on that wave, it would have put us straight back on the rocks, we would have been dumped. How we got out of that corner, I will never know.

'I was standing on some high-density foam, and the minute that got wet, it was like being on oil, it was so slippery. At one point I fell and hit so hard the kill switches came out, and I had to scramble to get them back in and restart the engines.'

Jerome says there was no way they could have attempted a rescue from the sea: 'At Kranshoek that day it became immediately clear that a boat couldn't come anywhere close, not within a mile of where Terrance had fallen, and a helicopter was the only way.'

Graeme Harding says, 'It was a very sad story. Terrance had walked down there with his friends, they were deeply devout Christians, and there was this raging sea behind them, and he wanted a photo of himself with the sea behind him.

'So he walked down, turned around to face the camera and this wave just came and took him. His one friend still jumped in and tried to grab him, missed him, and then luckily for him he got washed up onto the rocks. They never saw Terrance again.'

Fellow student Ellie Gunderson, who was with Terrance, told friends that 'he was reading his Bible, and as he was walking down to the rocks, he was singing gospel hymns.'

Chris van Staden sums up what it means to be a Knysna Sea Rescue volunteer: 'When you get the call-out, and get asked to go, when you're trying to get out the Heads, you go. That's what we do, we go.'

17 'Excuse me, are you Wayne Bergstrom?'

Tony Weaver, Andrew Ingram and Jo-Ann Bekker

THOMAS HOLMES LEANED OVER THE side of the rescue boat and asked, 'Are you Wayne Bergstrom?'

The exhausted man had been swimming and treading water for five hours. He looked up wearily, but still managed a sardonic reply: 'I'll be anyone you want me to be right now.'

It was 4.03 pm on the afternoon of Monday 30 March 2009, and Wayne Bergstrom was one of the luckiest men alive. He had been the equivalent of the proverbial needle in a haystack. Since 11 am that morning, Wayne had swum and drifted 11 km in steadily deteriorating sea conditions. And yet he was found, thanks to NSRI volunteers Thomas Holmes and Andrew Aveley on board the little 4.2-m rescue boat *Spirit of KYC* (named after the Knysna Yacht Club), aided by some masterly sleuthing work by Graeme Harding, then Knysna (Station 12) Station Commander.

Johannesburg-based Bergstrom, then 40, left the family holiday house on Knysna's East Head just after breakfast for a day's fishing from his 16-ft ski-boat, *Blu 2*. An experienced skipper, Wayne had taken *Blu 2* out many times off both Mozambique and Knysna.

He waved goodbye to his wife, physiotherapist Belinda, and his daughters Anna Blu, 2, and Lulu Rose, 15 months, telling Belinda that he planned to fish until 3 pm, and that he would call her when he was on his way home.

It was a perfect morning. The estuary was glassy and the sky clear. But as he entered the Heads, Wayne saw that the sea was bigger than he had expected. So he nudged the throttles a little harder, and powered the ski-boat into the channel.

Once clear of the Heads, the sea was flat and glassy, so he set his lines and began trolling his lures, looking for warm water and hoping to get into some big fish. Out past Buffalo Bay, he turned and headed 15 km out to sea to anchor at the well-known bottom angling spot, the Dalgleish Banks.

But at about 10 am, there was a sudden change in the sea and weather conditions. A westerly wind came up hard, and the glassy, mirror surface of the sea changed almost instantly into a mass of white chop. *Blu 2* bucked against its anchor, chop began to break over the boat, and Wayne decided to call it quits.

Worried about the return trip through the Heads, he called Belinda on his cellphone. Estimating that the return trip would take him an hour and a half, he asked her to be at the lookout on the East Head to guide him through at around 11.30.

Back at Station 12, Graeme Harding was watching the rapidly deteriorating weather and said to crewmen Holmes and Aveley, 'I hope nobody's out there.'

Wayne finished stowing his anchor, powered up the engines and turned to head for home. While at anchor, the boat's transponder had stopped operating. Frustrated at not being able to get the GPS and trip log working, Wayne slowed the boat down and, with the engines ticking over, moved to the stern to push the transponder down.

And then it happened. 'It was almost as if I was bumped off the boat. Obviously, I hit something or a bit of a swell hit me, and it literally just knocked me straight off the back.' His 'dead man's kill switch', which would have automatically stopped his motors as he fell, wasn't attached.

'I fell between the two motors and, since the motors were running, there were bubbles everywhere. By the time I came up, came to my senses and turned around, the boat was gone.

'It was just gone.

'And that was me. It was a moment of absolute panic and terror. My immediate thought wasn't about how far the shore was or anything like that; it was literally just … shit!'

That was it. His boat was gone, he was 15 km away from the shore, he hadn't been wearing a life jacket, and his cellphone was on the boat. He was dressed in shorts, shirt, shoes and a rain jacket.

'The first thing I thought of was sharks and I took my Leatherman [multi-tool] out.'

As a fan of TV survival programmes, Wayne knew he should keep his shoes on, even though he knew they would interfere with his swimming. 'They were my security in case of something attacking me,' he said.

For the next hour, he trod water in a circle. Then he decided he had to try and swim to shore, so he removed his shoes, took off his shirt and trapped air inside his rain jacket to use it as a flotation aid. Bad move.

'Immediately I bared my back a million seagulls started flocking over me. I thought, "If they're picking me up from above, what's picking me up from below?" They were landing next to me. That freaked me out. If I was getting so much attention from the sky, I must be getting attention from underneath. It was as if they knew I was going to be food. They were waiting around for me to be broken in half, so that they could get their share.

'It was like something out of a Stephen King movie. I was so freaked out that I put the jacket back on, and the birds flew off.'

The waves were now constantly crashing on his head, pushing him under, so he decided to move. 'I started swimming my heart out.'

Wayne was pretty fit from working out in the gym and playing squash. And in his favour was the fact that he had phoned Belinda to tell her when to expect him through the Heads.

'I knew Belinda would have alerted the NSRI, but I was terrified they wouldn't find me before dark. I figured I had seven hours to get to shore. I kept on checking my watch; every half an hour I would swim breaststroke, and then for half an hour I would lie on my back and kick my legs to relieve the tension in my neck from swimming with my head raised.'

But after so long in the water he was exhausted. 'I was finished. I had swallowed so much water when I was swimming, and I was having permanent diarrhoea.'

By 12.45 pm, Belinda, who had been waiting at the lookout on the East Head, knew he was in trouble. Wayne was always punctual; for him to be running this late was a bad sign.

Belinda's mother, Jo McDonald, recalls: 'Belinda and I stood alone in the biting wind at the viewpoint at the top of the Eastern Head in Knysna. We had been scanning the stormy seas for over an hour, first during a light-hearted walk to the beach at the Heads with the little girls, then with mounting anxiety when Wayne didn't arrive as scheduled, and wasn't answering his cellphone. We took the children home, and drove to the viewpoint, fully expecting to see Wayne's boat approaching the sand bar.

'Apart from the misleading white horses, which kept raising our hopes, the empty sea stretched desolately to the horizon. The only sign of comfort was the phone number of the NSRI on the small hut next to where we were standing.

'So Belinda made the call. In answering, Graeme's first duty was to ensure that his team was not being called out on a false alarm. After Belinda had assured him that Wayne was habitually so punctual and reliable that something must be wrong, the amazing NSRI rescue machine swung into action.'

Because of the weather, Graeme decided 'to get the guys imme-diately, and we launched our 8.5-m rescue boat, *Colorpress Rescuer*'. He phoned Station 14 (Plettenberg Bay) to get their backup plus air support, and the Plett Station Commander, the late Ray Farnham, activated his crew. Ray told them to start searching while motoring down to Knysna, then organised to get a plane in the air.

Guessing that Wayne had probably capsized *Blu 2* shortly after phoning Belinda, Graeme started working out a search pattern based on the likely drift of the boat. But one key element was missing from his equation: the rescue crew thought they were looking for a man on an upturned hull, not a swimmer.

By now, Wayne was exhausted. He kept his spirits and his mental strength together by thinking of Belinda and his two daughters. 'I felt like they were on a stick in a current that was pulling me along towards them.'

After about three hours of swimming, 'the shoreline was becoming bigger and I started panicking that I'd be stuck in the water in the dark. I kept on wondering when Belinda would have called the NSRI. I mentally shouted at her, "My babe, send those red boats!" I was praying I would see them coming through the water.'

Graeme had decided to send the *Spirit of KYC* to join the search, a decision not taken lightly. The little single-engine boat shouldn't be out in a rough sea without support. But the clock was ticking.

Volunteers Thomas Holmes and Andrew Aveley knew it was a risk they needed to take. Graeme says, 'I was worried about *KYC* in those sea conditions, and we said to them we want to hear from them every 15 minutes.'

Sitting in the NSRI's radio shack on top of the Eastern Head, about two hours into the search, Graeme decided to act on a hunch that he later couldn't fully explain. He got on the radio.

'That was the biggest turning point. I said, "Okes, we're not looking for a boat, we're looking for a person in the water." They came back to me and said, "We'll never find a person in the water, how do you know it's a person in the water?" And I said, "I've just got a feeling, a hunch."

'I knew where Wayne had been fishing, I knew where they were searching, and it would have been almost impossible for them not to have spotted a boat. I knew it had to be a person in the water.'

With Belinda and her mother sitting on a bench a few metres from where he was directing the operation, Graeme couldn't afford to be negative.

Jo McDonald remembers: 'Once Graeme realised there was no way Belinda and I were going to wait at home, he had to deal with the task of directing a rescue where there was a good chance of failure, as well as deal with the emotions of a very anxious wife sitting on a bench nearby.

'I was aware that he didn't want to upset us. At the same time, he was not going to give us false hope. I want to thank Graeme and all of the crew who spoke to us that afternoon for being so coolheaded, professional and sensitive … there's no doubt the quiet efficiency of the whole team inspired us with confidence so that we were able to endure three hours of waiting with relative calmness.

'Belinda was shivering uncontrollably, in spite of wearing a warm jacket provided by a kind supporter, Michelle. Neil was concerned that she was going into shock and he arranged for drinks and food to be brought. Despite all the kindness, Belinda dissolved into tears whenever someone spoke to her.'

Acting on another hunch, Graeme asked the *Spirit of KYC* crew if they were able to go past the Western Head down towards Buffalo Bay.

For Thomas and Andrew, this was bad news. They were taking a pounding from the horrible sea conditions. If they were looking for a man in the water, they would need to pass within 15 m of him. They were indeed looking for a needle in a haystack.

Graeme: 'We had been searching for nearly three hours and I was preparing myself for the worst. I asked Thomas and Andrew if they would go to Castle Rock and then return to base. We shifted to a one-minute radio check to make sure they were okay. On the third call, I couldn't get them.'

The boat had moved into a radio shadow, and so Thomas decided to move further out to sea so they could confirm they had finished the last pass and were calling off their search.

And that's when Andrew saw something way out at the edge of his vision. Both men strained to get another sighting. And then Thomas saw it: a head that kept disappearing.

By this stage, Wayne was so exhausted, he didn't think he could go on for another five minutes. He knew he was losing it. The current was fierce, and he doubted that he'd be able to swim through the surf, which was breaking a kilometre out to sea.

'After five hours of swimming, from the top of a swell I could see the beach between Buffalo and Brenton. I knew that I was getting closer. But I was exhausted, totally finished.

'And then I heard it, this distant little buzz. A little rubber duck was a few hundred metres away. I went berserk. Thomas and Andrew came flying over and Thomas leaned over the side and asked me if I was Wayne Bergstrom. I did see the funny side of it. I said, "I'll be anyone you want me to be right now."'

'The moment they grabbed me I was totally finished. They pulled me into the boat and I huddled between them. From that moment on, I've never felt safer in my life. I felt like a wrapped-up baby. All I wanted to do was go to sleep.'

The radio communication electrified all who heard it. 'Base, this is *KYC*. We have the casualty.'

'Confirm that the casualty is Wayne Bergstrom,' Graeme said.

'It is him.'

Jo McDonald says that minutes before the radio call came through, 'The cloudy sky was bringing the evening closer and a note of desperation crept into Belinda's voice as she begged for the plane to appear.

'While giving my attention to Belinda, I thought I heard Graeme say "Wayne" from the hut. Then he was standing in front of Belinda: "They've found him, he's okay."

'Belinda didn't hear properly. "Is he alive?" she asked. "He's alive."

'Belinda crumpled into a heap of sobs.'

It was 4.03 pm when Graeme walked out of the radio shack and told Belinda that Wayne had been found, alive.

'And that was it. It was pretty emotional. It was pretty hectic,' Graeme recalls. 'This rescue has been testimony to a great human will to survive.'

Thomas and Andrew rendezvoused with the much larger *Colorpress Rescuer*, which rushed Wayne back through the Heads, where an

ER24 ambulance crew picked him up and took him to hospital in Knysna. He was severely hypothermic and dehydrated, and secondary drowning was a real threat. Wayne spent three days recovering in the intensive care unit (ICU), helped by the head of the unit, Emily Burgess, also a Sea Rescue volunteer.

Former Knysna Station Commander Rein Hofmeyr reckons that 'of all our rescues, that was the rescue where I got the most incredible feeling of satisfaction, when we saw him reunited with his wife and his two young daughters, and you realise how close they were to not having a dad and a husband.'

On Friday 3 April, Wayne was discharged from hospital and met the rescue crew. He commented that 'I feel like I'm on permanent endorphins, like I've run the hardest marathon.'

He was also reunited with his boat, which had been found several kilometres from the search area. Ray Farnham said at the time that if they had spotted the boat during the rescue, the search area would have been changed dramatically and Wayne would never have been found.

There's one more twist in this extraordinary tale: back in the 1960s, when it was first decided to build an NSRI base for Station 12, Knysna, the land on which it was built was donated by Belinda Bergstrom's grandfather, JP Burls.

'Its amazing how that circle has come around,' says Wayne.

How did Wayne survive?
Dr Cleeve Robertson, NSRI CEO and former Director of Emergency Medical Services in the Western Cape, talks about the many factors that aid casualties in the sea.

Sea conditions and the temperature of the water are clearly primary factors in determining whether someone will survive in the sea. The presence of floating aids and the physical and mental condition of the casualty are secondary but no less important factors.

In this case, being immersed in water of moderate temperature along the east coast was an advantage, but the same person in the

Atlantic Ocean would not have survived. The lower the water temperature, the shorter the period of survival. I've had a case where seamen capsized off Dassen Island and the subsequent two-hour swim to shore resulted in the deaths of two of three initial survivors.

Water drains the body of heat 25 times faster than air, and movement through the water accelerates this loss. The advice is always to huddle or crouch and to stay as still as possible, but in practice this is not always easy to do. The survivor must weigh up the chances of being found against attempting to swim for shore. If there is a chance of climbing up onto a boat or floating object, the survivor should take it. Life jackets are an important factor and many victims perish simply because they didn't fasten the jacket properly. Securing a life jacket in the water with cold hands can prove to be an impossible task, so doing it up properly before embarking on any water activity is very important.

Wind and rough seas also hamper survival. In conditions of constant spray, chop and winds, the survivor will cool quicker and is more likely to aspirate water and drown. In cold, rough climates, boats carry life jackets with hoods to protect individuals from this kind of exposure.

Physical condition is also important, and the fitter and stronger the casualty, the greater their chances of resisting hypothermia. Body composition may likewise assist in resisting hypothermia, although body mass and fitness may not always match up. Perhaps more importantly, mental strength and the will to overcome will result in survival.

Treading water can very quickly cause exhaustion. The survivor should float or swim slowly with minimum effort to conserve energy and reduce heat loss.

And wearing bright orange clothing or a life jacket will help the searchers to find survivors.

We're always taught in the rescue discipline that search is an emergency – because at the end of that search is a human life ... if you don't search now, you won't find the casualty.

I don't believe in miracles. I believe in the NSRI and other rescue services in South Africa that will respond, as they always do, if I end up in trouble.

18 The Kiani Satu *saga*

Tony Weaver

WEDNESDAY 7 AUGUST 2013 WAS a foul day at sea and on land. It was pouring with rain, there was a five-metre swell running, and the wind was gusting at 45 knots (83 km/h). So when Knysna (Station 12) Station Commander Graeme Harding's phone rang at five minutes to midnight, he knew there was trouble.

'It was the Transnet National Ports Authority to say that there's this ship that has lost its engine and it's drifting pretty close to our coast, but just relax, we are monitoring it, so go back to sleep. After a call like that and with that massive storm that had come through, there's no way I was going back to sleep.

'I immediately put all the guys on standby. Then the distress call went out three hours later, and at 3.30 in the morning we all rushed down to the base because we were told that it was now imminent. Then we were put on hold; we were told, "You mustn't go, you mustn't go."'

Drifting offshore without power after suffering mechanical failure was the *Kiani Satu*, a 168-m German-owned bulk carrier. It was en route from Ho Chi Minh City, Vietnam, carrying a cargo of 15 000 tons of Vietnamese long-grain rice, worth almost US$7 million, heading for Tema in Ghana.

The ship was drifting in foul conditions, six kilometres west of the Goukamma River mouth, between Knysna and Sedgefield. Not only were the lives of the 19 crew members in serious danger, but an environmental disaster of epic proportions was also looming; in the ship's tanks were 330 tons of heavy fuel oil, and the *Kiani Satu* was drifting towards shore right in the middle of the rich series of estuaries that stretch from Plettenberg Bay to Mossel Bay. The environmentally sensitive 'Lake District' between Wilderness and Sedgefield was facing ecological ruin.

Graeme and his crews knew that it would be impossible to launch through the notorious Knysna Heads in seas that big, and it would be equally dangerous for the crew from Station 23, Wilderness, to launch from their beach, so both crews towed their boats round to Buffalo Bay. It was pitch dark, and the weather was wild.

'We went around the dunes with [current Station Commander] Jerome Simonis's vehicle and mobile. We had to pull the bakkie across the river on the pont. We got up there on the dunes and we were monitoring the radio,' recalls Graeme.

Meanwhile, the well-oiled machinery of sea rescue and disaster management swung into gear. The South African Maritime Safety Authority (SAMSA), ordered the salvage vessel *Smit Amandla* to set sail from Cape Town, but it would reach Knysna only by nightfall.

A Dutch tug, the *Fairmount Glacier*, was in the area and also steamed to the scene, but was unable to get a towline on board the *Kiani Satu*, which began to drag its anchor.

The tension was mounting, as evidenced by a pre-dawn press statement issued by NSRI media spokesperson, Craig Lambinon: 'Fog has descended, further hampering the standby rescue operation. There are no direct access points for media on the scene, and media are respectfully requested to hold back and not approach, as the coastline in the area is dangerous and the ship cannot be viewed from shore.

'The captain is not willing to have his crew leave the ship at this stage and NSRI on-scene commander, Graeme Harding, NSRI Knysna Station Commander, is in agreement that unless the situation turns worse it is unnecessary to evacuate crew in the dark under these sea conditions.

'Media are respectfully requested to NOT call NSRI by phone on the scene and to liaise only via NSRI Communications at [cellphone number]. This is a tense situation and our NSRI rescue resources on the scene cannot have communications tied up.'

Meanwhile, NSRI Wilderness (Station 23) volunteer rescue swimmers Donald Olivier and Torsten Henschel had raced to George airport, where they met up with pilot Jaco Steinberg, copilot Andy Crawford and engineer and 'patterer' Rob Woodrup from the Titan Helicopter Group, who had already been placed on standby. They got ready to fly out to the *Kiani Satu* in Titan's Sikorsky S-76 helicopter at first light.

When the helicopter got airborne, it quickly became clear that this was going to be a very tricky operation. The *Kiani Satu* was rolling heavily as it was hammered by the swells, and, with the waves breaking right over the ship, it was clear that the only feasible evacuation zone was a three-metre by three-metre section of deck above the bridge. Two of the NSRI 5.5-m RIBs (rigid inflatable boats) had powered through the swell and wind to take up station as safety standby beyond the breaking back line.

Donald Olivier got ready and they began lowering him onto the deck, but as he was about to make contact with the ship he was yanked upwards and became airborne again. A massive wave set had come through, forcing the helicopter crew to take swift evasive action. If the Sikorsky's engines ingested salt water, the crew would be literally dead in the water, and several times they had to accelerate upward to avoid being hit by a mass of spray.

And then the whole ship started to move. The anchor chain had snapped.

Graeme, Jerome and the NSRI crews were anxiously monitoring the scene from the shore. Graeme said, 'The next minute the captain of the *Kiani Satu* came on the radio, and I'll never ever forget, my whole life, how calm he was, dead calm as he said, "I think we have hit the ground."'

'That was as the ship hit, and she came stern-on towards the coast.

It was pouring with rain, just after first light. It took just three waves to put that ship from bow out to side on, then it was beam on and the waves were breaking right over it.

'Our boats couldn't get anywhere close to them; they had to stand off beyond the back line. The sea was so bad that the Wilderness crew launched but they were just vomiting and vomiting, so they headed back,' Graeme said.

As the *Kiani Satu* settled on the reef it had struck, the helicopter prepared for a second attempt. Donald Olivier made it onto the slippery deck and unclipped. He entered the bridge, where the crew were assembled, and faced his next hurdle: the crew were from the Ukraine, the Philippines, Montenegro and Venezuela, and he could only converse with them in broken English.

Donald divided the crew into groups, and explained as best as he could how the underarm harness hoist worked. He looked out and saw Torsten signalling to him that the helicopter was coming in for a hoist. Outside, conditions underfoot were becoming dangerous as the anti-slip rubber matting covering the steel deck was steadily ripped away by the sea. Donald later said he felt like he was on a muddy rugby field sidestepping his opponents as he tried to keep his footing on the rapidly disappearing non-slip matting.

The hoists had to take place in the short intervals between the massive set waves, typically 13 to 15 minutes apart, with 13 to 15 seconds separating the swells in each set. Three or four sailors could be hoisted at a time, and the timing had to be immaculate; after one hoist, Donald only just made it back inside the bridge before a set wave slammed into the door behind him.

After a couple of hoists, he realised that progress was slowing because of the number of bags the sailors were taking with them, and so he ordered them to take only one bag each. Then it was sprint, secure, lift, sprint, take cover – all in rapid succession on the slippery, heaving deck.

There was a short breathing space while the helicopter landed the sailors on the beach, where NSRI 4x4 vehicles picked them up and ferried them to the parking lot in the Goukamma Nature Reserve, where the CapeNature office had been taken over as a rescue operations control point.

In the helicopter, everything had to be done with silky precision. Torsten kept a hawk eye on the waves, and coordinated with Donald by means of hand signals. Engineer Rob Woodrup controlled the winch and kept up a running 'patter' so pilots Jaco Steinberg and Andy Crawford knew exactly what to do next. (To 'patter' is helicopter parlance for talking the pilot through a tricky descent when he or she is unsighted; because the hoist cable hangs directly below the machine, the pilot cannot see how far there still is to go to the casualty, and so 'pattering' him or her in is a highly skilled and very precise operation.)

Finally it was just Donald and the captain left. The captain kissed the wheel, turned and, at two minutes past 10 in the morning, he and Donald were hoisted to safety.

An NSRI statement, from spokesperson Craig Lambinon, reported that, despite the extreme conditions, 'only minor injuries were sustained to two crew members of the ship, a laceration to a hand and one with a minor ankle injury, but they do not require to go to hospital and were treated on scene by paramedics. None of the remaining crew of the casualty vessel were injured and all 19 crew are accounted for and safe.'

But that was just the start of the *Kiani Satu* saga.

Graeme recalls: 'That turned out to be a ten-day epic, 12 hours a day, launching every day at high tide waiting for the tug, the *Smit Amandla*, to try and tow her off, on standby for them.

'If she had broken up in that place I think Knysna would have shut down. If all that oil – 330 tons of bunker oil – had been dumped out there, these towns on this coast would have been destroyed, there would have been no tourism season at all. These towns would not have survived that.

'I'm not sure people fully understand the implications of us getting that vessel off. Once we got everybody off, the next two days it calmed down and we could get nice and close with the boats, but all the *Smit Amandla* salvage crew were flown on by helicopter, so we always had to have a rescue swimmer on the chopper and they would lower him onto the deck of the ship first, offload all the crew, then take the swimmer off, then they would do their day's work and we would repeat the process when taking them off the ship.

'And every time the chopper was operating, we had to have one of our boats on standby out there for safety. So for 10 days we had boats out there almost all the time, and boats on standby every time the tug started towing, which was half an hour either side of high tide. So we were launching one, two, three in the morning, every high tide we were out there.'

Former Knysna deputy Station Commander Mike Jacobs says: 'That was the biggest bargain for us old toppies that had been chucked off the boats because we were now too old – the crews were so overtaxed that they asked Chris van Staden and myself and Rein Hofmeyr to please come and coxswain the boat because the okes were so tired, so we had sea time again for a change.'

Chris van Staden says that it's never too late to teach an old sea dog new tricks: 'The most amazing thing there, and it shows that in Sea Rescue you never stop learning, was to work with the *Smit Amandla*.

'I was in absolute awe of the power of it, the precision with which they could position that tug, no matter what the sea was like. We were sitting there trying to maintain position in our 5.5- and 8.5-metre boats, and this captain comes in, turns the tug around, and puts the stern towards the beach and towards *Kiani Satu*, and at the hit of a button, using the GPS and the computers, he stays right on that position; it didn't matter what the sea did. It was phenomenal to work with, one of my favourite memories.

'I'll never forget the first time they started pulling, the engines are going flat out and the captain says, "The dogs are barking, the dogs are barking," and there's black smoke and he says again, "The dogs are barking but we're not moving."'

But then, on 17 August, nine days after it first ran aground, the dogs barked loud and clear and the *Kiani Satu* was refloated on the high tide and towed out to sea. The plan was to get the ship as far away from land as possible and sink it as deep as possible.

Graeme says: 'They towed her out to sea and, four days later, in the early hours of 21 August, just over 100 nautical miles from land and in 1 000 m of water, she finally went glug glug glug, she went down on her own.'

More than 330 people from various organisations were involved in the rescue and subsequent salvage. For his part in the operation, Donald Olivier was awarded the NSRI Directors' Thanks. Jaco Steinberg, Andy Crawford, Rob Woodrup and Torsten Henschel were awarded the NSRI CEO's Letter of Appreciation.

Their citation read in part:

During this process, with huge swells racing at the ship, which regularly smashed over the stern, the helicopter had to often break away and rapidly gain height and the crew and rescue swimmer had to move into the safety of the superstructure for fear of being washed overboard. Despite this grave danger all 19 men were winched to safety.

The whole operation was an extremely demanding rescue that involved excellent team work, steel nerves and communication amongst all who were on board the aircraft and the NSRI volunteer on the deck below.

The team's actions were in the best traditions of the National Sea Rescue Institute and we are delighted to be able to recognise their efforts with this vote of thanks.

19 *The Italtile disaster*

Tony Weaver

TUESDAY 8 FEBRUARY 2011. IT's a date that is etched deep into the memories of the rescue crews from Station 14, Plettenberg Bay, and Station 12, Knysna.

At 4 pm that afternoon, a single-engined Pilatus PC-12 turboprop aircraft, en route from Queenstown to Plett, went missing in heavy mist somewhere between Plett and Knysna. The Pilatus was owned by Majuba Aviation, a subsidiary of the ceramic tile giant, Italtile.

They were due to land at Plettenberg Bay airport at 4.30 pm. Just before the Pilatus disappeared, a cellphone call went out to say that they were diverting to George airport as the mist was too thick in Plett.

At 4.33 pm, the plane vanished off the radar.

On board were nine people: the CEO of Italtile, Gianpaolo Ravazzotti, and six of his colleagues and business partners – Gia Celori, Marilize Compion and Aletsia Krause of Italtile; Sava di Bella of Prima Bella Bathroom Accessories; Simon Hirschberg of the joinery and shopfitting company Grainwave; and Jody Jansen van Rensburg of CTM Alberton – along with pilot Bronwyn Parsons and copilot Alison van Staden.

They all died that afternoon in a terrifying, catastrophic event that left very few clues as to what went wrong. The subsequent Civil Aviation Authority (CAA) investigation found that the crash was 'not considered a survivable accident due to the high kinetic energy associated with the impact sequence that was well above that of human tolerance'.

The NSRI were left to, literally, pick up the pieces.

It turned out to be one of the most harrowing operations ever carried out by the volunteer crews of the service. I met with the Plett and Knysna crews five years after the disaster. At the end of the interviews, I felt like a trauma counsellor still debriefing them all those years later.

I am a relatively hardened journalist, with many years of war reporting and combat experience behind me, but still, the stories I heard that morning – a beautiful late summer's day in the magnificent Plett NSRI base (rebuilt with very generous funding from Italtile) – chilled me to the bone.

I have had many internal debates with myself as to how this story should be told. What is the morality of once again exposing the families to the horror of what happened that day? What are the arguments in favour or against telling this story in all its graphic detail?

And after weighing it all up, I realised that the families already know all this detail. They've read the report of the CAA investigation. They were on the beach in Plettenberg Bay when the body parts were recovered. They know the process involved in matching up little pieces of flesh to piece together a DNA picture.

They know what the NSRI crews went through.

The story that has never been publicly told is the story of the NSRI men and women who were tasked with collecting the aftermath of one of the worst civil aviation disasters in South African history.

I have left out some details that are simply too graphic to record.

* * *

Sitting around the table at the Plett base are four men who were part of that operation: coxswain Robbie Gibson, crew member (and the station's marketing person) Sean Searle, another coxswain, Brad Thomas, and the current Station Commander, Marc Rodgers.

Two more key people – former Plett Station Commander, the late

Ray Farnham, and former Knysna Station Commander (and now the NSRI's training officer), Graeme Harding – added key information, both in a video shot by Andrew Ingram.

Marc Rodgers begins the story.

'We got this call that this plane was missing, and from the calls we were getting from people who had heard the plane, we surmised that it was between Robberg and the Kranshoek viewsite. People could hear it powering up, and we assumed they were doing that to miss the mountains, so we started cordoning off areas, and sent out search parties to each area.

'We put a major focus on the side of Robberg, the south-facing side. That narrowing-down of the search area was happening as the sun was setting – not that we could really tell. It was eerie. I have never, ever seen mist that thick in Plett, and it was that thick when the plane went down.'

Sean Searle chips in: 'We picked up the radar track, so we knew it had to be on that side of the mountain [Robberg]. The plane was due to land at 4.30 pm; at 6 pm we had a briefing at the fire station, and by 8 pm everyone was on search duty.'

The NSRI crews split up into four groups and began searching the Robberg Peninsula. Robbie Gibson says: 'We were hiking up through the bushes, anywhere we could to try and find wreckage. We went up to the top of the lighthouse and were firing off illuminating flares but getting nowhere; the mist was just too thick.'

The mist was so thick, Marc says, that the crews were shuffling along in single file, hands on the shoulder of the man in front of them so that they wouldn't lose the track – or each other.

With no visuals available, the crew had to rely on their hearing and their sense of smell. The mist deadened all sound, and, ominously, there were no cries for help.

But NSRI crews are trained to rely on their sense of smell – to detect diesel, petrol, Jet A1 aviation fuel, paraffin, even the smell of dead bodies, of vomit, and of blood.

Robbie Gibson recalls: 'We kept getting waves of what smelt like jet fuel, that paraffin smell of Jet A1, and we'd walk past it, then come back around again, but it could also have been the milkwoods – the smell is similar when you crush the leaves. We did this many times, and eventually we just sat there in the dark seeing if we could pick up this smell, or hear anything.

'We decided we were smelling milkwoods. But, in hindsight, we could just as easily have been smelling jet fuel. We walked to the point of the island, and we could also smell the jet fuel there. We didn't know it, but we were very close to the crash site, but we couldn't see a thing.

'We were trying to shine our torches eight to ten metres into the water but the beams just couldn't penetrate the mist; it was too thick. The next day, we found a seat from the plane right there where we had been, in that exact spot. It was floating, suspended in the water.

'We were 90 per cent confident we had found the place, but we just couldn't see anything. We searched until after midnight, way past; we carried on until 3.30 am, we didn't want to give up.'

The crew were desperate. They just wanted to find out it was all a false alarm, that the Pilatus had made it to George.

Marc Rodgers described that feeling: 'That night with the search, because we could smell this fuel we had this feeling that we were so close but not managing to find them, and we just didn't want to give up, it was 10, 11 o'clock, the coordinators were saying, "Come guys, off the mountain, you've got to get a night's sleep and we'll get this search going properly again in the morning." But we kept pushing it and pushing it. The mayor of Plett brought us Steers takeaways to eat on the mountain at half past one in the morning; it was so unreal. We were the last to walk off the mountain that night, I remember getting home at 4 am, and we launched at 5.30 am again.'

Robbie adds: 'Marc, you still said to me, "Dude, we're going home now and there could be someone out there hanging on a wing." It was hectic, it's a horrible feeling.'

Marc: 'There are a few rescues that never leave you, phew, where you just keep going until you physically fall over but you can't stop, you don't want to go home.'

By now the guys are in debrief mode, chiming in one after the other. I put down my pen because I can't keep up and I make sure the voice recorder is running. It's the only way I can keep track of their stream-of-consciousness recounting of a horrifically traumatic recovery.

Brad Thomas says: 'No one really wanted to believe this had really happened. We were in denial. We launched the boats at first light and it was a perfect day, flat sea, getting around the point the sea conditions were amazing, flat, flat, flat.'

Sean Searle: 'We were in mist all the way to the point, I was still 100 per cent convinced the plane had crashed into the side of the mountain, and we had discussed that all the way round, and as we went around the corner, we were all looking up at the mountain then we came around the corner and then I looked down and I saw this white piece of plastic, and I said "Oh fuck." I picked it up, and then we all looked down and we saw debris floating in the water, everywhere, just everywhere.'

Graeme Harding's team had been put on standby the night before, and they set out from the Knysna rescue base at first light. They were hoping for the best, and that they would meet up with the Plett crews, 'have a jibber jabber', then find out the plane had diverted and that all aboard were fine.

'Or maybe, because the sea was so flat, they had managed to belly flop the plane and we'd find survivors out there.

'That's what we expected until we saw the first debris, and then we knew.'

'We had launched at five in the morning into thick pea soup, thick fog. Often we get called out to go and look for things. You get used to it, and it's quite jovial on the boat – bit of tension because of the fog – but we put the radar on and we get out there and our orders were to search from Knysna all the way up to Robberg. Four miles out, the fog lifted, sun's coming up, so the spirits lifted, everybody's pretty jovial, we're going along, then I noticed a lot of flotsam in the water.

'As we went into the area where the plane went down, the whole demeanour on the boat just went down. Suddenly we realised just what we were dealing with by the size of what we saw floating in the water.'

They headed to Robberg, still hoping against hope that they might find survivors, and met up with the Plett boat there. Then they found the first body. 'Unfortunately there's no other word for it but "gruesome"; we came across gruesome discoveries. Everybody did what had to be done; the radios were quiet, it was a sombre, mind-blowing experience.

'It was then, in the middle of the whole lot, that I got hold of our base quietly on my phone, not on the radio, and I told them, "I need someone at the base when we get back," because as big heroes as we are, as tough as we guys like to think we are, the guys were taking strain; they were taking immense strain out there on the boats, and we've never dealt with anything like this before.

'Normally on a rescue there almost isn't time to think, the adrenaline is pumping. This one, there was no adrenaline, the sea was calm, everything was relaxed, and we suddenly came across the scene, and the radio comms just went quiet, nobody wanted to speak about the kind of destruction we were seeing because you just weren't sure who was listening on the other side. It became very difficult for the controllers – long silences – and after not getting responses, they realised as well what we were dealing with.'

Brad puts his head in his hands, and on my recording I can hear that his voice has gone quiet as he talks into the table: 'The things we found were indescribable really, it was terrible.'

Plett Station Commander Ray Farnham was interviewed on video by Andrew Ingram: 'Our crews were on scene at first light, and within 10 or 15 minutes started recovering wreckage parts, and then of course we started retrieving bodies, and that's when the reality hit home, that the aircraft went into the water, and that we were dealing with something completely different.

'You could hear the mood start changing on the radio, from the normal chirpiness to the more serious mode, and the feedback came from the coxswains on the boat telling us that we were dealing with something that we weren't prepared for. We didn't expect to see something like that.

'As the day progressed, you could see the expressions on the crews' faces: they went into a strange zombie mode, executing the task, retrieving the bodies. Later in the evening, when I met them all at the base, there was just this silence, their heads down, they were all in a state of shock.

'They just shut off, they became zombies. They did the job, recovered the bodies, but through the day you could just see that the mental state of the crews was just sliding down into a hole.'

Marc Rodgers says it was the most traumatic recovery any of them has ever done, but after a while, it became strangely clinical: 'It just never leaves you, it was radical, insane, the recoveries – there was no smell, it was almost clean, sterilised, no blood, no smells. We've all had to do body recoveries where it's a week or two old and you can smell it for weeks afterwards, but this was just clean.

'As the day progressed, we started following the birds and the sharks to recover more body parts.'

The recovery was relentless. The crews would find debris floating, pick it up, mark the spot on the GPS and move on, then come back to that spot and find the area filled with debris again as more floated up from below.

Brad Thomas says, 'It was a long couple of days because we were instructed to pick up every piece of debris and every body part we could, every bit, so that they could do DNA testing to identify the nine bodies. They said we had to keep all the body parts separate to avoid cross-contamination, but it was nearly impossible. They set up a sterile area here in the Beacon Island car park, the mortuary tents, where they were literally trying to match body parts.'

It was an intensely traumatic few days, and the memories haunt them still. Rodger Foster, CEO of SA Airlink, recognised what they were going through and sent down a trauma counsellor to debrief the crews.

Ray Farnham: 'I got a call from Rodger Foster and he said to me, "Look, Raymond, I've had a look at the crew and I've seen things, I would like to send down a professional counsellor." And he did: he chartered an aircraft and flew the counsellor to George, booked him in at the Beacon Island Hotel.

'Of course me, macho boy himself, decided I don't need him because I'm strong enough. Big mistake, huge mistake. It hit me a month later and it flattened me.'

Graeme Harding says they all learned an enormous amount from the disaster. 'We've picked up drowned, complete bodies, put them in the body bag, but we've never dealt with the destruction that we saw on that day. In all our training scenarios that we've had with aircraft ditching, we've never had someone say, "Guys, you need to understand what you might come across." I had to say stuff to the guys like, "Don't look, just get it in the boat, we need to get it in the boat."

'If the guy in control, the coxswain of the boat, gets too emotionally involved in a situation like that, the crew will fall apart very quickly. They need to have that person, the coxswain, trained, adequately trained for the kind of trauma he may be going through; he has to keep that strong composure.

'Afterwards, I went out to the Spar and I walked past the newspapers, and I just had to sit down on the ground. One of the local Knysna guys came up to me, and said, "Graeme, are you all right?" I said, "I'm a bit shaky at the minute, just give me a few minutes." It was a photo of one of the women, and I'd seen the utter devastation, and here was this beautiful picture in the newspaper. It was very hard for me. I had to actually sit down and compose myself.'

Sean Searle recalls: 'It was hectic; quite a few guys joined Sea Rescue because of the disaster, but quite a few also left because of the trauma. A lot of the guys felt they didn't need trauma counselling, but there were a couple of guys who said they really needed it. It was an event that brought people very close together, and we all spoke of it, often, for days and weeks afterwards, and that was the counselling that was most effective for me. Talking about it, you come together and have a few drinks, you all feel shit together but you can walk away and go and be normal at home. That is what really helped.'

Marc Rodgers agrees with Sean: 'I think that's the case with all our rescues, there's definitely a point where you need trauma counselling, but the worst part is that it's something you can't talk to just anyone else about. People who weren't there, they're not going to understand; the only way you can sort it out is by talking to the buddy who was next to you on the rescue, supporting each other.'

And often it is the NSRI crew members who find themselves taking over the role of trauma counsellor. As Sean puts it, 'knowing the families is also quite something. A lot of the work we do is dealing with family members who are sitting with our guys, like this last plane crash [in December, 2015, when pilot Johan van den Berg was seriously injured, and his wife, Aurora, and his mother-in-law, Elicia Morrison, were killed when their Cessna crashed near Koukamma], we had family members sitting at the airport and some of the crew were giving them counselling.

'You are watching them fall apart, break apart, you have to be so careful what you say on the phone, on the radio. They want answers, now, but you can't until you have full confirmation.'

Brad Thomas says that is one of the most traumatic parts of rescue operations. 'It is absolutely draining, you are giving away part of your soul to that person.'

Postscript

Italtile subsequently donated R1.8 million to the NSRI, which used the money to renovate and upgrade the Station 14 base into a state-of-the-art facility. A further R857 132 was raised by Italtile through sponsorship of a team of staff, family, friends and NSRI members Marc Rodgers from Plett and Darren Berry from Knysna, who climbed Mount Kilimanjaro in memory of the deceased.

Marc says, 'I was expecting to be cornered somewhere along the line on that trip and asked some tough questions, but what ended up happening is that we had a lot of quiet nights in little tents with 20 people in the freezing cold, just looking at each other and understanding what had happened.

'Following all of that is the connections we have made and have still got with those families. They phone, and we phone them, we see each other, and there's this kind of understanding – we have been through the whole thing together. The CEO's niece says we are now her extended family, she can never forget about us. It's so true – you get so connected to people and you are linked for life.'

20 *Storms warning*

Dominique le Roux

The Storms River tragedy, in which 13 people died on 25 March 2000, was the worst disaster ever to hit the South African adventure tourism industry. The dangerous and intricate rescue involved 50 people from the emergency services, among them the police, the Mountain Club of South Africa's Cape Town team led by Lester Coelen, NSRI volunteers from Plettenberg Bay (Station 14) and Knysna (Station 12), and helicopter crews from the SAAF's 22 Squadron. But the terrain and the conditions were so dangerous that it was impossible to get rescuers down into the narrow gorge on foot. So Major Gees Basson flew an Oryx helicopter, dangling Mountain Club member Douw Steyn from a rope, to search the gorge. Some of those who died that day worked for Engen, and the company donated a rescue boat, Spirit of Engen, *to Station 14, Plettenberg Bay, in their memory.*

Shortly after the tragic event, Dominique le Roux spent time with the survivors and wrote this harrowing report for Out There *magazine. It is reprinted with her permission.*

ASHLEY WENTWORTH WAKES AT 4 am, as he does every morning. It's a big day for his company, Storms River Adventures (SRA). And he's a hands-on operator who's involved in every aspect of his business.

Today he has three separate 'black water tubing' trips down the river, one of them a corporate hospitality event: Port Elizabeth legal firm Stulting, Cilliers and De Jager has sent fake summonses to senior Engen employees, inviting them and their families for a day of fun.

Wentworth and his team have been doing a corporate drive over the last year, and this is a great opportunity for the company. Not that SRA lacks business, mind you. Backpackers and tourists from all over the world know there are two must-do adventures on the Garden Route: you go bungee jumping at Gouritz or Bloukrans, and then you go 'black water tubing' on the Storms River (tubing is when you go down a river seated in an inflatable tube similar to a motor car inner tube). Wentworth's permit allows a maximum of 60 clients per day; some days, SRA turns down another 30. Today is one of those maximum-capacity days. It's all hands on deck.

'Flight plans' were drawn up a week ago, with every member of the team already briefed on exactly what to do, and when.

Daniel Syme's alarm clock rings well before sunrise. The weather outside is cold and rainy, as it has been for the last 24 hours, and he hits the snooze button, hoping today's trip will be called off. He loves water; he was a lifesaver as a kid, and swam for Natal. Now that love has translated itself to tubing, a newfound passion he indulges even on his days off. After deciding the IT world was not for him, the trendy 18-year-old has been living a life many would envy: since October, he's been a tubing guide on one of the most dramatic pieces of earth imaginable.

Today, however, the weather has temporarily dampened his enthusiasm, but his good spirits quickly return. How bad can it be? And besides, he's scheduled to work with his best buddy, Herman Swart, whose brother Jaco will be the lead guide.

Reluctantly Syme finally hauls himself out of bed and heads for the SRA adventure centre at the end of the only tarred road in Storms River village.

Wentworth has not wasted a second. He's a man who likes order, who believes in systems, and who is intent on doing things by the book. This morning he's already been out twice to check the water levels of the river – at 6.30 and again at 8.00 – and defined it as a 'medium top sector'. In other words, the top section of the river will be run, not the narrow gorge lower down.

The runnable section of the Storms River is broken down into four parts: sectors one to three are what Wentworth describes as an 'eco wilderness experience'. But it's the gorge – sector four – that people come for. The gorge that Pieter Cilliers has done four times before. It's the gorge that he had in mind when he booked this trip. But when the water's high, as it is today, Storms River Adventures clients put in at the top of sector one and take out at a wire ladder with wooden rungs laid out up the slope just before sector four. Just before the rock walls suddenly close in to form a magnificent, narrow, sheer-walled gorge that ends in the mouth of the river in the Tsitsikamma Nature Reserve (today a unit of the Garden Route National Park).

It's 9 am when Andrew Gay and his wife, Lorna, arrive at the SRA centre. Gay is an adventure-seeker and outdoors-lover, but, with a demanding corporate job as Engen convenience manager, he doesn't have much time for the wilderness, and has to settle for an occasional Sunday morning cycle with boss and mentor John Boyd, who will also be joining today's trip.

A private group is being briefed as the corporates straggle in. They're moved to the old backpackers' lodge next door, where lead guide Jaco Swart takes them through their safety briefing, outlining river hazards, demonstrating hand signals, discussing their equipment, and explaining that life jackets are optional, helmets and wetsuits not.

He also requests that any of the party with any medical conditions or with claustrophobia, and those who can't swim, notify the guides, if necessary in private, after the briefing.

Lorna, who sits in on the safety talk, even though she isn't going on the river, notices Wentworth mentioning three times that, if he's unhappy with the level of the river when they get to the put-in point, he'll have no qualms about calling off the trip.

Then, just when they think they're ready to go, each participant is asked to sign an indemnity, which starts with a description of the nature of the activity: 'Black water tubing takes place in a rocky, remote, rapid-filled gorge where slipping and falling can happen and where people may be carried downstream in strong currents with hazards that to them are unforeseen. The gorge is dangerous and conditions may worsen at any time,' it reads.

Having signed away all right to claim 'even my death arising from negligence', the corporate group – paddlers and their partners and children – climb onto the tractor trailer to tootle off down the gravel road, through the indigenous forest, to a low cement bridge over the inky Storms River.

Most of the members of the group know one another, so it's a chatty ride out to the river, taking a little longer than usual because they've combined it with an informative forest tour. Daniel Syme and Herman Swart sit right at the back, imitating the guide, who's renowned for the thoroughness and length of her narration.

Finally they get to 'Oubrug', the low-water bridge that is the put-in point. Here there are two rocks whose shape Carel van der Merwe knows by heart. He's the local chief forester for the Department of Water Affairs and Forestry (now the Department of Water and Sanitation), and the man who makes the call on whether the river can be run or not. He takes two factors into account: the rainfall of the previous 24 hours, and the water level as evidenced on these two rocks. Today the level's slightly high – not disturbingly so, but high enough for him to call off a private trip that has been booked through his department.

Private trips have been run on the Storms River for years; in fact, Van der Merwe did his first one 23 years ago. Private trippers, however, have to run the whole gorge, all four sectors of it, as they cannot take out at the SRA 'escape route' at the end of sector three. When the water level is too high to run sector four, the 1.8-km gorge, as is clearly the case today, private trip permits are rescinded by Van der Merwe.

Storms River Adventures, on the other hand, has had to cancel only about five per cent of its trips. The company has had about 700 black water tubing river-days to its name since Wentworth took over in May 1998. That's about 8 000 people, all in all. Of those, about 82 per cent have done the gorge, with the remainder limited to the tamer top section when water levels have been too high in the gorge.

Now, as Van der Merwe's practised eye measures the water level again, it's about 10 to 15 cm over the two marker rocks. It's 10.30 am, and the forester gives the thumbs-up.

Cilliers is disappointed. He's had his heart set on doing the gorge, not just this somewhat tamer wilderness experience. As it turns out, he'll do just that. He'll find himself at the centre of one of the most remarkable survival stories South African adventure sports has ever known. Of the 15 people who will eventually be flushed into that narrow ravine, he and guide Jaco Swart, who'll sit trapped in a tree with a broken kneecap for 27 hours, will be the only two to emerge alive.

The paddlers grab their purple, pink, blue and yellow tubes, wave goodbye and jump in, grinning and happy, despite the rain.

Jaco Swart, the trip leader, has a shaved head, a huge handlebar moustache and a friendly, confident personality. The 33-year-old opted out of the corporate life and moved to quiet little Storms River village with his wife and two children when his father became ill the year before. He's happy with the simple life he's chosen, though it doesn't pay much, and he's been guiding on the river for about a year. Part of the joy of this simple life is working with younger brother Herman, who, together with Syme, began guiding in October the previous year. The two were assessed and passed as tube guides by the Southern African Rivers Association (SARA) chief instructor for the Cape, Andrew Kellet, just under three weeks ago.

The last guide on this trip is Stanford Skosana, who exemplifies the opportunities afforded to locals by SRA's investment in the community. He too is qualified, though not a strong English speaker.

One client falls out of his tube in the very first rapid. The Swart brothers discuss his abilities with him, and together they decide he should not continue, as it transpires that an accident a few years ago left him blind in one eye and damaged one of his arms. There are now 19 clients and four guides.

Lead guide Steve Brouwer has put in slightly downstream with a different group. It being a smaller bunch of only ten, who all seem fairly fit, he reckons he doesn't want to be caught up behind the big crowd. His group makes fairly fast progress, though they still get caught on the rocks at times.

Further down, Angus Stembull has a group of 13 that is well on its way. Having started first, they're quite a bit further ahead, and are having a ball. Stembull is SRA's abseil lead guide and a tubing veteran. With him is his sister, Ronelle, who at one point calls her brother over and points out an interesting phenomenon: water is pouring down from the banks of the river near the confluence with the Witteklip River, but the tributary itself seems as dry as usual.

The Stembull siblings take note and continue for approximately 300 m past the confluence of the two rivers to the big, calm pool at the end of the top sector, with a stream on the right and the takeout on the left. It's been a good, positive trip, all in all.

Angus has two deaf girls with him, and has tried to make a 'train', with each one holding on to the other. But it's been a frustratingly bumpy ride over the exposed rocks.

Brouwer's group follows. They're having such a good time that some of them stay on at the end to play and splash about in the pool after the last rapid. The rest of the group all gathers on the big sandy beach, laughing and joking about a great day on the river, before they all set off up the steep 900-m 'escape route'.

The corporate group is also all smiles, although one member falls out fairly early on and takes fright. He's not keen on running any more rapids, but is determined to continue, despite Syme's offer to walk back with him. Skosana is designated to portage around each rapid with him instead. This, of course, is a slow process, so when the group gets to what they call Bar One island, where there's a seven-metre jump into the water, they decide to push on.

At the next rapid, a place called Bums Up, Daniel Syme catches a glimpse of the last member of the previous group. It's not far to go now, and then the day's trip will be over. Everyone is in high spirits, with 33-year-old client Bartholomeus Duminy describing how he did this when he was in the army. In those days, he explains, they took almost none of the impressive safety precautions in evidence today. No, back then, he and his buddies had little more than shorts, takkies and a liberal dose of Dutch courage.

At the confluence with the Witteklip, conditions are looking rather different from normal. Usually one must get up and clamber over the rocks, where the river flows in on the right. This time not so. The Witteklip has started flowing strongly.

Herman is in the habit of comparing the Storms and Witteklip rivers every time he passes this confluence. He and Syme have even walked up and tubed the last few of the Witteklip's rapids in the past, but he's never seen it like this before. 'Even on a very, very flooded Storms River, when we don't take clients down and only we go down, the Witteklip is not nearly as fast flowing,' the Swart brothers agree later. 'When you looked up, it was just a mass of brown water,' explains Syme. 'At least we won't get stuck,' he thinks now.

The rapid after this confluence is to be the last. While Syme takes the throwline and heads down the rapid to get into position at the bottom to help anybody that might need a hand, Jaco Swart briefs the clients about this last rapid, just as he has every other one, gathering the group together and telling them what to expect. It's nothing major – what the guides call a 'freelance rapid', i.e. not really the real thing. In fact, it looks 'lekker'. It should be little more than a slight increase in gradient that washes people through and lands them in a big pool at the bottom, where the rapid seems to peter out completely. There's a lovely sandy beach on the left, the inside bend, where people will take out. And there's always a guide there, because the takeout point is not that obvious, marked only by two small signs pointing vaguely in the right direction.

That's the theory, the way it's happened every other time. ('In all my experience over the years,' says previous SRA owner Robert Birch in a statement later, 'there has never been a problem exiting at this point. I have run the river in high conditions and have never had a problem in getting clients out with minimum of effort.') That's the way it's happened for Stembull's and Brouwer's groups. This time, however, things are very different. Syme finds himself flushed much further than usual, and only with a desperate struggle does he manage to pull himself out onto the bank.

The water is a far cry from its usual inky black. Brown and churning, it's thick with leaves and, as he notices as he pulls himself out, his wetsuit is covered in the splinters of snapped tree trunks.

Syme gazes round in bewilderment. Where's the beach that should be here? Where's the pool that's always been here? Now there's only a river so swollen, it's devoured every feature usually associated with this spot. A river that's throbbing and pushing, grabbing hungrily at the forested banks.

Back round the corner, upstream and out of sight, Swart is preparing to send clients down. The standard operating procedure had always been to count 30 seconds after the safety guide before sending the first person. This has always worked in the past. It takes about 20 seconds for the safety guide to get into position, plus another ten seconds as a margin for error …

This time, however, Swart is disturbed by the water that seems to be rising, pushing the group onto him. 'Don't be so overeager,' he tells them.

'We can't help it,' they counter. He's concerned to see that Duminy is nowhere to be seen – he's been sucked down the rapid already.

Syme, in fact, is standing helplessly by, watching Duminy being washed past him, way out of reach. Clutching at the bushes, metres above the now-submerged sandy beach, the young guide desperately flings out his throwline to people careening past, well out of reach.

This is the stuff of nightmares. Imagine that feeling of helplessness and disbelief, when all you can do is watch and shout and keep throwing out your little yellow rope. There's even less Syme can do

The first Sea Rescue crew – the Originals – got together at Bakoven in 1967, and consisted of *(left to right)* Don Nicholls, Pieter Pienaar, Mitch Brown, Bob Selman and Trevor Wilkins. The green shed in the background is the original Sea Rescue shed, with the modern rescue base next to it. *(NSRI)*

Table Bay Sea Rescue volunteers move in to take crew members off the *Eihatsu Maru*, a 50-m Japanese-registered fishing trawler hard aground at Clifton in May 2012. *(Paula Leech/NSRI)*

Following the rescue of the yacht *Llama Lo*, skipper Jean Sitruk *(right)* and crewman Kyle Castelyn *(left)* recount their experiences at the Table Bay Sea Rescue base in the V&A Waterfront. Between them is Kyle's father, Raymond. *(Andrew Ingram/NSRI)*

Hout Bay Sea Rescue volunteers aboard the *Albie Matthews* stand ready as a Metro rescue diver brings a woman to them after swimming her out of the hull of the capsized whale-watching boat *Miroshga*, 13 October 2012. *(NSRI)*

The Hout Bay fishing boat *Claremont* ran aground on Robben Island on 12 August 2013. In a dramatic rescue, the crew were plucked to safety by NSRI volunteers from the Table Bay, Bakoven and Melkbosstrand rescue bases. In this photo, the skipper of the *Claremont*, Marcelino da Silva, is helped ashore at the V&A Waterfront. *(Andrew Ingram/NSRI)*

Crewmen from the fishing boat *Claremont* come ashore after their ordeal, strain evident on their faces. The 11 men, all from communities in Hout Bay, were rescued by NSRI volunteers after the *Claremont* lost power in heavy seas off Robben Island. *(Andrew Ingram/NSRI)*

On 13 December 2012, NSRI Simon's Town volunteers were activated following a request for assistance from David Black, 26, of Newlands, whose surf ski had broken while he was on a downwind run from Miller's Point to Fish Hoek. Shown here is Black's broken craft. *(Chops Craig/NSRI)*

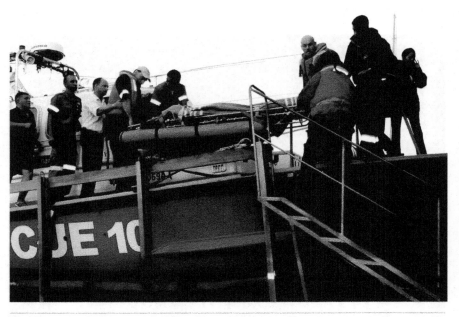

Medics and volunteers transfer David Black, warmly bundled up on a stretcher, from the NSRI rescue boat *Spirit of Safmarine III* to shore. Black's body temperature had fallen to just 32 °C as a result of his immersion in the bitterly cold waters of False Bay. *(Chops Craig/NSRI)*

The bulk carrier *Kiani Satu* ran aground on the environmentally sensitive coastline between Knysna and Sedgefield in August 2013 after suffering mechanical failure. Despite horrific sea conditions, all 19 crew members were airlifted to shore with the help of NSRI volunteers from Station 23 aboard an S-76 helicopter operated by Titan Helicopters. *(Bianca Bezuidenhout/NSRI)*

The dramatic rescue of Wayne Bergstrom by volunteers from the Knysna Sea Rescue base in March 2009 was the result of dedication, commitment and a bit of old-fashioned intuition. Shown here are *(left to right)* the late Ray Farnham, Chris van Staden, Graeme Harding, former Knysna Station Commander, Wayne Bergstrom and his wife, Belinda. *(Liza Wigley/NSRI)*

On 27 September 2015, the NSRI responded to a Mayday call from the fishing trawler *Lincoln*, reported to be taking on water in heavy sea swells 20 nautical miles south of Cape Hangklip. *Spirit of Safmarine III (right)*, from the Simon's Town Sea Rescue base, participated in the rescue operation, together with the tug *Imvubu (centre)*. Sadly, 12 fishermen lost their lives during the tragedy. *(Matthew Melidonis/NSRI)*

Senior crew member Mike Patterson *(left)*, now Deputy Station Commander, and former Station Commander Mark Hughes *(right)* at the controls of *Spirit of Richards Bay*, the 12-m rescue boat used by Station 19 (Richards Bay) since 1986.

Agulhas volunteers *(left to right)* Jaco Louw, Reinard Geldenhuys and Darryl Moon, with their Directors' Thanks, awarded for the rescue of five people from the yacht *Redfin* in August 2010. *(Andrew Ingram/NSRI)*

Witsand Sea Rescue volunteers *(left to right)* Quentin Diener, Attie Gunter and the late Leon Pretorius with the life raft from the yacht *Gulliver*, June 2011. The *Gulliver* was later found washed up on rocks on the shores of a farm in Eerste Rivier. For their heroic work in rescuing the yacht's crew – Greg West, Frans Strung, Mike Morck and Shaun Kennedy – the Witsand volunteers received the NSRI's Gallantry Award Silver class. *(NSRI)*

Nadine Gordimer, the ten-metre rescue boat operated by Station 8, Hout Bay. *(stefansmuts.com)*

A joint training exercise with crews from various rescue bases is an opportunity to build camaraderie as well as to hone skills and techniques. The NSRI is deeply rooted in the communities it serves, and volunteers liken it to being part of a family. *(Chris McCarthy/NSRI)*

when the bag gets snagged and he can't even haul it in for another attempt. He concentrates on remaining calm, and takes the time to tie off the throwline to a sturdy branch with a good, solid knot.

Herman Swart has been paddling with one of the women. Wilma Woest has been struggling a bit, so he's holding on to the handle of her tube with one hand, and paddling with the other. They flush through the rapid in tandem, and the next thing he sees is carnage. There's no way he can control these two tubes in the churning, growling water … All seems hopeless. Until a guardian angel joins the fray. For a split second in that brown chaos, Herman glimpses a little yellow piece of rope. He yells to Wilma to grab hold of it. Miraculously, they both manage to do so.

Hanging on grimly with both hands, Herman feels the water tearing at his body, tugging him downstream. To make matters worse, his tube has somehow landed on the upstream side, and is being pushed against his face by the force of the swollen river. There's nothing he can do but fight to stay on top of the water; fight for air; fight for life. Syme comes to the rescue, wading into the current to give his buddy and the client a hand out. It's his throwline that has saved these two lives.

That same throwline – or at least Syme's frantic attempts with it – has indirectly saved another. Andrew Gay bobbed through that rapid at quite a speed, and now he can't see any takeout spot above the churning brown water. But he does hear a guide screaming 'Come left!', which he tries to heed. And, when he sees that guide desperately casting his throwline, Gay realises the situation is dire. 'I ditched my tube and swam,' he recalls.

Gay manages to get to the side about 40 m past the escape ladder. Hauling himself out on a rock, he has no idea quite how close he's just come to death. Just a single metre beyond that rock, and he would have had almost no chance at all.

Gay looks around. On the other side, he recognises colleague Neville Areington. He sees some empty tubes. And he searches for 15-year-old Richard Wagner, Areington's stepson, who only moments ago was bobbing happily along, 'still sitting on his tube with a big grin on his face', unaware of the danger that was about to consume him.

In an attempt to rescue Gay, three guides jump into the heaving water and half-float, half-wade towards him. Oblivious, it seems, to the extent of the danger they're putting themselves in, so intent are they on rescuing their client.

Brouwer's group has made its way up that steep hill. It's still raining, so they don't bother taking off their wetsuits. They just stand shivering under a tarpaulin, enjoying the snacks provided. It's been a mellow trip. Angus Stembull's group, the first of the day, is already back at the SRA centre, having a drink, looking at all the photographs of previous trips, and laughing about their own.

The partners of those in group three are not quite so cheerful or full of smiles. Wives are frustrated that their husbands are taking so long to get back. The miserable weather has meant their planned boat ride in the mouth of the river has been cancelled, and they're all cooped up in one small room with some increasingly antsy children.

At 2.30 pm, they decide they've had enough hanging around. They're not going to wait for the guys to arrive before going ahead and having lunch. Sometime after 3.30 pm, one of the Storms River Adventures office staff tells them the group will still be a while longer, as they're now doing the gorge after all. Just typical, think the wives.

Jaco Swart has been trying to reach Dawn Boggenpoel. She's floating down about ten metres ahead of him, but he can't narrow the gap between them. His thought is to catch up with her, hook his foot through one of the handles on her tube and paddle her to the bank and its exit route. It's the way he's done it so many times in the past. 'But then I realise I'm not gaining on her.' They're both just being swept towards that narrow gorge, where a 20-m-wide river must compress itself into about a fifth of that width.

Instead of finding himself near the left bank and its exit, Swart finds the whole surge of the current now pushing to the right. At lower water levels, there's a position named Point of No Return a bit further down. In reality, he has passed his already.

Washed directly over a section that tubers would normally wade through knee-deep to begin their gorge trip, he finds himself plummeting over a vertical drop of about five metres. Freefalling. Then he lands. On his knee. He feels the crunch. Feels it shatter. But there is no pain yet.

Swart is in a cauldron of chaos, yet his mind remains lucid. There's a distinctive spot just further downstream where on usual gorge trips you pass beneath a log that's jammed across the gorge about four metres above your head. He knows where that log should be. But this time he's swept over it. His mind registers that his dangling, damaged leg doesn't even touch the log – a measure of how much higher the water is than at any other time he's been here.

The other thing he notices quite clearly is the quiet. The absolute silence in his head. 'Like playing a video with the sound shut off.'

He spots a little eddy on his right. Boggenpoel and young Richard Wagner are sheltering there, with their tubes. He can't get to them but, as he's swept past, he indicates to them to stay put. He even has the presence of mind to look up to ensure the gorge is clear all the way to the top, so that searching helicopters will have no trouble spotting them.

But Jaco Swart is the last person to see those two alive.

'I believe they either panicked and tried to follow me or, with a change of water level later …'

Further down, Swart spots George Stulting, one of the senior partners in the law firm that initiated this trip. The elderly man has no tube, but he is floating with his head above water. Swart manages to grab him and the two clasp each other's shoulders across the single tube, all the while being swept downstream through the narrow, sheer-sided gorge.

There's a place in the gorge where a section of the cliff juts out into the stream. Usually the water just flows round it. Today it's pummelling into the cliff. Swart and Stulting are swept into the rock, where they spend a good while being recirculated in a triangular death trap. Swart tries to get a foot into the corner each time to push them away, but they're being tumbled at such speed that his one good foot just keeps glancing off the wall. The two seem irrevocably trapped in this cycle of aerated water, water-saturated air. Then the old man just seems to give up.

'Uncle George just smiled at me. He had a very friendly face. And he let go of me. I couldn't hold on to his wetsuit ... It twisted out of my hand and I just lost him. He went under ...'

This changes the dynamics. Next time a lateral wave hits Swart, it lifts him high into the air. In fact, it tosses him into the corner, where an old tree branch is lodged in a crack. 'I've never caught anything that valuable,' he recalls. Mercifully, his tube is lodged between his body and the branch. Frantically casting around with his one good leg while hanging on with his arms, he finds a small foothold. With a bit of weight on this, he can hook his elbow over a fork in the branch.

Jaco Swart will hang like this for 27 hours. At one stage he will manage to put his one leg through the deflated tube, which he hangs over the fork as a makeshift sling. Once in the night, the branch will shift in the pitch dark. He will taste terror again. Exhaustion will seep in, but he cannot afford to fall asleep. In the night he has no idea whether the river is rising or falling. Swart will pray throughout the night. He'll pray without ceasing. He will go through every scene from his life, forgiving those who have wronged him, asking for forgiveness from those he has wronged. 'A real cleansing of the soul,' he remembers. At 6.11 am on Sunday morning, the first light breaks through. 'Things always look brighter in the light,' is his thought at that point. Scrutinising the wall opposite, he notices from the lichen growing there that the water has dropped about two and a half to three metres. He notices a pillow-sized rock a bit lower down, and manages to climb down to it. It's chilly; he urinates in his wetsuit to keep warm.

At 9.35 am he decides to look for a sign: if the water drops exactly a foot in the next hour, he'll know it's God's will that he jump in and try to make his own way out of this death trap of a ravine. Perched as he is under an overhang, he's coldly aware that he's invisible from the sky.

By 10.35 am the water has dropped only six inches. He must stay put. At one point he thinks he hears a helicopter nearby. Nothing comes of it, and he decides the sound must have been a delusional mind's confusion with the noise of water beating and echoing off rock walls.

More interminable hours.

Finally, at about 1 pm, he hears it coming closer and louder. In the small piece of sky that's visible, he sees the ends of the rotors. It's definitely a helicopter.

Swart leans out and waves his tube. The sound remains static, but he can feel the downdraft from the rotors. He sees fern leaves being blown downward, and spray upward.

Then a person dangling on the end of a cable hovers into view. Rescuer Douw Steyn gives Jaco Swart a big thumbs-up. 'I was cold, my knee was sore, but I was singing and crying and laughing,' he remembers afterwards.

The rescue takes five more hours. Climbers have to be dropped by helicopter on a nearby cliff. They abseil down to the tuber and help him climb up to an exposed outcrop that the helicopter can access. Steyn talks the helicopter pilot in. The two are so accurate, they drop a 40-kg sandbag on the end of a 180-m line. The sandbag, which stops the line being whipped up into the chopper blades, and stabilises it for accuracy, lands directly on Swart's knee. The pain is unbearable, but he doesn't care. He's winched up and carried off, still dangling below the chopper, on an unimaginably scenic ride. There's only one thing he wants to see: his brother, alive and well. It's the first sight that greets him as he lands.

There's an ambulance waiting nearby. It already has someone in it – the only other person who went into that gorge and came out alive. Pieter Cilliers has also been trapped on a tiny ledge all afternoon, all night and most of today. He's also been praying non-stop. He's also praising God for miraculously saving his life.

Swart asks about the rest of his group. Are they all okay? Thirteen people are missing, he's told. He passes out.

Postscript

The Port Elizabeth legal firm of Stulting, Cilliers and De Jager lost senior partners Bertus de Jager and George Stulting and colleagues Erich Knoetze and Charles Wait. Pieter Cilliers was the only survivor.

Engen employees who died were Dawn Boggenpoel, retail manager John Boyd, Estelle Grobler, Bartholomeus Duminy and Quinten van Rensburg. Others who died were family members Jan Grobler, Richard Wagner and Marie and Keisha Pieters.

A year and a half later, Magistrate Theresa Bothma, sitting in the Humansdorp Magistrate's Court, found that no one was guilty of negligence in the disaster. She found that the deaths were the result of natural elements and not negligence on the part of the guides, the adventure company or the Department of Water Affairs and Forestry.

21 *The other Cape of Storms*

Andrew Ingram and Tony Weaver

MOSSEL BAY ON THE SOUTHERN Cape coast officially marks the start of the Garden Route, and is reputed to have the healthiest climate of any town in South Africa. For centuries, it has provided a safe haven for mariners; the Portuguese navigator, Bartolomeu Dias, and his crew were the first Europeans to land there, on 3 February 1488 (after he managed to sail right around the Cape of Good Hope without realising it), followed in 1497 by his compatriot, Vasco da Gama, by when the bay had been charted as *Aguada de São Brás,* (the Watering Place of St Blaize).

Archaeological explorations in caves in the area, notably those at Pinnacle Point, have revealed that the area gave shelter to our ancestors more than 164 000 years ago.

But as balmy as its climate is for some of the year, the coast also gets lashed by fearsome storms. One of those storms hit the Portuguese navigator Pedro d'Ataide in 1501, when he lost contact with the three other ships in his fleet and put in to Mossel Bay. He wrote an account of his woes, which he hid in an old shoe in a milkwood tree, now a national monument called the Post Office Tree.

Some 528 years after Dias put ashore, Andrew and I are sitting very close to where he landed, at NSRI Station 15, perched above the Mossel Bay harbour, listening to some more history. With us in the Ops Room are Mossel Bay's first Station Commander, Ian Hamilton, who helped establish the station in 1969; the Station Commander from 2000 to 2012, Dawie Zwiegelaar; current Station Commander André Fraser, who also served in that position from 1994 to 2000; and coxswain Roger Brink.

Their stories mostly centre around the fearsome storms that smash their way through here, like the one on 21 November 1997, which saw two boats, the *Dankie Pa* and the *Betta Luck*, disappear without a trace, with none of the nine crew members ever found. Roger was the coxswain (and was awarded a Meritorious Service Certificate for his role), and he says that 'it was just a freak force 10 wind (89 to 102 km/h) that came up very quickly, with swells of over 10 m; we never found anything except for a tiny bit of debris.'

But there is one operation that they all kept coming back to as one of the most epic ever, because the conditions were so appallingly bad: the wreck of a local fishing trawler, *Mandi*, on Monday 26 October 2009.

The 12-m *Mandi* had sailed from Mossel Bay the previous Wednesday, 21 October, to trawl for sole off Still Bay. It was a good trip; the team worked well together and enjoyed being at sea. They had about three tons of fish on board before the weather started to deteriorate on Sunday, and when the skipper, Christopher Diedrichts, announced he was running for home, the crew was in high spirits. Soon they'd be back with their families.

But the weather steadily deteriorated. Early on the Monday, near hurricane-strength winds began to lash Cape Town, causing major damage and killing at least two people, and by mid-morning, the Southern Cape was starting to feel its full force, with the swell building to a scary eight to ten metres.

By midday, the usually calm waters of Mossel Bay had turned gunmetal grey and had become a foaming mass of huge waves. Gusting at more than 110 km/h, the wind made it hard to stand upright. One of the worst storms in living memory had landed.

Sea Rescue volunteer Quintus Deacon, 25, visited Station Commander Dawie Zwiegelaar around mid-morning, and while they were chatting asked, 'If there's a call-out, would we go out in a sea like this?'

Dawie said he replied: 'Ja, you know, if you take it head-on, you can go out in almost any sea. But I never thought that there was going to be a call-out.'

The first alert came from the supply tug *Seacor Achiever*, which called Mossel Bay Port Control on VHF channel 12. It was 12.09 pm. Dawie said, 'I got the call and I went down to The Point and saw the capsized trawler floating there, and I thought there is no way anybody can go out in those conditions. I rushed to the boathouse, put out a code red and another coxswain arrived and said, "You can't go out in this," and I said, "We need to do something." We couldn't just sit back and do nothing.

'I asked for volunteers and, of course, there were quite a lot of them. So I picked the three youngest and fittest guys.'

Corné Wessels was one of those three. He later wrote that 'we launched the nine-metre *Vodacom Rescuer 1* – we managed to do it all within three minutes. And then we went out into that wild sea. When the first wave hit us, just outside the harbour, we realised just how massive the swell was. We tried to head for the capsized trawler, but after the fourth wave hit us, we realised our boat's engines simply couldn't function properly. With waves bigger than nine metres, it was simply impossible for us to operate.

'Every time we hit a wave, it felt as if the boat had exploded, and we had to hang on for life and death. It was a matter of survival, and we headed back to port.'

Dawie said that 'as we left the harbour, I could feel that the one motor was cavitating [when aerated water causes the propellor to spin too fast, thereby losing traction and thrust], so we turned around and sorted it out, then went around The Point and three or four monster waves, nine, ten metres, were coming for us, and I said to the guys, "There is no way we can carry on in this boat."

Inspector Arno Cloete, of the police's Border Unit, was standing on the balcony of his office watching the little trawler battling the seas at the moment it foundered. He glanced down at his cellphone, and when he looked up again *Mandi* had capsized.

'I ran for the VHF radio and called the Port Office,' he says. Things became a blur as the experienced young policeman shouted for his colleagues, Inspectors Francois Joubert and Hugo Jordaan. They hooked up their new six-metre rigid inflatable boat (RIB) and, with lights and sirens on, raced for the slipway at the Mossel Bay Yacht Club. In the bouncing boat, they struggled to get their uniforms off, and wetsuits and life jackets on, and to secure any loose gear on the deck.

Huge waves breaking onto the yacht club slipway made it impossible to launch from there, but Arno thought there was a chance that he could get in at the municipal slipway 150 m away. He had seen the trawler crew in the water and knew that every minute was an eternity in those conditions.

With two-metre waves smashing onto the ramp, the men managed to get the boat into the water and, gunning the powerful engines, headed towards the open water. 'A trip that normally takes two minutes took us 17 minutes. It was so bad that our engines were sometimes totally under water,' says Arno.

'At the harbour mouth, the first really big wave hit us. A gas cylinder came flying past my head and there was a lot of rope in the water. We went up, and then it felt like we were falling into eternity. The wind was so strong that I was scared we would flip, so Francois and Hugo moved to the bow,' Arno said.

Eventually the police boat battered its way to the upturned hull, and Arno manoeuvred up to the life raft tethered to it. 'There was nobody inside,' Arno said. They spotted two bodies close by, and while trying to recover one, a huge breaking wave slammed into them. The boat was thrown up and pushed over to the port side, and for long seconds it seemed that they would go over. 'By the grace of God we didn't, but the starboard engine cut out,' said Arno.

After this narrow escape, they ran back to the harbour to reassess their options. In the safety of the harbour, they pulled up alongside Sea Rescue's *Vodacom Rescuer 1*.

Dawie continues: 'The police boat had also turned back. He had got all the way out to the casualty boat and almost flipped, and came back in. We did a couple of runs in front of the bay area to see if we could see some of the crew, and then they called us on the radio to say that, incredibly, there was this guy, Robert Pace, who is hugely experienced on a jet-ski; he had gone out on a ski, and he had found a casualty alive, but he couldn't load him onto the ski.

'We said to the harbour captain, we're going out, but we need the support of the tug, the *Arctic Tern*. And she went out, and was about 200 m out and the first wave hit her right on the bow and I swear I saw the keel of that boat, it almost overturned, and they made a 180-degree turn and rushed back to the harbour. They had to treat the tug's skipper for shock.'

Robert Pace later told Andrew that 'I did a crisscross over the swells, didn't find anyone, and came back. It was on the second run that I found the oke floating in the water.' He had found the only survivor, 30-year-old Wilhelm Isaacs. 'I went closer and asked him to grab the back of the jet-ski, but he was too weak. He looked up at me and said, "*Meneer, moet my asseblief nie hier los nie*" [Sir, please don't leave me here].'

Then the police boat came racing towards him. 'It was just the greatest feeling,' said Arno. 'We jumped three or four huge waves and then landed right next to him; Francois and Hugo leaned over and pulled him in. He was completely exhausted; Wilhelm was unable to help them.'

Looking Francois in the eye, he said, '*Die Here het julle gestuur*' [God sent you]. Then he passed out.'

The conditions were, almost unbelievably, still deteriorating. The only way that the police crew could keep Wilhelm in the boat was quite literally to stand on him. Despite this, after handing him over to an ambulance crew, the men took their boats back, hoping against hope to find more survivors.

To the roar of the wind and waves there was added the 'whup-whup-whup' of a helicopter. Kobus Crous, legendary Mossel Bay pilot, had arrived in his little four-seater Robinson 44 to help. When most pilots would be strapping their machines down, Kobus had not hesitated to assist after hearing about the disaster.

Kobus is well known in the area for being an exceptional pilot with a keen sense of judgement, so nobody was surprised to see the machine. In these weather conditions, only a pilot with vast experience and natural ability would dare to fly. Kobus is just such a man. He is one with his machine.

'We did a couple of runs, but the sea conditions were shocking,' Dawie said. 'I was standing on top, I didn't want to be inside the boat, I said to the guys, "Don't sit inside, so that if we capsize, you can get out." The spray was being driven like needles by the wind, it was like sand blasting on our faces; we couldn't see a thing.

'That was the worst sea I have ever been in in my life.'

André Fraser says, 'I call it a kotch sea, a vomit sea, completely *deur-mekaar* [confused]. There's no regular swell, just huge waves, typical westerly, southwesterly short sea, the waves just too close together.'

By now the sea was so wild that the two skippers decided it was just too dangerous.

'Waves were breaking randomly, the sea was unreadable. We were at our limit and it was now about our survival,' Dawie said. 'I would have loved to have done more and was deeply disappointed that we had to turn around. But I couldn't put these guys' lives at risk any more. It's more difficult to turn around than to carry on, I can tell you.

'The waves were just too close to each other. You couldn't turn around in an emergency. It was breaking right across the bay: one hand was on the steering, the other on the trim and tilt just trying to keep those engines in the water.'

Mossel Bay's grizzled veteran, Ian Hamilton, said that 'when you think of the conditions that day, it takes more courage from the coxswain to turn around than to go forward. It's not just his safety, it's the crew's as well.'

Dawie says that 'two of those guys on the crew grew up in front of me. I thought to myself, how can I look their parents in the eyes if something bad happens to these kids? So I turned around.

'They brought Wilhelm into the harbour, where the ambulance was waiting for him. He was the only survivor; five guys died that day.'

Meanwhile, Kobus Crous was in the air acting as a spotter for the rescue crews, trying to find the five bodies in the maelstrom. But there was a problem: the gawkers.

Corné Wessels says that 'at De Bakke, a volunteer had already recovered one body. But it was chaos in all directions. The road and whole area was blocked by curious onlookers and cars. We were trapped in a huge traffic jam, and battled to arrive at our destination. We raced to Diaz Beach, where Kobus had spotted another body, with screaming sirens and lights.

'But spotting was very hard: the crew of the *Mandi* had all been wearing green oilskin suits, and it was very hard to distinguish the bodies from all the floating green fish crates that were drifting across the whole bay. We then spotted a body, but because of the impossibly huge waves no one could enter the water. We had to wait until the bodies washed ashore.'

Eventually all five missing crew members were recovered, and the shattered volunteers returned to the base to debrief and recover.

Corné later wrote that 'back at the boathouse, there was an atmosphere of exhaustion, sadness, shock and relief. Such a tragic day will stay with all of us who were involved for years to come. But we are proud of the service that we all delivered. From the crew of the police boat to Kobus Crous – who risked his own life braving the gale-force winds in his helicopter. And to my fellow NSRI volunteers: I salute you.'

Quintus Deacon went back to where he had abandoned his bakkie, the hazard lights still flashing, window wound down, the interior of the cab soaked from the driving spray. 'The indicators were still on, flashing against the building in front, and it was like there was that "freeze" moment, like, "Sheesh, actually five people lost their lives when that trawler capsized,"' he remembers.

The extreme danger of the operation had hit home.

For jet-ski hero Robert Pace, it hit when he got into the shower back home: 'I just started shaking.'

* * *

Four months later, sitting in his little one-roomed house in the township on the outskirts of Mossel Bay, survivor Wilhelm Isaacs told his story to Andrew in a staccato monotone.

'It was like a daydream. There was this bang on the keel, spray over the boat, and then I was in the water. I prayed, I prayed, I prayed, I asked God to help ...'

He puts his head in his hands and his body starts to shake. Tears run down his face and splash onto the bare concrete floor, forming a puddle between his feet. He tries to compose himself.

'Sometimes I struggle to breathe; it's like I am in the water again. I haven't told my wife about that. I don't know what to do, I'm too shy to tell them that I am scared. I tell them all the time that I am alright, I am good. I don't want to look like a lady or something, I am a man, *mos* [right]?'

Wilhelm's wife, Nicolene, 28 at the time, quietly walks out of the house with the child that she is minding to help support her husband financially. He sits alone on an old couch, his shoulders shaking and the tears flowing freely.

'I married her to look after her. How can I help her without going to sea? I thought to kill myself. I pray. Sometimes we don't even have food and I must run to my mother's house, there is no money.

'You put your face in a washing machine and you hold your breath. You can't hold your breath long. I am talking about eight-, nine-metre swells. I was just too cold. But what could I do? You see a friend of yours drown, and you try, you try to go and help him but you can't get there. The chief engineer, Christopher Gurner from Cape Town, he was my best friend.'

Wilhelm can't talk any more. He lifts his tear-streaked head from his hands and says, 'The friends that I lost, they were my family. I miss them. I am alone here.'

- *The men who drowned that day were Christopher Diedrichts, Christopher Gurner, Edward Hunter, Edward Stoltz and Winston Michaels.*
- *Kobus Crous, Robert Pace, and Inspectors Arno Cloete, Francois Joubert and Hugo Jordaan all received the NSRI Directors' Thanks for their bravery.*

22 Twelve men died that night

Andrew Ingram and Tony Weaver

THE TOWN OF WELLINGTON, IN the Boland, is home to a close-knit community of fishing families whose menfolk have been going to sea for decades. When disaster strikes, word spreads quickly among friends and neighbours.

Thus it was that, late at night on Sunday 27 September 2015, word spread fast that the 42-m fishing trawler MFV *Lincoln* was possibly in trouble and might have sunk.

Rosemarie van der Heever was one of those woken at around 11 pm that night by a neighbour, who told her that 'something terrible' had happened to the *Lincoln*. Her husband, Derrick, then 39, was a crewman on board the vessel. 'He was a man who did not know how to live on land. He lived and breathed the ocean,' Rosemarie told *Die Burger*.

She tried calling the owners of the *Lincoln*, Viking Fishing, in Cape Town, but at that late hour there was nobody answering the phones. The next morning, she heard the news: 'I was told that Derrick died, but it did not feel like he was gone,' Rosemarie said as she stared at the wall.

Jacobus Juries, then 44, also died. 'My brother had the biggest heart,' his sister Lucinda said. Jonathan Diedericks was the third man from Wellington among the 12 dead that dreadful day.

On Monday 28 September, there was still no finality about casualty numbers, and fear gripped the Wellington community. Bianca Julies was due to celebrate her 19th birthday that day, but instead the family sat around in despair, convinced that her father, Peter, was dead.

The news wasn't good. They had heard that nine fishermen had died, nine had survived and three were still missing after the *Lincoln* had taken on water in heavy swells 20 nautical miles south of Cape Hangklip and 35 nautical miles southeast of Cape Point.

Peter's sister, Lena Welkom, said as they waited for news that Peter's wife, Salomé, was in agony.

'On Sunday night, close to midnight, Salomé's daughter got a call that Peter has died at sea. You can imagine that everybody went in shock. Now, this morning [Monday] someone from Viking called to say Peter was okay.

'We said, let us just talk with him, so we can know he is really okay. But till now, we are still waiting. We can't take it any more. If he really is alive, why won't they let us talk to him?'

Lena was at work at an old-age home in Wellington on Monday morning when she got the news.

'Peter is my baby brother. This was only his third week on this boat, but he has worked on fishing boats for seven years. He always said he can't manage on dry land. The sea is his home.'

And it wasn't just Peter that they were worried about, Lena said. 'We know all the men on the boat, because they are all from Wellington. They are all friends. I start crying every time I hear the name of another person who has died or has survived on that boat.'

She rattled off the nicknames and names. 'There's Mr Big, Vlam (because he turns pink in the sun so quickly), Jonathan, Aiden, Derrick, Brandon, Jacobus ... They are our people, now we don't even know where they are. We just want the boat people to tell us where they are,' she told *Die Burger*.

And then came the good news for the family: Peter was one of the survivors.

Slowly the story of that terrifying night emerged.

Peter was lucky to survive: 'The weather was very, very rough and the boat started taking water on the port side. Soon the boat was leaning completely to the one side and we knew it was time to save ourselves.

'I jumped from the starboard side into the freezing water. Soon I couldn't even feel my legs. The rain was pouring down and the gale-force wind had no mercy. Luckily help didn't take too long, but it was too late for some of my friends,' he told the *Cape Times* the next day.

He narrowly escaped being dragged under and was almost sucked into the vortex created by the still-turning propeller of the *Lincoln*, but managed to kick off his sea boots and swim away to safety.

Earlier on Sunday, in Hermanus, Petrus Hendrikz shut the door to his restaurant above the Old Harbour and stood for a while looking at the sea. It was wild. Huge swells were marching across Walker Bay and slamming into the cliffs. The water was slate grey. Wind blew the tops off the waves in a shower of spray. It was not an evening to be out at sea.

Petrus and his wife, Estelle, both volunteer fundraisers with the Hermanus NSRI (Station 17), had been invited to have supper with Station Commander Deon Langenhoven and arrived at around 5.30 pm. They told Deon how bad conditions were.

'I have never seen it so rough,' said Petrus.

With a laugh he added, 'If there is a call-out there is no way that you will be able to launch either of the rescue boats.'

It was Deon's night to cook and he had prepared pork chops. Shortly after 6 pm he took them out of the oven and was putting the last touches to the gravy when the SMS came through.

'NSRI Station 17, contact Port Control.'

As his guests detected the change in Deon's mood, conversation stopped. His wife, Jane, had seen this many times before and she watched as he dialled Cape Town Port Control and listened intently.

'Activate the crew,' he said before cutting the call.

Looking at his guests, he excused himself. 'We have a situation. There is a vessel in distress 20 miles south of Hangklip. She's taking water in heavy seas. The crew is abandoning ship.'

It was 6.06 – exactly 40 minutes to go until sunset.

For people who live on, and love, the sea, there is nothing quite as electrifying as a Mayday. For the person transmitting the call, it is their final hope. They need help. Desperately.

'MAYDAY, MAYDAY, MAYDAY, this is the Fishing Vessel *Lincoln*. Mayday.'

As the Hermanus Sea Rescue volunteers were scrambling to their base, fishermen and even the captain of a bulk carrier answered the call for help.

'*Lincoln* this is Fishing Vessel *Sistro*, three hours to distress position … *Armana* … four hours from position … *Trust Agility* … estimated time of arrival six hours … *Fuchsia* … 1.5 hours estimated time of arrival … *Harvest Rising* one hour from position.'

Navigators put the *Lincoln*'s position into the chart plotters of their vessels and, if they thought they could help, swung their bows around and nudged the throttles forward.

It's what you do at sea. In a Mayday situation you don't ask questions. You just get there as fast as the sea will allow.

Harvest Rising, the ship nearest to the *Lincoln*, is a 189-m, 27 000-ton bulk carrier. Realising that they were closest to the *Lincoln*, the captain slowly swung the bow of the huge ship towards the floundering 42-m trawler. Conditions were foul and the sea was huge. Swells of up to six metres were being whipped by a gale-force southeasterly wind.

It was 40 minutes before sunset as the 21 fishermen, all wearing life jackets, abandoned ship.

Darren Zimmerman, Simon's Town (Station 10) Commander, had seen a call-out message for the Gordon's Bay volunteers, and then the call for Hermanus: 'I thought to myself … mmm, something is brewing. So I called Anton Prinsloo (Station Commander at Gordon's Bay, Station 9). He said that one of his coxswains was dealing with it and he would call me back. Minutes later he did.

'It sounds like a vessel going down on the Hermanus side. Deon at Hermanus is handling it,' said Anton.

Darren had seen that Deon was on WhatsApp and sent him a message: 'We are available if you need us.'

Deon, knowing that there were 21 people on board the *Lincoln*, answered that Simon's Town should please launch.

Darren activated his crew.

About 20 minutes later, as the ten-metre Simon's Town rescue boat, *Spirit of Safmarine III*, was backing off its cradle, the Hermanus crew gave them the position of the *Lincoln*.

'Our plot put the vessel 46 miles from us, so we knew we were in for a long run,' said Darren.

'We zooted around the wall doing about 20 knots on to a course straight on to the position, but within five miles we were down to eight or nine knots and running into a big sea.'

By now the Hermanus rescue boat, *South Star*, was pounding into huge swells. The boat would come off the top of a wave and slam into the next, sending green water rushing over the deck and white spray flying high over it, climb up the next swell and slide down the other side.

'I told the guys just hang on. Don't try and do anything,' said Deon, who was at the helm. The doors and hatches of *South Star* were battened down and Deon had to judge how fast he could go, how hard he could push his boat and the crew.

While the two rescue boats were racing for the *Lincoln*, the SAAF/NSRI Air Sea Rescue unit (Station 29) had been called out. With so many people having abandoned ship, eyes in the sky would be crucial. The 22 Squadron ground crew readied a Lynx helicopter for the operation as the aircrew and the NSRI rescue swimmers reported to Ysterplaat Air Force Base.

The SAAF base security had been briefed on the call-out, and were expecting the Sea Rescue crew. Rescue swimmers Lourens de Villiers and Davide del Fante were first to arrive, followed by Ernesta Swanepoel.

They stopped at the security gate and showed their IDs.

'Be careful. Be safe out there,' Ernesta remembers the guard saying as the boom swung open.

Under the floodlighting and full moon, the Air Sea Rescue crew went through their equipment checks, with each person responsible for specific tasks. In the final briefing, the Lynx commander decided to take only one rescue swimmer, Davide del Fante. The weight saved by leaving a second swimmer behind would give them more time in the search area.

Harvest Rising was the first vessel to arrive on scene, and, despite the enormous size of the ship and the terrible sea conditions, the captain and crew managed to rescue three people. They also dropped their life raft in the hope that survivors could climb aboard.

Next to arrive were the *Armana*, the *Fuchsia* and the *African Queen*, all using their lights with the full moon to try and find survivors.

It was 9.30 pm when the NSRI's *South Star* arrived in the search area.

'We saw the lights of the vessels, all in a line, and as we approached the first one, the *Armana*, they called. They had seen something in the water,' said Deon.

'They had crew up on their bow, which was a great vantage point. Following their signals we saw the first body.' Hermanus rescue swimmers were chosen for their strength and agility. Wearing full protective gear, André Barnard and Alwyn Geldenhuys went out on deck and moved up to the bow of *South Star*.

'They had a hell of a ride,' said Deon. As the rescue boat bow dropped into a trough, freezing water washed over the two swimmers. Signalling to Deon at the helm to bring the boat alongside, and then moving back to the stern, keeping pace with the person in the water, they gave Deon the exact position of the casualty until they could grab him and pull him aboard.

They carried him into the cabin and checked carefully for vital signs. There were none.

Using this search method, with the crew of the *Armana* spotting from their elevated position, the Hermanus volunteers found another two bodies. By now the crews on both *Spirit of Safmarine III* and *South Star* were battling seasickness. The little rescue boats were being tossed around like corks.

'I heard that the helicopter was in the air and 15 minutes later they flew over us,' said Darren.

'That was a mixture of emotions. It was so frustrating to hear what was unfolding on scene. And we couldn't get there faster … as hard as we tried.'

There was phosphorescence in the water, which allowed Darren to see the tops of the waves and throttle back to prevent the boat from crashing into the hole between the wave crests.

'The boat would ride up a wave and then dive down the other side. If we didn't get it right, we would fall. Everyone was braced in, and after every fall each would call, "I am okay," so I didn't have to turn around to check. Those were the worst conditions that I have ever been out in,' said Darren, who at the time had been with Sea Rescue for 25 years, and a coxswain for 21 of those years.

For the four controllers at the two rescue bases, it was difficult to know that their boat crews were taking such a hammering. And for most of the operation, the rescue boats were out of radio range of the bases. They had to talk to their vessels via Cape Town Radio.

'We were well aware of the hammering that they were taking. They are heroes, man,' said Simon's Town controller John Sleigh after the rescue.

At about 10.15 pm the SAAF Lynx helicopter arrived in the search area and in quick succession found a life ring and life raft. Both had lights switched on, which stood out like beacons to the aircrew.

Both were empty.

As the Lynx started to run a search pattern, the crew spotted two life jackets. 'Our light picked up on the reflective tape on the jackets,' said Davide del Fante.

The helicopter went into a hover and radioed *South Star* to come across to their position. Two fishermen, about 70 m apart, were lifted onto *South Star*. But it was too late for them.

As each of the rescue boats and helicopter reached the edge of their fuel endurance, they were released from the search area. In all, nine of the 21 lives were saved by the vessels that responded to the Mayday.

Nine bodies were recovered and three fishermen were lost at sea.

On Wednesday afternoon, Deon got a call from the family of one of the fishermen who had died on that terrible night. They had come to Hermanus to identify his body and wanted to meet the Sea Rescue crew who went out to try and save him.

'They were at the New Harbour, so I called our crew and we invited them into the base,' said Deon.

'The whole family was there: his wife, brother, two sons, his daughter and his sister. They showed us a picture of their dad.

'His was the first body that we found.'

'They wanted to know what the water conditions were, what it was like out there. The children had lots of questions ...' Deon's voice trails off.

'It was very emotional to meet the family. And to know that we brought their father back. It's closure for them. They could say their last farewell. It's not always that we can do that.'

23 The sea was chocolate

Tony Weaver

KwaZulu-Natal is the South African province that gets nailed by severe floods more regularly than any other. And it's a double whammy. Tropical storms and cyclones tend to make landfall in the first quarter of the year, and cut-off low pressure systems hit the province in the third and fourth quarters. Cyclone Domoina (sometimes also spelled Demoina), which struck on 28 January 1984, leaving 242 people dead in then Natal province, Swaziland and Mozambique, is one of the more famous of these storms.

But it was a cut-off low pressure system that hit Natal on 28 September, and for the next five days, in 1987 that is remembered as the most disastrous storm ever to hit South Africa. It caused far more damage than Domoina and killed 506 people across the province. More than 50 000 people were left homeless, infrastructure damage amounted to around R400 million (at 1987 rates) and some areas received up to 900 mm of rain – just short of a metre – in four days.

Mark Hughes, currently the NSRI's Executive Director of Operations, and then one of the coxswains at Station 19, Richards Bay, remembers the floods as being one of the most challenging operations the station was ever involved in.

'We had more than 700 mm of rain in a couple of days, and all the rivers came down in flood. The sea turned into this mass of floating vegetation. There were hippos and crocs everywhere, cattle on the beaches, human corpses on the beach, dead and living dogs, there was

172

so much debris about we couldn't even use our vehicles on the beach.

'A friend of mine, Johan Blignault, was driving to work and the bridge had been washed away. He drove off the end but survived the crash.'

Mark describes it as being a 'bizarre time'.

'We got a call from a ship to say they had come across a papyrus island the size of a rugby field and there were a whole bunch of people on it. We rushed out there in our six-metre boat, *Aberdare 2*. The "humans" were baboons and monkeys and there was nothing we could do; we couldn't load them on the boat. Luckily they washed back to shore.'

The crews came across cattle that looked as though they were swimming two miles out to sea.

'But when we came alongside, they were dead and bloated; it was just the way they were bobbing in the waves that made them look alive. We had ships recovering bodies way out to sea and there were dead animals everywhere.'

In the middle of it all, the station got a Mayday call from a solo yachtsman who was desperately battling his way to Richards Bay through giant swells. 'The seas were horrendous, the swell was bigger than ten metres, it was unbelievable. There's an area we call the Dance Floor off the South Pier of the harbour where the wave action gets messed up by the effect of the South and North Pier and you get very confused seas, and that's where he was heading.

'We were powering our way through to get to him and I had my head down checking the radar screen, and the next moment it felt like I was being pushed down by a jet thrust, I looked up and we were completely airborne. We crashed down, breaking the one engine mounting. Mike Patterson was the coxswain that day, and he came down so hard on his chair that he compressed his vertebrae.

'Crew member Ubaldo Faranacci was dumped down so hard he broke his leg and I had whiplash. Ubaldo was screaming, and Mike couldn't move. We strapped him to his chair and he drove the boat like that, only just able to reach the throttle.

'We got hold of the yacht on CB radio and told him that he would have to come in on his own, we now had to take care of our own injured crew. Our other boat, the *Aberdare*, tried to get to him but couldn't. The yacht started to run aground in a ten-metre swell. We told the yachtsman to jump overboard and strike out for the shore, where we had a crew standing by.

'He was washed all the way around the South Pier and washed up on the beach. He was in shock, hypothermic and completely exhausted. He hadn't slept for four days and he had lost everything.'

But the Sea Rescue crews weren't just deployed out at sea. The entire region was under water, bridges were washed away, and entire villages were in danger of being destroyed.

In Durban, drinking water was rationed after the four supply aqueducts from the Nagle Dam were washed away, and the port was shut down as 80 km/h winds and a monster swell battered the harbour. The airport was closed, as were schools and many industrial plants and businesses, and 11 people died when two houses in Durban's Chatsworth township collapsed.

Five cars were dumped into the Tugela River and their occupants drowned when the 410-m John Ross Bridge over the Tugela River was washed away, and Richards Bay was completely cut off from the rest of South Africa, by rail, road, sea and air.

Mark says that 'it was a hectic, hectic experience. All the bridges were washed away, we were carrying out rescue ops on the Tugela River. It was chaotic, people were stranded all over the place. We ferried 300 to 400 people across the Umfolozi River. We pulled telephone cables across the rivers so that communications could be re-established, and set up radio relay stations using CB radios for the emergency services.

'It was very, very tense. Empangeni was cut off because the Mhlatuze and Nseleni Rivers were in flood. After the storm had abated, the hostel students in Empangeni were trapped, so local farmers and others who had light planes set up a ferry service to fly them to Mtubatuba. The hospitals ran out of medical supplies, there was no fuel, there was livestock wandering around all over the place.

'The sea was chocolate for weeks afterwards.'

24 *South into darkness*

Tony Weaver

BACK IN THE 1980s, A vast stretch of South Africa's most dangerous coastline, between Durban in the north and East London in the south, was without any Sea Rescue protection. That included the popular KwaZulu-Natal South Coast holiday resorts, and the entire Wild Coast southwestward from Port Edward – 460 km of coastline, and 640 km apart by road.

So a bunch of locals lobbied the NSRI for support in starting a station at Shelly Beach, 129 km (66 nautical miles) south of Durban. In April 1985, the NSRI board approved the setting up of Station 20, 'provided it was self-funding'.

Steve Reimers, Station Commander from 1990 to 1997, says that 'when we started, there wasn't any money. We didn't have a base until May 1989, when we built the boathouse next to the ski-boat club. In the early days, we really had to beg, borrow and steal.'

Their very first rescue boat was handed down to them from, of all places, the Bronkhorstspruit rescue station, in what was then the Transvaal.

'It was a six-metre wooden Robcraft with a deep V hull, with two 90-hp Mercury engines. We towed it down on a trailer that was half-broken, sanded the whole boat down, repainted it – we did it in a workshop miles out of town – and every single night the crew would pitch in, wives, kids, girlfriends, doing stuff we didn't really know how to do. And that's where the strength of a station really gets built, that togetherness.

'That boat was a dog; it was so unsuited to the Natal coast. That hull would have been fantastic in the Cape waters, but with the swell pattern off the Natal coast, that boat became a complete animal. But we did some good rescues with it until someone took pity on us and gave us a better boat.'

In old *Sea Rescue* magazines, there are photographs of a very strange-looking vehicle that they used to launch the boat. It was a rusty old scrapped Toyota Land Cruiser that the crew rebuilt with fibreglass, made some seats, and fitted a homemade winch made by a crew member who owned an engineering works. 'The winch had a 16-mm cable and we ran it off a five-horsepower Honda motor. Later we got a tractor, and that made it a lot easier.'

It was nearly a decade later that rescue stations were established at Port Edward and Port St Johns, with Port St Johns at first more of a satellite station. So Shelly Beach, whose first inflatable was a five-metre boat, covered the coast past Port Edward and into the then Transkei.

'Being a surf launching station made it enormously difficult. Besides Port Edward now, we were one of the very few true surf launching stations in the country, and that scared away a lot of crew, but also attracted an equal number of guys who were looking for that kind of adventure. It made life interesting for us.

'Almost all our injuries to crew were during shore-break launches, but our crews got really good at it. On weekends it was a circus: some of the ski-boat crowd would be back at the club in the pub having a drink, the parking lot would be full of people waiting for the boats to come in to see what they'd caught, so you've got this crowd watching your every move.'

Night-time launches were particularly challenging.

'We've launched off the beach at the Wild Coast Sun many times at night, and it's a terrifying bloody experience for some of the crew. You have to evaluate whether or not it is essential to launch, because you do put crew in danger.

'It is through hundreds and hundreds of hours of daytime experience that you work it out. We've launched when things have gone wrong, although we haven't ever flipped a boat, but we've had some bad experiences.

'There was one launch where I hit a wave, the boat got airborne, and old Fred Jollands, who was well into his sixties, also got airborne. We came down and he came down afterwards. He went right through the bloody hatch.

'Fred was a sea dog of note; there weren't many rescues he was left off. His navigation skills were superb; you didn't need a chart on the boat if Fred was there. He was old school, hugely experienced, ex-Royal Navy guy, who had a big calming influence on all of us when we were younger.'

With the night-time launches, especially with no moon, there was a fair amount of guesswork involved, and that's where experience paid off. It was virtually impossible to see unbroken waves because there was no white water or phosphorescence, and the channels would shift from storm to storm.

'So we launch with absolutely no lights on the boats, everything blacked out. We made special covers for all the instrumentation to block them so they don't impact on our night vision.'

While the initial support for the station came from the local community and organisations such as Lions, Round Table and Rotary, it was only when petrol giant Caltex came on board as a sponsor that they were able to buy a bigger boat. Steve recalls: 'Their deputy managing director, Jock McKenzie, was the point guy there and they sponsored the seven-metre RIB [rigid inflatable boat], *Caltex Endeavour*. He and his wife, Liz, launched the boat on 31 January 1988 in massive surf. It was pretty hair-raising stuff – you don't really want to lose a sponsor overboard.'

But there was one major design flaw: they'd built a wheelhouse on the boat. 'That's fine in the Cape, but insane in these waters. We are launching into surf; if that boat turns over in the surf, there is no chance of getting it back upright with the wheelhouse in place, so we took it off. We tried it for a while, but it was incredibly dangerous.'

Because of its location, Station 20 is renowned for doing long-distance rescues, although not quite in the league of sister station to the north, Richards Bay, Station 19, whose members often venture as far as the Mozambique border on operations that stretch over 24 hours and longer.

Two of the most interesting and challenging rescues Steve was involved in were both in the 1990s. The first was the rescue of renowned South African yachtsman John Martin, the second a medical emergency on a log-carrying freighter, the *John N*, off the Wild Coast.

'John Martin was over a weekend. I was on duty and opened up early. I heard some banter on the high frequency radio, and it was Dave Sievwright from Durban.

'We listened for a while, and then they started giving coordinates, and we started plotting them, and realised it was a yacht and its keel had fallen off. When we plotted it, we saw that it was directly off Margate, about 30 miles (55 km) out – might have been further out, I know it was far because I got into trouble over that one.

'Those days we only had the old Decca triangulation system to plot on, so I phoned Durban and said, "What's up?" They said they had been in touch since the early hours with John Martin, who was sailing this yacht to Mauritius for the Beachcomber Race. They had hit some heavy weather, and the bolts on the retractable keel sheared and the keel had fallen off.'

It was a foggy day with very bad visibility, and it was agreed that Steve and his crew would try to find the yacht, as it was drifting south with the current. They would try to rendezvous with the much bigger 13-m keelboat, the *Urban Campbell*, from Station 5 (Durban).

But then a complication hit: the whole Durban crew, except for coxswain Brian St Clair-Lang, were desperately seasick somewhere between Durban and Margate. So a relief crew were driving down to Shelly Beach to be put onto the *Urban Campbell*.

They set off at 1 pm that afternoon with crew in the base control tower plotting their course and directing them, because they couldn't take the Decca receiver on the boat.

'We went straight out, reached the line we thought he would be on, and we headed due north on that line for about half an hour. That fog was so thick that we literally drove up the yacht's arse. John was sitting on the coach [cabin] roof playing dominoes with a crew member, and he said "What the hell?" He couldn't believe that this orange boat had come up on him out in the middle of nowhere.

'We hooked him up for a while, and slowly began towing, but we couldn't tow him back all the way. I had started out with 600 litres of fuel in those rubber tanks on the decks. I had 200 litres below the deck, and that wasn't enough to get back to Shelly Beach with a tow attached. And we were so far out that we had lost comms with the base, and the only people we could comm with was the *Urban Campbell*. So we waited for them to arrive, changed crew, and they then took up the tow.

'We escorted them for a while towards Durban just to make sure everything was fine, then we headed back to base. We reached Protea Banks about two the next morning, after leaving at 1 pm the previous day, and we picked up a radio call from commercial fishermen on Protea Banks who couldn't start their motor. So we went alongside them, fixed their motors at about two in the morning, then hit the beach in the early hours of the morning. It was an epic, a great joint rescue between two stations.'

But it was another epic, the freighter *John N*, in the mid-1990s, that stands out as one of the most memorable operations ever. Steve took a call from the Port Captain in Durban late that evening to say there had been a fire in the freighter's engine room 'somewhere off Margate', and the chief engineer had been badly burned.

Caltex Endeavour launched at around eleven that night in very heavy surf, with a northeasterly of about 25 knots (46 km/h) blowing, and headed towards Margate, but there was no sign of the freighter.

'So we kept going south and started to make comms with the ship, and we said to the guys on the control tower that they needed to establish where this boat was before we get to the point in the south where we lose comms. We also sent a vehicle down towards Port

Edward to act as a radio relay station because we had no resources between us and East London.

'I also knew that once you've passed the Port Edward light, after that it is just black, there are no shore lights, nothing. When it's that dark, it is very difficult to get a perspective between land and sea to work out the distance you are offshore. By then we had got a better fix on where they were, and they were a lot further south than we had thought, drifting without power down past Mzamba and towards Mkambati and Msikaba, towards Port St Johns.'

In the early hours of the morning, Steve and his crew finally found the ship, nine kilometres off Port St Johns and 122 km south of Shelly Beach. Steve and paramedic Daphne Sprouse climbed the gangplank, and were taken to the master's cabin.

'It was terrible. The Russian chief engineer came in; he had a sheet around him and he opened it up and the skin was just hanging off him, everywhere. This poor guy was burned to smithereens.

'There were two other guys who were burned, but not too badly. By the time we had got the engineer sedated and in a reasonable condition to try and get him onto the *Caltex Endeavour* and back to shore – and at this stage, they were still a dead ship, just sitting there – we looked down the passageway and the whole crew was lined up. Some were burned, some weren't, but they all wanted first aid from Daphne. It was a sad, bad situation on board that vessel.

'There was another Russian guy, smartly dressed, unhurt, who also insisted he was coming ashore with us. We were about halfway through getting everything stabilised, when the pitch of the vessel started to change and the doors were clanging, and I said to Daphne, "I'll go and look what's happening."

'Gavin Staats was standing by alongside on the rescue boat, and I went to the starboard side where the gangplank was, and he'd had to duck for cover. The wind had suddenly switched from northeast to southwest – a real buster had hit us. It was busting a gut.'

They carefully transferred the engineer to the rescue boat, loaded up the second Russian, and set off for Shelly Beach. But by now they had drifted even further and were some 139 km from base, and their fuel situation wasn't looking great.

'We took turns helming it back to Shelly Beach. The sun started to come up when we were near Port Edward, off Palm Beach. The painkillers were starting to wear off. We had the engineer lying just in front of the console to try and keep the impact of the boat on him down, because going in a southwesterly, the boat's yawing all over the place and we were taking water over the transom. We were trying not to go too fast because every time we pounded, this poor guy was screaming at the top of his lungs.

'We packed all the life jackets around him to pad him. But as we ran lower and lower on fuel, the boat became lighter and the more we pounded and bounced. That just exacerbated the situation terribly for this poor guy. By the time we hit the beach at Shelly, at about nine that morning, when we came through the surf, he was constantly screaming at the top of his lungs from pain, it was horrendous, it was really hardcore.

'We hit the beach running and the ambulance was waiting and took him off to hospital with this other Russian guy. And that's the last we ever heard of them.'

25 Squid pro quo

Tony Weaver

LOOK OUT TO SEA AT night when the squid are running off the Eastern Cape coast and it looks like rush-hour traffic out there. Or maybe a new gold rush. Dazzling halogen lights bob from side to side on top of the boats as the fishermen from Port St Francis cash in on *Loligo vulgaris reynaudii* – calamari to most of us, 'white gold' to the fishermen, 'chokka' in the vernacular. The halogen lights are used to attract the different fish species the squid feed on, which in turn lures the squid from their usual habitat on the seabed to just a few metres below the surface.

That's when the chokka fishermen, as tough a bunch as any found on the South African coast, fish their hand lines, 50 m of 19- to 22-kg breaking strain line wound around a wooden handle and tipped with multi-hooked, coloured lead jigs and plastic floats. Each boat has a crew of between 12 and 26 men. The very experienced guys can handle up to four lines at once, and when the squid are running the crews can easily haul in up to five tons each in just a few hours of fishing.

The catch is sorted by size, and blast frozen at -40 °C on board the boats, which are essentially floating factories that can spend up to three weeks at sea. Then the catch is packed into plastic bags ready for offloading at journey's end in St Francis Bay.

Ironically, almost all the catch is exported to Europe; the calamari we eat in South Africa is imported from places like the Falkland

Islands. Go figure the carbon footprint on that one. But the theoretical economics of globalisation don't impact the day-to-day lives of the chokka crews.

'They're a tough crowd, and it's a really rough and hard job. I'd like to see the guys from that TV show, *Deadliest Catch*, spend a few weeks on the boats; they'd never cope,' says the former Station Commander of Station 21 (St Francis Bay), Marc May. 'Probably 80 per cent of our call-outs and rescues involve the chokka fleet.'

'When that rescue phone rings and you can hear that engine hammering in the background, you know it's game on; the skipper is not at anchor, he is running to get the dead or injured guy inshore as fast as possible so he can get back out to the fishing grounds.'

It can be the real Wild West out there. Tensions can run high in such close living quarters. 'We have done rescues for amputations. Just the other day we had a guy who lost three toes on one side and two on the other.'

The permanent St Francis Bay community is a small one, which swells over weekends and the holiday season as upcountry property owners commute. But out of season the economy revolves around the fishing fleet, and everyone knows everyone else. Marc and all the NSRI crew members have lost people they knew well.

'We've had a chokka boat at anchor here, right here just off the harbour, lying towards the south and there was a massive swell running. The boat went right over and upside down, sank to the bottom with the crew inside. We lost six fishermen. I knew most of them.'

Marc has great admiration for the chokka crews, but wouldn't for a moment even think of joining them: 'I would rather go and mine in the middle of Siberia at 400 feet underground and minus 30 °C than actually go and work on a chokka boat. It's a hard, hard life, and it's very labour-intensive and competitive.'

And every now and then things just go pear-shaped for the chokka boats, an inevitable occurrence given the huge storms that lash this coast. There have been wrecks with major loss of life, but sometimes it is the less dramatic stories that linger, the stories where it gets personal.

'The *Sikelela* was one of our more dramatic recent chokka boat rescues. We got the call-out at 7.41 am, on Wednesday 27 August 2014.

'The skipper was Hugh "Hudge" McKenna, and Hudge taught many of us everything we know about sea rescue. He is the former NSRI coxswain here. He had been out squidding and was returning to port, but there was a very big swell running. Hudge did a few turns at the mouth of the harbour, checked it out, picked his swell and tried to run the entrance, but, even with all his experience, well, shit happens. As he came in, he touched sand; it slowed down the boat and turned him sideways, he lost power and he wound up on the *dolosse* [the interlocking concrete blocks used to protect harbour walls].'

The swell was running at five metres, and there was a 10 to 15 knot (19 to 27 km/h) westerly wind blowing. As the *Sikelela* ran aground, waves began crashing right over the top of her. During a brief lull in the swell, the *Sikelela* miraculously rolled side-on to the *dolosse*, and eight of the 13-man crew were able to jump off. Residents from the neighbouring marina and other locals helped them scramble to safety.

Both the NSRI's *Spirit of St Francis II* and the Balobi Fishing Company's rubber duck, *Ricochet*, normally used as a harbour tender boat, were activated.

The *Ricochet*, skippered by Lafran Troskie and crewman Kevin Bremner, managed to get alongside the *Sikelela*. They pulled two more crew on board, and, with immaculate timing, got to safety before the next big swell hit. That left two crew members, plus Hudge McKenna, still on board.

The crewmen were hanging on to the side being battered by the swell, while Hudge was standing on top of the boat. Just then a huge wave hit, and he fell, badly lacerating his right arm.

Spirit of St Francis II, with Coxswain Neil Jones and Marc on board, together with rescue swimmers Tantum Dace and Stuart Obrey, came in as close as they dared. Neil handed the helm to Marc so that Neil could direct the swimmers.

Marc says conditions were extreme: 'It was in the face of a very big swell coming in there. I had to pick my turn very carefully. We sent two swimmers out, and if I had had half a second to think, I wouldn't have sent them out – but then they wouldn't have helped save the crew. They were brave enough to go and face that sea. As they dived and hit the water, my warning bells were just ringing and ringing, but I still had to look after the boat. The concentration is intense in a situation like that.'

The two swimmers swam up to *Sikelela* and ordered the two crewmen to jump into the water. Both were dragged by the rescue swimmers, through breaking swells, debris, ropes, fishing lines and flotsam from the chokka boat, while Marc timed the sets to bring the rescue craft into the danger zone. 'Facing towards the waves, and punching through, they managed to rescue both casualties on to the rescue craft, where they were received by NSRI coxswain Neil Jones and NSRI crewman Sara Smith and hauled onto the rescue boat while Marc helmed the boat through the incoming wave sets.'

Marc says, 'Hudge stayed on board until every single one of his crew were off. I remember him hanging on, and the blood was pouring down his arm. When the swimmers went in, they shouted to him, "Come, jump, jump now; if another wave comes and takes you off, you're finished." He hung on till his crew were all off. He's just that type of guy.'

Meanwhile Lafran Troskie, skippering the *Ricochet*, had dropped off his casualties and crewman Kevin Bremner, and picked up a new crew member, Craig 'Short' Humbee. 'They again managed, while timing the incoming sets, to bring their boat up against *Sikelela* and rescue the skipper of *Sikelela* off the chokka boat,' an NSRI media release later said. 'The rescue was made difficult because he was tangled in fishing lines.' Fishing lines with multiple hooks on them.

The 12 crew were treated for shock and put under observation for secondary drowning. Miraculously, the only injury was to Hudge McKenna, who, in the best maritime tradition, stayed on board his vessel to the last. His right arm was stitched up, and he and the four crew who had jumped into the water were treated for possible diesel inhalation.

The final act of bravery that eventful morning belonged to coxswain Neil Jones, who was deployed into the surf to try and get a towline onto the *Sikelela*. But the swell was just too big and too dangerous, and the operation was aborted. The NSRI media release said later that, in an 'incredible feat', the crews of the *Ricochet* and the *Spirit of St Francis II* had 'certainly averted a maritime disaster' that day.

'Ja,' Marc reflects as he finishes the story. 'That was an epic.'

26 Fire in St Francis Bay

Tony Weaver and Andrew Ingram

THE TWIN EASTERN CAPE HAMLETS of St Francis Bay and Cape St Francis go dead quiet during the week and out of season when many of the wealthy property owners commute to Johannesburg and other major centres. 'It becomes a "mommy town" from Sunday afternoon on,' says Marc May, who was St Francis Bay (Station 21) Station Commander until 2015.

'Often, when there's any kind of emergency, like a car crash, a snake in someone's house, a fire, anything, the first people the residents ring are Sea Rescue, because in a small community they know they'll get a fast reaction.'

We sit chatting with Marc in the NSRI base's meeting room, perched above the fishing and recreational harbour, surrounded by swanky restaurants, and looking out over multi-million-rand homes on the marina. Sixty years ago, there was almost nothing here.

In 1954, Zululand sugar farmer Leighton Hulett and his wife, Ann, saw an ad in *Farmer's Weekly* offering 234 ha of coastal land for £1 750. They visited the site and found an enormous dune field and a sheltered bay fringed by a lovely stretch of beach. They bought it.

They sold their property in Zululand and moved down to the bay a month later, carrying their belongings across the Kromme River and the sand dunes by ox-wagon. Leighton set to work building a fishing camp with seven rondavels, a kitchen and an ablution block.

Their regular guests soon started to pester them to free up some land for sale, and in 1956 they proclaimed a township of 51 plots. From the start, Hulett insisted on a uniform building style of whitewashed walls and thatched roofs.

Ten years later, Hulett acquired another 153 ha of land with 2.8 km of river frontage and set out on his most ambitious project yet – Marina Glades. Again, the rule was that the building style had to be whitewashed walls and thatched roofs. In 1967, he started pumping and digging the first of the 12-km network of navigable canals that is today the signature feature of St Francis Bay, creating a village in which many of the homes have their own bit of waterfront.

Not only was Hulett the founder of St Francis Bay, he also established the NSRI station there in 1971, just four years after the Institute was formally launched, and today the base is known and registered as the Leighton Hulett Station 21. The first base was a corrugated-iron shed on the canals, and rescue boats had to negotiate the often difficult river mouth passage in bad weather. In the early 1990s, a new boathouse was built at Granny's Pool with a slipway providing direct access to the sea, and in 1997, with the building of the harbour at Port St Francis, the NSRI moved to their current state-of-the-art rescue base.

Sunday 11 November 2012 was an out-of-season day. Marc and the then coxswain (and now Station Commander), Paul Hurley, were having a braai just after 5 pm that afternoon.

Leighton Hulett's thatched-roof rule was about to translate into a 24-hour nightmare.

Marc's phone rang. The call was from Calibre Security that there was a timeshare unit on fire. 'We jumped into my car and got there at 5.20. We said, "This is still containable," and I thought, *sjoe*, I've been here before, I've done a fire at this house before. We said we can save this house. It's a timeshare unit at Royal Wharf Marine Resort, and the people who had hired it were busy getting the hell out of there.'

Marc had put out an NSRI alert, and most of the local volunteers had pitched up by then. Marc divided them up into teams, some to fight the fires, some to help evacuate residents. 'The water pressure was really pathetic, because everyone was running hoses onto their roofs, and pipes were bursting as houses burned, so we got up on the roof and started pulling burning thatch off the roof. It's a good way to stop the fire spreading, but then the wind started gusting, and it started throwing sparks.

'I shouted to one of our crew members, Sara Smith, who was then a trainee coxswain, to run and warn people to get out and wet their roofs. Within five minutes she came back in tears; she was bawling and she says "Marc, there's eight houses that are burning." I sent the crews to warn more people to evacuate. Some of the people were saying, "Ja, we get it, we'll go wet our roofs," and the crew were saying, "You don't get it, your roof is already on fire." Some people didn't actually realise their houses were on fire.

'Then it just started jumping, house after house, jumping and jumping so quickly. Then there were ten houses on fire, then 12. We were battling with the low water pressure; we've been battling for years for decent fire equipment, right since the early days. I saw the first house collapsing, and then I could just see house after house going down. It wasn't about looking after the fire now; it was about going to warn those people up front that they've got to protect all their houses because it was just jumping so quickly.'

The whole community pitched in. Marc was panicking because he couldn't get hold of some key people, so he phoned Meriel Bartlett at NSRI headquarters in Cape Town. He said, 'I don't know who you can get, or what you can organise, but we need help, our town is going to burn down. I just saw the writing on the wall. Meriel did amazing work; she got NSRI crews from PE, J-Bay, farmers from Hankey, Patensie. They came with tractors, you name it.'

Marc called his NSRI counterpart at Oyster Bay (Station 36), Mark Mans, who raced across, and, working with former Station Commander Bob Meikle, helped set up a JOCC (Joint Operations

Control Centre) at the police station to help plan the firefighting operation.

'That fire burned down 75 buildings, right down to the bottom. If a house had burnt ten per cent, you just left it because it was going to burn down. You couldn't save it.'

Marc closes his eyes and relives the moment: 'It was pandemonium.'

'Houses just went down, one after the other. Some people lost pets that were locked up or forgotten. We tried to save as much property as we could; the guys would run into a house and carry out whatever they could, curtains, cutlery, crockery, couches, anything they could carry.

'The younger guys went house to house, grabbing gas bottles and throwing them into the canals. At one point, I was walking between a window, a wall and a garage wall, and a car exploded. If I'd been two seconds forwards, or two seconds back, I would have been gone, gone. We were lucky, we had a few guys with minor burns, a guy who fell off a roof, but nothing major.

'There were pieces of gas bottles that were embedded in wood; they were like shrapnel when the bottles exploded. It was absolutely bizarre to see so many houses burning around you. Eventually all you did, all you could do, was look after the house next door and try and channel the fire down towards the water, to the canals.'

Then the NSRI volunteers saw that people were getting trapped between the burning houses and the canals, so they commandeered a speedboat and began ferrying people to safety.

At the height of the fire, the *Herald* newspaper in Port Elizabeth managed to get hold of local estate agent Esmé Welman by phone: 'It is absolute pandemonium. There are not enough firefighters. The National Sea Rescue Institute has called for civilians who are able to come and assist.

'We tried to get firefighters from Port Elizabeth here but there were huge delays because we are "out" of their region. First we were wiped out by floods, now fire is destroying what is left,' she said. 'It is beyond tragedy. Everything that is here is going – and not slowly. You can see the flames destroying the houses, boats and businesses. You can see here and there houses and restaurants with gas exploding. It sounds like war. People are screaming and crying. They want to get to their homes, but they can't because of the danger.

'Volunteers have shut off the bridges, but there are still some people who have refused to leave their homes and could be trapped,' she said, explosions erupting in the background.

'I have had homeowners phoning me to find out if their houses are all right. I don't know what to tell them. I haven't got the heart to break the news to them,' Welman said. 'We are slowly being encircled. Soon there will be nowhere to go except to the sea and into the canals. Those fighting the fire are saying that it might be too much and that they should retreat to try and save what they can. This is terrifying.'

The NSRI crews fought tirelessly through the night and into the early morning, and helped run the JOCC throughout the crisis. Marc says, 'Our wives were on social media organising help lines. Social media played a huge part in fighting the fire, in organising it.'

After the call went out on Facebook, the response was overwhelming. People brought food and medical supplies. Church groups donated blankets, people donated water, B&Bs offered free accommodation. The local Spar opened up and gave free water to those who were fighting the fire.

Kelvin and Liz Atkinson lost everything. Speaking to the *Herald* from the St Francis Bay Golf Club, to which they had been evacuated, the Atkinsons said they were grateful to be alive. 'We just grabbed our two dogs and a few pictures of our children graduating. We didn't want to see our house burning, so we got in the car and left. We built the house in 1986 and moved in about eight or so years ago,' Kelvin told the newspaper.

Liz said they would pick up the pieces and start from scratch: 'Material things can always be replaced. I just hope that no one was killed. The people of St Francis Bay have been really helpful opening up their homes to us. We also lost our chronic illness medication, but the chemist came and gave us a month's supply,' she said.

Marc says that, with hindsight, it was 'incredible that no one was badly hurt or killed. We lost a couple of pets, but no people. There were people that were in those houses that didn't even know their house was on fire. We were smashing garages open and hauling out jet-skis and things.

'That time of year, it was really an empty village – very few owners around. There were only a handful of guys around who could physically take on the fire. Most of the owners, we call them "swallows", they fly in for weekends and holidays. For the rest, it is very much just the wives and children of men working upcountry or overseas. That's one of the reasons our rescue crews are pretty small.

'It's great that we've had the Jeffreys Bay station [Station 37] formed, because in the past we would have to run to rescue a kite surfer or kayaker at J-Bay, and that's a bit of a haul. You just know that if you get a drowning, it is going be pretty bleak. It was great how, when the fire got going, the J-Bay and Oyster Bay guys just got in their cars and pulled in, they were on it.'

The fire was a wake-up call for St Francis Bay.

Marc again: 'That fire, it was straight through, 27, 28 hours with no sleep, I couldn't even sleep after that: my ears rang for days because of all the explosions. The fire was a huge game-changer for fire protection here. I never ever thought that many houses could burn, and to be in the middle of it, it was terrifying; you just hear "gwa, gwa, gwa" – a car or a boat or a gas cylinder exploding.

'You go into the canals now and you can see the houses that haven't been rebuilt yet, they are massive, multi-million-rand houses, and the amount of energy that burning thatch develops, those big roofs, it is intense, it's a fireball; they just went up like torches. The jetties were burnt; boats that were moored, we just cut lines and pushed them into the canal. Everything went into the canals – first were the gas cylinders. The younger guys, the surfers, they were the stupidest, craziest guys we could find – no fear, they were prepared to do it. They ran in to get the cylinders out. But you couldn't fight it: once a house was burning, you just had to leave it.

'And as the houses collapsed, they took the water pipes with them, and that was it, the water pressure was gone. So the guys literally stood on those roofs to protect the houses – as a piece of thatch started burning, you pulled it out and put it out until the water trucks could get there.

'The wind was gale-force westerly that night, 35 to 40 knots, and when that westerly hums, it really, really pumps. The west wind normally drops in the evening, but that day it just picked up and up near sunset.'

Marc says the houses that are being rebuilt will have slate roofs. There were major fights over this in the village, but the change was inevitable: 'This was originally built as an all-thatch village, but after the fire everything's changed; everybody is going slate. A lot of the houses are being rebuilt as super-mansions. The guys who had R10 million mansions are rebuilding R20 million mansions. It's rude.

'There goes the neighbourhood.'

27 A parent's worst nightmare

Tony Weaver

ONE OF THE ENDURING MYSTERIES in the annals of South African sea rescue remains that of three students who went on holiday to St Francis Bay, and were never seen again.

On Monday 6 July 1998, Marlise Schoeman – who had turned 20 that Saturday – and her friends Pierre van Vuuren and Darren Aitken, both 21, went for a boat ride on the Kromme River. The three, all studying in Durban, were on their winter break and were staying at a holiday house in Poivre Crescent.

On the Saturday, Marlise had phoned her mom, Marita Bruwer, in Port Shepstone to get a pancake recipe for her birthday party. On Monday morning, she had phoned her best friend to wish her happy birthday. Those were the last contacts the trio had with friends or family.

Monday 6 July was not good weather for going boating. There was an icy wind blowing, the deep-sea swell was running at up to 12 m, and the spring tides meant that there were strong rip currents at play. But all the indications are that the three friends had planned a short joyride in the St Francis canals and possibly up the Kromme River estuary. The house where they were staying is near a back canal just off St Francis Drive, but the rubber duck they used, Darren's dad's four-metre Gemini Manta Econo 400 with a 25-hp engine, was on a trailer.

The families of the three thought nothing of it when they didn't hear from the students for nearly a week. They were on holiday, after all. In 1998, cellphones were still a relative novelty and coverage was limited to the major cities. Call boxes were still widely used.

They had told their parents to expect them back home the following Thursday or Friday, and that they would be touring the Eastern Cape for the rest of the week, stopping off in Grahamstown for a day or two to attend the National Arts Festival.

Marlise's mother, Marita, told reporters six days after they went missing that, when she didn't hear from her daughter for a few days, 'At first I thought they were just occupied with the last days of their holidays, and couldn't be reached by cellphone. I left messages on her voicemail, but received no answer. Eventually on Friday I phoned Marlise's stepfather, Frik Bruwer, who is a policeman, to help me search for my daughter.'

It was a parent's worst nightmare come true.

Frik Bruwer said he telephoned 'every police station, every hospital and every mortuary' from St Francis Bay to Durban. But there was no trace of the three.

On Saturday morning, six days after they were last seen, the local police got a duplicate key for the house in Poivre Crescent and found everything neatly in order. There was food in the house, and all the signs indicated that the students were still on holiday: Marlise's identity document and the trio's wallets and cellphones were in the house. All that was missing was their vehicle, the rubber duck – and the three students.

At 11.45 am, the police found the Toyota Venture the trio had been using – Pierre's father's vehicle – parked at the slipway on the Kromme River. There was no sign of forced entry.

At the time, Frik Bruwer was quoted by *Die Burger* as saying, 'We are very worried that there is only a 25 hp engine on the boat, and that last week there were warnings of gale force winds in the area.'

The NSRI, the police and the SAAF immediately launched a massive search. An SAAF Alouette III helicopter and a Piper Seminole light aircraft from Port Elizabeth, the police's coastal patrol and air wing –

with reservist Flip van der Merwe, from St Francis, volunteering his private aircraft – along with the NSRI and Metro rescue searched until 10 pm that night, and began again at first light on Sunday.

Their search covered 30 km up the Kromme River and 12.5 km of canals, as well as an initial 120 km of coastline and 5 000 sq km of open ocean. All shipping in the area was alerted to be on the lookout for the dinghy, and plans were set in motion to patrol the coast by vehicle as far as the Transkei in the days ahead.

The then St Francis Bay Station Commander, Clive Shamley, said they called off the air and sea search at 2 pm on the Sunday when it became clear that everything had been done that could be done. He and the other rescuers were by then convinced that a combination of strong winds and the outgoing spring tide had sucked the boat out of the notorious Kromme River mouth and into the open sea.

Their best guess was that the winds and current would have dragged them up the coast towards Port Alfred, northeast of Port Elizabeth.

This fear was confirmed when the news of the search was broadcast on television news on the Sunday evening.

A farmer from Piketberg, holidaying in St Francis, contacted the NSRI that Sunday night after seeing the TV bulletin and delivered the bad news: he had seen the three young people in the rubber duck at about 10.30 am the previous Monday, six days ago.

One of the young men was barechested, Marlise was dressed in a tracksuit, and none of the three were wearing life jackets. The boat was heading out through the Kromme River mouth, and two hours later the farmer saw them again, out beyond the surf line in the bay.

The swell out to sea was running at up to 12 m, and there was an icy wind blowing, with the South African Weather Service saying temperatures had dropped as low as 3.4 °C on land, with temperatures out to sea expected to be even lower.

One can only speculate how different the outcome might have been if that farmer had phoned the NSRI and said, 'I suspect there might be a problem.' Possible false alarms often turn out to be real alarms, and hunches often turn out to be real calls.

Pierre's father, Piet, flew in from Gaborone on the Saturday to help with the search, and his mother, Lorraine, drove through the night with Pierre's cousin, arriving on the Sunday. As the parents rallied together to face the inevitable, Piet said, 'We are praying they are still alive. But if they are dead, we can only wish that their bodies be found so we can bury them and go on with our lives.'

In the weeks that followed, Piet continued the search for his eldest son and his friends after it had been officially called off. He hired a twin-engined plane and, helped by Clive Shamley, searched the entire area again, south and west to Cape Agulhas and up to 35 nautical miles out to sea. The total search area eventually covered a total of 20 000 square miles. They searched the Transkei coast, KwaZulu-Natal, up to Mozambique and even followed up on tip-offs from Zimbabwe.

Meanwhile, back in Gaborone one of Piet's friends, Jim Oxley, had unbeknown to Piet set up a fundraising committee to help the family sustain the search for the missing trio. Piet later wrote to the NSRI that 'we have been fortunate enough to finance the cost of the searches through our own resources'.

The family decided to split the nearly R25 000 raised by Jim's committee, donating half to Makoko Mahunga, a rugby player from Maun who had suffered a severe spinal injury while playing against Francistown, and had been rendered a quadriplegic: 'As Makoko's parents have no way of affording such an astronomical financial burden, a trust was formed ... and we wish to allocate 50% of the funds to the trust.'

In his letter to Clive Shamley laying this out, Piet said, 'Your branch at Cape St Francis was a great help to us, assisting us physically with the search and kept our morale and hopes high.' They donated the balance of R12 292.69 to the base 'for improvements to your station to assist with searches in such cases as ours'.

And that's where the twist in the tale comes in. The NSRI decided to use the donation to contribute substantially to the purchase of a new rescue craft, which they named *Pierre* in honour of the memory of Pierre van Vuuren. It was launched on 16 September 2000, two years and two months after the trio had vanished without trace.

NSRI veteran Allan Cramb – then the national Operations Director – recalls: 'As Ops Director, I was going around from station to station doing inspections and having a bit of social time with the crews, having supper with the station commanders, that kind of thing. Almost by coincidence I was on St Francis Station 21 rescue base for the launch of their new boat, and they have a scrapbook of newspaper cuttings, as most of the stations have.

'I was going through their scrapbooks and I saw a photograph of a boat, and a newspaper cutting of this boat that had gone missing two years earlier with these three young students on it, and they had never been found. I remembered the case well, it was one of the great mysteries of Sea Rescue.

'And I turned to Clive, and I said, "Hell, I've seen that boat some-where before, or at least a boat very similar to it." I suspected that it was in a photograph that had been sent to me in an email or fax or letter from SAMSA [South African Maritime Safety Authority] about a boat being found on the West Coast by a fishing boat.

'Not having the photo with me, I thought, naah, this is ridiculous, this is like 18 months, two years after the fact. Anyway, I told Clive, "That looks just like the boat in the photograph that SAMSA had sent out, let me do some digging."'

Allan went back to his files at the NSRI head office.

Four months went by before he struck gold. On 29 January 2001, he phoned Clive Shamley with the news. He had found a letter and photographs dated 23 October 1998 from Captain W Hoogendijk, one of SAMSA's representatives in Saldanha Bay. The letter had been sent to Andre Botes, manager of SA Search and Rescue at Silvermine in Cape Town, who had passed it on to the NSRI.

In the letter, Captain Hoogendijk explained that a local fishing vessel, the *Kalahari*, skippered by Ricky van Boom of St Helena Bay, had found a rubber duck adrift about 20 nautical miles northwest of Saldanha, off Cape Columbine, ten days earlier – 13 October 1998, three months and one week since the trio had disappeared. The skipper towed the boat to St Helena Bay, where it was photographed.

'I faxed the photos to Clive, and he checked them against the scrapbook photos, and then confirmed they were of the missing Gemini Manta, with the number 168 on the pontoon. I tell you, I had goose bumps.'

Clive immediately got hold of Piet van Vuuren, who flew down to the Cape to identify the boat. It was a definite match, and at least Piet and the other families finally had some sense of what could have happened, and realised there was no hope of finding any survivors.

Darren Aitken's father, Ian, donated the boat to Ricky van Boom as a gesture of thanks for his solving part of the puzzle.

'To this day they don't know what happened,' says Allan Cramb. 'It's an incredible, incredible story. It drifted from St Francis Bay all the way to Cape Columbine; that's 1 000 km away on the other side of the continent.

'My personal opinion is that they must have overturned and tried to swim for it after the engine broke down. We always say don't swim, stay with the boat.'

But the local St Francis Bay fishermen mutter darkly that '*Wat die Baai vat, gee die Baai terug*,' (what the Bay takes, the Bay gives back). The circular currents will spit out any wreckage back onto home shores.

Whatever happened, says Allan, 'It is a sad, sad, terrible story, very, very sad.'

28 The longest hours of my life

Tony Weaver

MANTEN MARINA OCCUPIES A COMMANDING position overlooking the wall of the Vaal Dam at Deneysville in the Free State, a vista across a vast expanse of water, green with algae and hovering just above half-full in the middle of one of the worst droughts in living memory. But even as we sit in the main office and command post, we can see the weather changing.

It is a stark reminder of just how dangerous large, fairly shallow inland bodies of water can be. As we finish the interview, Dicky Manten says, 'Hell, we may not be able to braai this evening; this is a big one.' The wind starts to pick up, huge cumulonimbus thunderclouds start building in the northeast, and by the time I get back to my guesthouse the rain is pouring and the wind is blasting. Hail starts to hammer down and I rush to get my hired car under cover. It's the best rain Deneysville has had all season, and the locals are rejoicing.

Manten Marina was born after Dicky's late father, master boat-builder Dick Manten, bought the derelict property in 1974. Dick and his family started renovating; the first objective was to raise the property above the flood level. Five years later, with the Vaal Dam sitting at just 13 per cent full, Dick Manten set about building massive 12-m-high harbour walls to create the Vaal Dam's first safe and secure berthing harbour.

'In a decent storm, we can get a two-and-a-half-metre swell running here,' Dicky says, 'and then you can't even stand on the harbour walls when the dam is full, the waves would knock you off.' The NSRI's Vaal Dam rescue base, Station 22, established by Dick Manten, Sr, in 1984, is housed in a spacious boat shed at the top of the marina's slipway, and Manten's main office is the command post. Dicky is the current Station Commander, and Station 22 is very much a family concern.

'We're very different to the coastal stations. Here the people we are rescuing are often our clients and our friends. We know this dam intimately; it's our living and our life. It's our home.'

That's something Manny Raposo would agree with. On 30 January 2002, he and some friends were out on the dam on two 26-ft Dragonfly trimarans when a highveld thunderstorm moved in. 'As the winds increased to an estimated 30 knots [55 km/h], I decided to lower the main and wait it out under genoa only. I then decided to sail back to Stilbaai. A second storm system approached with a little more breeze and we were sailing at approximately 12 knots [22 km/h], on a beat under genoa only,' Manny wrote later.

'I had been in similar situations before, and as I had dropped the mainsail, I believed that I was in control, and no danger existed for my crew or yacht. I was, however, proven wrong when a further gust lifted the boat to a point where the rudder blade was out of the water. I lost steerage; the yacht did not come up as there was no mainsail to push it to weather. It just powered up, accelerated and capsized. The estimated gust was well over 40 knots [74 km/h].'

The crew of three managed to clamber back onto the upturned trimaran, with the mast and still-rigged genoa acting as a massive sea anchor: 'I have never been on a more stable craft,' remarked Manny. The second Dragonfly managed to get into the lee of Groot Eiland, and raised the alarm. Dicky and Simon Farrington launched from Deneysville within five minutes of getting the call. They took the crew ashore, and then returned with Manny to assess the chances of recovering the craft.

After battling to tow the trimaran, Dicky called in diver Alan Stokes, who dived in and released all the halyards, side stays and running back stays. He also released the mast, which the crew loaded onto a second boat. They then towed the crippled trimaran back to the marina. 'The advantages of having yachtsmen, yacht owners and yacht builders on hand to assess all the possibilities of recovery cannot be overemphasised. I believe that damages were minimised due to the experience and competence of the NSRI crew,' said Manny.

Dicky says: 'This is a vast body of water – the shoreline alone is 1 300 km – and there are more sailboats on the Vaal Dam than on the whole of South Africa's coastline. We have 150 to 200 boats in our marina alone, and there are 11 clubs on the dam, each with up to 200 boats in them. So it's a very busy place, this.

'And because it is so busy, you get some pretty strange rescue call-outs. About 15 years ago, the dam was close to full and we had 17 sluices open, pumping 130 cubic metres of water per second per sluice. The river below the dam was probably running at 10 to 15 km/h. That changes everything when the river is pumping; there are a lot of eddies and whirlpools, there are huge rocks and you can easily capsize. You can imagine the vast amount of water that comes gushing out; it is scary down there even if you know the river.

'About two o'clock in the morning, pitch dark, I get a call from people who live on the river below the dam and they say they can hear people shouting for help. We geared up the 5.5-m boat, called the police, and then we had a fairly easy launch in a little backwater downstream. We knew that, even with two 60-hp engines, getting back was not going to be easy. Once we hit that current, it got very, very tricky. It felt as though we were being sucked in and over, and we had to chuck the guys about from side to side to keep us from capsizing.

'We heard them shouting – they were stuck in a tree – but in the dark it was just too dangerous to even think of pulling them off. So we told them to hang on, and we would be back at first light. As soon as it was light, we returned. And there were these two guys, stark naked, *kaalgat*, in a tree that they were sharing with a swarm of ants that were also escaping the flood and nibbling their butts.

'The two of them had jumped off the road bridge below the dam wall as a dare. They said they were 'trained swift water swimmers', and it turned out that the one guy was an off-duty cop. We were moeruvva unimpressed, I can tell you. It was a very, very hairy and dangerous mission to rescue two very foolish people on a dare.'

The areas just above and just below the dam wall have been the scene of most of the really tricky rescues that Dicky remembers.

'Another one, virtually the same spot, the river was also in flood. It was 29 December 2010. We got called out just after 6 pm.

'About four kilometres below the wall, there's a weir. Two guys from Germiston – Brad Edwards, 22, and Geoff Thompson, 21 – launched a tractor tube from the bridge that marks the Gauteng/ Free State border at Willow Rapids. I got a call from a local resident, Pat Lizemore; he phoned us and said, "These guys have gone over the weir and they've capsized and are trapped in an eddy." Then another resident phoned us and said, "Please hurry, Pat and his brother launched Pat's boat to try and get a rope to these guys, and now they've also gone over the weir." As Pat drifted past them, he managed to throw them two life jackets.'

The NSRI crew rushed to the scene, but there was nothing to be found. 'There was no boat, no young guys, no Pat, no brother. So we got hold of Water Affairs and got them to shut down the sluice gates and then started searching in four vehicles; we also alerted residents living along the river. At about 8 pm we finally found three of them in the dark, all floating together, clinging to the upturned boat another two kilometres downstream; they all survived, with one guy managing to get to shore a bit earlier.

'Those guys were nearly, nearly gone.'

But it was a series of rescues in early 1987 that stand out as among the most challenging ever on the Vaal Dam. The Manten family were finishing lunch one day when a storm of epic proportions hit. Dicky takes up the story: 'The dam was full to capacity, there were 23 sluices open and the amount of water going over was frightening. The wind was howling, a 30- to 35-knot southeaster

[55.5–64 km/h] and the swell was running at around one and a half metres.

'We got called out to rescue an overturned catamaran and some windsurfers in trouble, and were on our way back in on the five-metre inflatable, *Ruth Wise*, when we saw this yacht, the *Free Spirit*, a Theta 26, drifting towards the dam wall. There were eight people on board; as they came into their moorings they had cut their engine and then dropped sail ready to anchor, but instead the wind caught them and began driving them towards the wall, and the open sluices.'

The summer 1987/1988 edition of *Sea Rescue* carried a dramatic Tony Ribbon painting of the rescue, with a detailed – if somewhat lurid – account inside: 'Eight people aboard the Theta 26 *Free Spirit* watched in horror as the surging current and 35-knot southeast wind whipping the waves up to almost one-and-a-half metres swept them inexorably towards the open sluice gates of the Vaal Dam wall. Apart from two flimsy safety cables, they knew there was a mere 10 m of surging water separating them from certain and gruesome death.

'Panicking, reeling and staggering about the lurching boat, brutally knocked and buffeted by wind and waves, they frantically tried to start the boat's puny outboard engine or hoist sail as the terrible emptiness and fearsome drop beyond the dam wall rushed to meet them.'

By now, Dicky tells me, it was pouring with rain and starting to get darker. 'They first jumped into their dinghy, and the dinghy motor wouldn't start, so they jumped back on to the yacht and abandoned the dinghy. It went through the sluices and no trace of it was ever found. That wall is over 60 m high; it is a very big drop. There is no way any human could ever survive going through there; it's a maelstrom at the bottom and the turbulence will just keep you down. You will never be seen again.

'There are two safety cables with floats on them strung across the approach to the wall in case of something like this happening. But they were driven over the first safety cable, and by some fluke managed to get their anchor on to the second safety cable, and that was the only thing between them and going over the wall. At the time, our engine was a 90-hp Mariner, and if something had to go wrong with that, the crew and I would have gone over the wall. As it is, we had to cut the motor and lift it to get over the first safety cable, and then restart it.

'We managed to get a line to them and they secured it to their mast, then we had to get back over the safety cable with them in tow. But there was more mayhem going down. Another sailboat with four people on board was in trouble and also ran onto the safety cables, and then the Department of Water Affairs boat, with two guys on board, tried to rescue them. They were also swept onto the safety cables, and their two inboard engines stalled and they couldn't restart them.'

The NSRI crew, which included Colin Koen and Lee Stockenstrom, took 20 agonisingly slow minutes to tow the *Free Spirit* the one kilometre back to its mooring and safety, a trip that can usually be done in a couple of minutes. Then the crew returned to the danger zone in front of the sluice gates, first rescuing the sailboat and its four crew members, then returning for the Water Affairs boat.

All in all, the rescues took more than three hours. 'Those were three of the longest hours of my life,' says Dicky.

29 Trapped by a whirlpool

Andrew Ingram

THERE ARE FEW PARTS OF South Africa quite as beautiful as that stretch of coast known as the Garden Route. The wild coastline is interspersed with sublime beaches, and in many areas huge swathes of indigenous forest still cover the rolling hills.

This is also one of the country's most dangerous stretches of coast, and the NSRI crews all along here are kept busy throughout the year, even more so during school holidays.

But not all the danger lies out to sea. The craggy escarpment and rugged mountains that come close to the sea all along the Garden Route are intersected by scores of rivers, some just tiny streams, others more substantial. And one lesson the locals have learned is that if rain threatens, the rivers can become death traps, as many of them have huge catchment areas but then run through very narrow gorges where the flood waters get compressed and channelled into deadly torrents.

Get caught in one of those flash floods, and the chances of escape are slim.

It was two days before Christmas 2010, and Corné Edwards had slept over at his friend André de Goede's house in George. The family had been driving around looking at the rivers, all of them flowing fast after days of rain – welcome rain after a prolonged drought in the Southern Cape. By then the danger of a flash flood was past, as the water levels had stabilised and the rain was over.

On the way back from Wilderness, André asked his mom, Lieschen, if they could hire a canoe at the Kaaimans River crossing. He knew the river well, and his mom agreed – the two 15-year-olds were full of energy and the exercise would do them good.

André thought that it would be cool to show his friend the waterfall that plunges into the Kaaimans River from a feeder stream. It is a place that his family had paddled to often, and he knew it well, but he had never seen it after so much rain.

'We pulled life jackets on and were *lekker* amped. I told Corné about the waterfall and the rocks that we could jump off. But as we rowed out I saw, *jissie*, the waterfall is a little bigger than it was before,' said André.

Because of the heavy rain, the sluice gates of the dam upstream had been opened and the waterfall, normally quite strong, had been turned into a raging torrent. The approach to the waterfall is through a narrow and extremely high gorge. Five metres wide and 70 m high, it is only 150 m long. The waterfall plunges between vertical rock faces and races out towards the Kaaimans, and behind the waterfall is a pool, almost perfectly round, that is protected from its wrath. In these conditions, once you are in that pool it is very difficult to escape.

Under normal conditions, it is relatively easy to paddle between the waterfall and the rocks on the left-hand side, but on this day the water crashed all the way across the channel. The sound was enormous, it was impossible to talk and the force of the water falling created its own wind.

André realised that they were not going to be able to jump from the rocks as he would have liked to, but he really wanted to show Corné what it looked like on the other side of the waterfall. The big circular pool is beautiful and he was excited to see it in these conditions.

They climbed up onto the rocks opposite the waterfall and pulled the canoe up after them. They left their shirts and paddles with the canoe and sat watching the water in awe.

'It was *lekker*. The waterfall was so strong that we sat for ages on the rock. The spray was like a force that pushed us backwards.

'I told Corné that we wouldn't be able to get through, so we walked back to the canoe only to find that the current had pulled the canoe in. He grabbed it, but slipped on the rocks and went into the water. I grabbed him and he pulled me in as well. The water was very strong and we were knocked against the rocks and then swept in a circle to the back of the pool on the other side of the waterfall.

'We thought that it couldn't be *that* hard to get out, so we tried. We tried quite a few times. Perhaps for two hours. At first we pulled the canoe onto the rocks at the back and tried to swim out, but the current kept pushing us back. And we realised that that would not work.

'So we went back to the rock ledge, took the canoe, stood in it and held on to the rocks, slowly pulling ourselves around. But at the last bit the rocks slope down at an angle … and there was a whirlpool there. It just pulled the canoe from under us, and we fell in the water again, and got swept around to where we started.

'We kept trying that for ages before we knew it was not going to work. We had been sitting for a long time when we heard someone calling. It was one of the guys from Eden Adventures [a local adventure tour specialist]. We whistled and called back.

'The guy showed us that we must stay where we were and that's when we realised that we were in trouble. We didn't know what was going on on the other side and didn't know what our parents thought.

'We waited and waited … and then through the mist we saw the red colours of the NSRI.'

The sun was getting lower and the boys started to get cold. But their biggest fear was what their parents were going to say.

'We really started to get cold. We started shaking,' said André.

Hennie Niehaus, station commander at the Wilderness NSRI base (Station 23), had just got two calls for help – the second one saying that the teenagers were up at the waterfall.

'And that's when I thought, "Whoa, here is trouble."' He swung his crew into action. He and crewman Attie Hoffman were first on scene, and they launched the *Discovery Rescue Runner* jet-ski at the low-water bridge as fast as they could.

'I had no idea what to expect. And when we got up there, we could see nothing. I climbed up the rocks and saw that when the sun shone on the mist in there it prevented us seeing anything.

'It was just one thick mass of vapour.

'But just then a cloud came over and we could faintly see the children on the other side. I saw that they were all right and went back to tell Cliffie [Marlow] and them, who then went to tell the parents that they were okay.'

Clifford Marlow, deputy Station Commander, continues: 'Hennie came out and said that it was monstrous up there. "It's really rough," he said. I thought that he was exaggerating a bit. And then we got the Croc [inflatable canoe] ready and hooked it up to the *Rescue Runner*. I was on the back of the Croc and as we came around that last bend I really got a fright. It's something that I have never been exposed to before.

'We got in there and it was almost like a witch's cauldron. The river was really vicious and I thought, "We are in for a big thing here." It was two and a half hours of intense concentration. At no stage could you sit back and relax.

'The other thing was that I knew the De Goedes. I saw Derrick de Goede and he said to me that it was his boy, André, in there and suddenly it got very personal.

'So it was quite *lekker* to be able to tell them that the boys were safe and that they should take it *rustig* – we just had to figure out a way of getting the boys out.'

Hennie recalls: 'Richard Botha from Metro went with us, as we were the only two trained in swift-water rescue.

'There was no way to communicate. You struggle to see each other, and when you faced the waterfall you couldn't breathe properly. It was like someone had a fire hose trained on your face the whole time. We had to stand with our backs to the waterfall and actually lean back into the wind, it was so strong. And it was very slippery on the rocks.

'The whole rescue felt very short to me. When we came out we saw that it had in fact taken almost two and a half hours.'

Donald Olivier was the first rescue swimmer to get across, followed by Jaco de Jong. They checked that the boys were uninjured and then asked, 'How the hell did you get here?'

First to be taken across the pool was André.

'It was an adrenaline rush. I just hung on to the Croc and the guys pulled.'

André was transferred to the *Discovery Rescue Runner* and taken out through the gorge.

'By then I was flippen cold,' said André.

'When I climbed off the *Rescue Runner* I saw that the whole corner of the parking lot was full of people. There were cars everywhere. An ambulance. A 4x4 Metro rescue van. They took me to the ambulance and did my blood pressure, pulse and things and gave us huge blankets.

'My temperature was 34.9 °C and Corné's was even lower, 33.6 °C. We were blue.' Both boys were critically close to body temperatures of 32 °C, the point at which hypothermia becomes critical.

'Everyone gave us hugs. Corné's parents were there, my mom and them were there. Everyone was just glad that we were out and safe. We got goose bumps. And I thought, *jissie*, you don't know what a big thing it is until you are on the other side.

'It could have ended very differently if it had been an hour later. Sometimes when I lie awake at night, I think that it could have been the last day that I went for a swim.'

André's mother, Lieschen, said it took a while to understand what had happened: 'In the beginning it was just that they were going for an hour's paddle in the canoe, have a quick look at the waterfall and then come back.

'Then you realise after an hour, an hour and a half, that they are not back. People go to look and they can't find them.

'You start to wonder what could have happened. The insecurity and powerlessness ... it's terrible to stand there and all those emotions go through you.

'And in the end to see the guys from the NSRI, they were there to help. They were so kind, helpful and friendly. It was two days before Christmas and this huge team of people turned out to help.

'They gave us our children back. That is unbelievable to experience. I am eternally grateful.'

30 My foot was in the shark's mouth

Mathieu Dasnois

This account first appeared in the Mail & Guardian. *It is reprinted with the permission of the author.*

I TWISTED, AND SAW THE shark with my foot in its mouth. It was dragging me through the water. The shark – an eyewitness said it was a four-metre great white – was shaking its head from side to side to rip my leg from my body. But I felt very little pain. My mind was completely clear. I did a kind of sit-up in the water and started pushing and prodding the shark. Its skin was rock hard.

I noticed the eye and pushed my left thumb into it. I remember it felt squishy. I remember my thumb entering the eye socket. I felt the shark twitch. As it let go and swam away, I felt its teeth slash my foot.

I took stock. My leg was mangled and I had little control of my foot. My right fin was gone.

I had asked Rob Nettleton and Debbie Smith from Offshore Africa in Port St Johns if I could hitch a ride on their boat tour and jump overboard to look at a reef I'd seen from the shore at Sugarloaf Rock, with a view to coming back another time to spearfish. Rob is an NSRI volunteer, and Debbie is an instructor at the local NSRI WaterWise Academy, so I was in good hands. It was about lunchtime on 2 May 2015 and the weather was perfect – sunny, with little wind and calm seas. The boat dropped me off about 50 m from the tip of Sugarloaf, a conical headland that becomes an island at high tide.

I'd been in the water a few minutes and there wasn't much to see, so I was swimming back to the boat when the eight-metre-deep pebbled seabed gave way to a reef. This was what I'd been looking for! I stopped swimming and started taking slow, deep breaths, preparing to dive to the bottom and look around.

Then I felt myself moving. For a split second I thought the boat had hit me and I was being pushed by the hull. A shark attack seemed absurd, unreal.

When the shark let go of me briefly, there was a moment of relief. I thought maybe it had gone. But it turned around with an agility that was more terrifying for me than seeing my foot in its mouth. I was prey. I was being hunted. That's when I thought I was going to die.

Rob had seen the shark before I had and had already tried to get the boat to me, but I'd been dragged away.

He told me later that he saw me with my arm around the shark. He says the animal 'went ballistic on the surface, thrashing its tail and arching its back half out the water'. Rob said he thought: 'This is it, he's gone. We're not going to find him.'

I don't remember the second attack well. I remember my hand on the shark's nose, and I think I pushed myself away. It only got hold of my upper arm. Alison Kock, the research manager for Shark Spotters in Cape Town, suggests the shark may have attacked again more cautiously after I poked it in the eye, giving me time to react.

It dragged me through the water a second time. I remember thinking, 'Great. First a leg, now an arm. What's next?'

I managed to break free when the shark adjusted its grip on my arm. I surfaced and saw the bright red boat. Everyone was looking at me, including Rob at the wheel. I raised my arm and shouted, 'Help! I need help!'

Then I put my head back underwater to scan for the shark, and I saw it, straight below me, coming up fast. It had taken the time to line up from below, as if I were a seal. I could sense its desire. I was food. It had no vindictiveness, no hatred, no animosity. Nor had I. It wanted to consume me and I wanted to survive.

I saw it slowly opening its jaws, I saw the rows of razor-sharp teeth that I had felt tearing my flesh and muscle earlier. I was eye to eye, nose to nose with the creature hunting me.

I dangled my right hand to one side, to give it a target. As the shark shot up, I pushed against it with both hands. It twisted, jaws open, and burst out of the water with the sheer speed of the attack. It breached – 'nose to belly button', according to Rob – both pectoral fins out of the water, and almost fell on the boat, which had come closer.

I swam to the boat, feeling my useless, dangling right foot, concentrating on my left leg, which still had a fin. I reached out to Eddy Johnstone, a guest on the boat, saying, 'Help me. Please help me.'

He pulled me out of the water in one go, leaning out of the boat. He came face to face with the shark. It had already turned around for another attack.

On the boat, I could finally stop moving, but I was still full of adrenaline. I kept looking around, moving my limbs, telling people: 'That was a shark! I was attacked by a fucking shark!' as if they hadn't seen it breach, metres from the boat.

Debbie and Eddy were calming me down, telling me it was over and I would be okay.

I couldn't feel my right foot or move my toes. I was spurting blood.

Eddy was holding my head in his hands. Rob was on the phone to shore, while 'at the same time taking out our massive first aid box that we always carry and telling clients to rip open the packaging and pass it to Debbie'. Rob added: 'I was sitting ... seeing this enormous amount of blood flowing down the back of the boat and out through the scuppers.'

Debbie says she told herself: 'Just work, just get it sorted, just get it fixed, help, talk to Matt, ask for more sanitary towels, more bandages ... I remember my fingers sinking into the gaps in his wetsuit by his calf.'

Three arteries in my leg were severed. 'The boat was full of blood,' says Rob. Tendons and nerves were ripped, and both my hands were slashed when I fended off the shark. Eight hours of surgery and 187 stitches later, I knew I would make a full recovery. I was lucky. Lucky that Offshore Africa always carried that big medical kit on board, and that Debbie bandaged me up so well.

Right now I'm just recovering. The nerve pain in my mangled leg is constant, but it's good to have it still attached, and my arm and hands have finally healed.

I still have a cast on my leg and there are months of physio ahead.

Friends have asked me if I will ever dive again. Yes, but only in very clear water, from a boat, with a buddy like Rob and a dive master like Debbie.

Also, I have a new respect for the ocean and a new understanding of our place in the ocean's food chain: somewhere in the middle. I am both predator and prey. I must behave like prey, watchful and careful.

31 Rescue from the air

Andrew Ingram

Phil Ress, like so many Sea Rescue volunteers, doesn't boast about his achievements. Or about the recognition he has received from his NSRI peers. In his 37 years of service he has received five awards, something not many people can equal.

In 1992, he was presented with the NSRI Distinguished Service Award by President FW de Klerk for two helicopter rescues that saved 20 lives; in 2001 he received Directors' Thanks for the rescue of the crew from the fishing vessel Chia Ying no 6 *that was wrecked on the* dolosse *of the Port of Cape Town's container basin wall; in 2005 he received the Marmion Marsh trophy for dedicated service to Sea Rescue; in 2013 he received a Letter of Appreciation for serving 17 years on the National Operations and Training Committee; and in 2015 he was presented with his 35-year service award.*

As I WALK INTO PHIL Ress's office in Milnerton, there's a set of framed photographs on the wall. One shows a much younger Phil, incongruously wearing a tuxedo, shaking the hand of then President FW de Klerk. It is an old press photograph of Phil receiving the NSRI Distinguished Service Award.

'Tell me the story behind that picture,' I say to him.

The citation framed next to the picture is an impressive one: 'For his courage and determination in playing a major role in two

Court Helicopter rescue operations, on each occasion being asked to participate because of his Hi-Line experience and medic skills. On the 30th of October 1991, he was lowered onto a fishing vessel 150 nautical miles south of Cape Agulhas and successfully evacuated the skipper who was seriously ill.'

'The other rescue was the *Jenny Lee*,' Phil says.

It was 18 February 1992 when Phil got the call to report urgently to the Court Helicopter base, at that time located near the Paarden Island entrance to Cape Town harbour, near the container terminal.

'The *Jenny Lee*, a Namibian fishing boat with 19 crew on board, had sunk about 180 miles from Cape Town and 70 nautical miles west of Lamberts Bay. We didn't have an exact position for her. And it was close to the helicopter's maximum range, but there were 19 men in a life raft. So we went.'

The Sikorsky S-61, a huge machine that can carry up to 30 people, took off with pilot John Pocock, copilot Roger Watt, engineer Pete Phillips and Phil as the NSRI Hi-Line specialist on board. A Dakota from the SAAF's 35 Squadron was also dispatched to help search for the life raft.

'We were starting to get low on fuel and the Dak was on her last sortie when they spotted the raft and guided us in.'

John Pocock put the Sikorsky in a hover over the life raft. The wind was around 20 knots from the southeast and there was a three-metre swell. Phil, clipped into his harness, leaned out of the machine's door and was lowered straight into the life raft by engineer Pete Phillips. Unclipping from the line in the raft, Phil looked up and saw the reassuring sight of the huge machine above and Pete's helmeted head looking down at him from the open door.

'It wasn't pleasant in that raft. Nineteen seasick men had been throwing up all night. We lifted the first two in a double strop [padded harness], and then the next two. The helicopter was now low on fuel, but there were four survivors in the helicopter. And the strop came down again.'

The fifth and sixth survivors were halfway up to the helicopter when suddenly the winch stopped. Phil knew instantly that it had overheated. This was a fairly common problem with these winches in those years, and the flight crew were not particularly concerned. The helicopter slowly decreased altitude, with Pete hanging out the door 'pattering' – talking – the pilot through height and direction, and the two men were put back in the life raft. Phil took the harness off them, knowing that the Sikorsky would fly a circuit hoping that the winch would cool down so that they could use it again.

But that old trick didn't work.

When the helicopter was back above the life raft, it was obvious that they intended to try and manually pull the survivors one at a time into the helicopter using the Hi-Line rope.

'It wasn't good,' remembers Phil.

'They really battled to get the first guy in. His boots came off, and Pete signalled that they would fly away again.'

All this time the Air Force Dakota was flying high above the rescue team, keeping a watch over their operation.

The helicopter flew another circuit and Phil, knowing the machine intimately, saw that the overheating winch had been removed in order to rig a manual hoist system. The machine again went into a hover above him.

The Hi-Line, now passing through a D-shackle, was lowered to him with a single strop. Understanding what the plan was, Phil helped another crewman into it and he was pulled out of the life raft.

Phil shakes his head and laughs. 'The engineer had got the four survivors already on board the chopper to hold the rope and, using the extraordinary length of the Sikorsky, the men walked to the back of the machine, tug of war style, pulling the remaining fishermen into the helicopter, one at a time.

'It was fantastic flying by John,' remembers Phil. 'As the guys moved to the back of the machine the weight distribution obviously changed radically and he had to compensate for that.'

It took a total of 45 minutes to get everyone safely into the helicopter, and Phil, last out of the life raft, looked down to see it skipping away over the waves. With no more weight inside, it was blown away by the helicopter's powerful downdraught.

But the ordeal wasn't over.

They were now critically low on fuel. Cape Town was out of range, and so John turned for Lamberts Bay. Flying with great care to conserve every drop of fuel, the team and the survivors were greatly relieved to touch down in front of the Lamberts Bay Protea Hotel.

'They were great. We got lunch from them and then a lift to the hardware store where John used the company credit card to buy their entire stock of paraffin. It was just enough to get us to Langebaanweg Air Force Base, where we could refuel properly,' says Phil.

* * *

There are a few ideas that, over the years, have dramatically changed how rescue operations are carried out. The use of helicopters for rescues and the invention of cellphones are two prime examples. I ask Phil how helicopter rescue started in South Africa.

'The *Seafarer*,' he says without hesitation.

The wreck of the *SA Seafarer*, on 1 July 1966, off Mouille Point, was the result of a series of errors by its officers, operating under very severe storm conditions. If it hadn't been for three SAAF Alouette helicopters and their 12 crew members, 75 people on board – including a six-month-old baby – could have lost their lives.

The *Seafarer* was owned by the Springbok Shipping Company, and its home port was Cape Town. When the ship arrived home on the evening of 30 June 1966, there was a cargo of 7 800 tons on board, including a lethal consignment of tetraethyl lead (TEL) – a widely used fuel octane booster – and thousands of bottles of whisky.

A series of errors throughout the night resulted in the ship running hard aground on the reefs off Green and Mouille Points at just after midnight. The engines were shut down in case of an explosion. It was far too risky to attempt a rescue in the pitch darkness and foul weather, although the tugs *FT Bates* and *CG White* stood by the stricken ship in case the crew attempted to launch the lifeboats.

Attempts to send lines across by rocket and to rig a breeches buoy were foiled by the high winds and mountainous seas, and at 4.42 am the *Seafarer* broke its back. For the first time in its history, the Green Point lighthouse's revolving mechanism was stopped, and the beam switched to continuous and focused on the stricken vessel.

At first light that 1 July, six young South African Air Force pilots, flying three brand-new Alouette III helicopters, winched 75 people to safety from the *Seafarer* in a rescue operation that captured the world's attention. On the front pages of newspapers, and played on newsreels in cinemas around the world for months afterwards, the *Seafarer* rescue was a seminal moment in international air-sea rescue, putting the spotlight on the extraordinary skills of South African helicopter pilots.

In his book, *Chopper Pilot*, Peter 'Monster' Wilkins, later brigadier general but then a humble second lieutenant, wrote of the incredible flying that they pulled off in horrendous conditions. Their winch ropes were 'only 50 feet long' but the spray from the nine- to ten-metre swells was reaching up to 110 feet, blowing well over the top of the choppers. His flight engineer, Sergeant Bill Oosthuizen, was soon soaked, perched as he was in the open door of the Alouette.

'Due to the difficult conditions, and the very intense flying, which required high levels of concentration and much perspiration despite the cold, pilots alternated in doing rescues. Thus I would take every second rescue for Alouette 53 and [Lieutenant] Brian [Palin] would then call the waves. It is supposed to be every seventh wave that is the big one, but here every wave was big, and every seventh was colossal!

'The three Alouettes worked efficiently in a shuttle service to lift off the entire complement of 76 people, including a baby which came up in a seaman's arms, making it 75 hoists!'

It is a modestly told story, but the *Seafarer* rescue went down in international sea rescue history, and radically changed the way in which future rescues would be approached.

Phil recalls: 'In 2002 the same helicopter which was flown by Monster Wilkins in the *Seafarer* rescue, Alouette 53, became the first helicopter to be used in the Western Cape dedicated to mountain and sea rescue. That machine, painted white with big red crosses on her flanks, had the call sign Skymed II.'

Because the NSRI's Table Bay rescue base was close to the Court Helicopter base, and because Phil and Howard Godfrey were particularly interested in helicopter rescue, they worked closely with the specialist marine helicopter group.

From 1991, the Sea Rescue volunteers, part of the newly formed Court NSRI Hi-Line team, responded on the Sikorsky S-58 and S-61 helicopters to help mariners who needed evacuation from ships on both South African Search and Rescue (SASAR) and commercial calls. It was about then that the new rescue system was introduced, which changed the way that the helicopter crews evacuated patients from vessels. It is referred to as 'Hi-Line', and I asked Phil where it came from.

'Howard Godfrey,' he replies, without hesitation.

'Howard was visiting a friend in London, where he read a *Popular Mechanics* magazine. In it was a story on Hi-Line rescue. He thought it was a great idea, and brought it back to Cape Town where it became the rescue technique of choice that gave the team its name. The rest is history,' says Phil.

The Hi-Line rescue method involves a rope that is tied (with a weak link) on to the helicopter winch arm and lowered on to the boat below. The rescue crew then use that line to guide the patient, who is either in a stretcher or a harness attached to the winch cable, up to the helicopter. The Hi-Line method helps to reduce the swinging around of patients and makes it much easier for the aircrew to get rescue crews on to a small deck area and safely get patients off a small area.

Court Helicopters eventually became part of CHC Helicopter and was later acquired by the Titan Helicopter Group, and unfortunately their base in Cape Town is no longer active. This means the NSRI Hi-Line team and their rescue method are no longer used, but in the decade that they were active Phil and the team flew on over 900 calls and logged 3 000 hours in helicopters.

Meanwhile, across at Ysterplaat Air Force Base, the home of the legendary 22 Squadron and the base of the SAAF/NSRI Air Sea Rescue unit (Station 29), casualty evacuations are still done by Oryx helicopters using the Long Line method, a similar system to the Hi-Line, which allows the patients to be safely guided from ship to helicopter. The Long Line differs from the Hi-Line in that a rope is tied to the helicopter strop, instead of the winch, and is then lowered to the deck of a ship.

During Phil Ress's time as a coxswain at Station 3, Table Bay, he was involved in almost all of the 'inshore surf rescue' helicopter operations. Starting off with the John Rolfe helicopter, a combination of NSRI rescue swimmers and Surf Lifesaving Association of South Africa (SLASA) volunteers, which operated in the 1980s, the helicopter rescue service soon became a household name.

'In the third year of operating we were doing about 120 calls a year, until the sponsorship became a casualty of the ban on advertising of cigarettes,' says Phil.

Hunters Gold then came forward with sponsorship, and Lifesaving SA, Metro (Medical Emergency Transport Rescue Organisation) and the NSRI joined hands for a helicopter rescue operation that was run in Durban and Cape Town over the summer season. SLASA then found funding from cellphone giant Nokia, and when that sponsorship ran its course Win helicopters stepped into the gap in Cape Town.

Unfortunately, shortly after the Win operation was sponsored by supermarket chain Pick n Pay, two helicopters crashed during filming for the TV series *Fear Factor*. Press pictures of the two crashed helicopters lying on their side at the Waterfront helipad ironically echoed the Pick n Pay advertising tag line emblazoned on the aircraft: 'We are on your side.' Miraculously, no one was injured in the mishap.

The crash ended that sponsorship. Then came Vodacom, which

was followed by the Discovery ER24 helicopter rescue programme, which ended in 2010.

During his time in the NSRI air rescue teams, Phil was part of a team that pulled off many hazardous rescues, saving and helping hundreds of people. Like so many people who work in rescue, Phil developed a sixth sense for danger. And learned to listen to it. So it was that in 2009, when his daughter Isabella was born, that Phil decided to call it quits.

'I had passed my envelope of safety,' he said. 'I had done it all and it was time to stand down, to make way for the youngsters and spend some time with my family.'

Phil Ress is still a Sea Rescue volunteer, but he is now more involved in a training role at the Table Bay Sea Rescue base than in physical rescues. Phil keeps his hand in on rescue boat helms now as project manager for the building of all Sea Rescue's rigid inflatable boats (RIBs), as well as sea testing them before they are handed into active service at the rescue stations.

Like so many of the old hands, the pioneers in rescue, you wouldn't know the amazing contribution that he and others have made unless you take the time to sit and listen to the stories of grit and determination – stories that involve so many people being given another chance at life. Or perhaps if you saw the framed awards on the wall, or had the luck to hear firsthand of the bravery that is talked about by the older Sea Rescue volunteers as if it were all quite normal.

32 Time to leave

Andrew Ingram

At the Sea Rescue AGM in mid-August 2010, coxswain Jaco Louw, from Station 30, Agulhas, was presented with a Gallantry Award, and his crewmen Reinard Geldenhuys and Darryl Moon received Directors' Thanks for the rescue of five people from the yacht Redfin *on the night of 14 June 2010. These awards are not handed out easily.*

THE WEATHER OFF CAPE AGULHAS was dreadful. Huge seven-metre swells were driving towards the shore, it was pitch dark, and the wind was onshore. Skipper Lars Strydom had sailed from Hout Bay, bound for Port Elizabeth, with a crew of four, in his yacht, *Redfin*, which was also his home.

He knew the vessel intimately; he had spent 11 years building it. He knew how the old-fashioned junk rig handled, and he knew the strength of the steel hull. He had done his weather checks before sailing and knew that a big cold front was coming. He had worked out that by the time it hit he would be safely around Cape Agulhas.

But the front moved faster than he had anticipated and Lars found himself in huge seas being forced closer and closer to the land, his junk rig preventing him from forcing the bow closer into the wind. (The junk sail is very inefficient when sailing upwind, as the rig cannot 'point' as close to the wind.) And then things started to really go wrong. The headsail was damaged, which Lars quickly repaired, and then the tiller arm broke – in three places.

Being a practical person, Lars jury-rigged the tiller, 'but in the process I chopped off the tip of my pinky.

'The biggest problem was that, due to the motion of the yacht in the big swell, one of my batteries had shorted out, and I lost all my onboard electrics. I couldn't start my engine to get clear of the coast,' said Lars.

'That's when we discussed calling the NSRI, but then the wind, which had dropped while we were making repairs, came up favourably and we realised we could sail for Struisbaai.

'But as we made our approach to Cape Agulhas, the wind went 90 degrees from west through to southeast, and we were blown onto the wrong side of the Cape.

'I turned the boat around to head back up to Quoin Point. Then the tiller socket broke and I lost steering, the wind shifted again to the south, and we were being blown towards the land. We knew now that we were in the shit and called the NSRI.

'While the NSRI got going, I used the sails to steer, allowing the rudder to freewheel. I was amazed at how well she handled, but I couldn't "drive" the boat into the wind because I couldn't put pressure on the rudder.

'So I used a *bobbejaan* [monkey wrench] and pushed with my feet. It worked well, but eventually I broke that as well,' said Lars.

At 18 minutes to midnight, the NSRI's Station 30, Agulhas, was activated and the 8.5-m rescue craft, *Vodacom Rescuer VII*, was launched, with Jaco Louw at the helm. The swells were reaching seven metres, and the wind was gusting at 45 knots (84 km/h). It was so dark that it was nearly impossible to read the sea, and Agulhas Station Commander Shane Kempen called for backup. Simon's Town (Station 10) launched their deep-sea Breede-class rescue vessel and Hermanus (Station 17) towed their 5.5-m RIB (rigid inflatable boat) towards the danger zone.

Nobody said it, but if the Agulhas team got into trouble, help was far away. But, as Jaco said, 'If we didn't go, there was nobody else.

There was no option. I just stayed calm and off we went.'

The conditions were so foul that it took the Sea Rescue volunteers two hours to reach the *Redfin*. One small mercy was that, when they reached the stricken yacht, the sea conditions were marginally better than those they had fought through to get there, as *Redfin*'s position was partially in the lee of the mainland.

Jaco approached the yacht at an angle of 45 degrees on the lee side. It took the crew 20 minutes and three passes to get the four crew members – two women and two men – onto the bow of the rescue boat.

And then an emotional Lars refused to leave his boat. It was just too much for him to give up.

Jaco, at the helm of the rescue boat, decided he could spend no more time with the rudderless yacht. The wild sea conditions prevented him putting a towline on *Redfin*, and he had four hypothermic patients on board. He radioed his base to say he was leaving the skipper behind.

Shane Kempen was horrified. He called Lars on his cellphone and 'explained a few things to him'.

Lars said later: 'I thought I could make it, but the guy said if I come short in those breakers, I am tickets. He very calmly explained my situation. He was sympathetic to my feelings but firm about explaining my situation, and I agreed to get off.'

Jaco turned the rescue boat around, and headed back to find the yacht for a second time, this time taking Lars off.

'I was devastated to leave my boat floating,' said Lars. 'The last I saw was her sailing away into the dark. It broke my heart.

'Those [NSRI] guys did a sterling job. They are a really nice bunch of people. It was scary and tricky and they had no real reason to be there other than for us. I really appreciate that.'

Redfin later smashed into the rocks ('It sounded like gunshots,' said Lars). A Struisbaai local, Sarel Vermeulen, brought his excavator out to the stranded yacht and pulled it ashore. There the mast and rudder skeg were removed before fellow sailor Stuart Davidson took the yacht, free of charge, via flatbed truck to Port Elizabeth, where Lars was working for the Algoa Bay Sailing Marina.

33 The angels had their hands full

Tony Weaver and Andrew Ingram

As WE DRIVE FROM MOSSEL Bay to Witsand, near the mouth of the Breede River, Andrew turns to me and says, 'The story you're going to hear now is the story of a rescue that was the most amazing mixture of inexperience, big balls and great seamanship.'

Witsand Station Commander Attie Gunter, 32 years old when I interview him but just 27 at the time of one of the most epic sea rescues in recent history, comes to meet us at the Witsand rescue base straight from the fields of his farm on the Breede River, his work boots covered in mud.

'I remember that night better now than I did just afterwards because I was so traumatised back then. It was 15 June 2011. At about 7 pm – 7.22 to be exact – we got the call from Still Bay; their boat was in for repairs, and there was a yacht in trouble. We spoke to the ship-to-shore radio communications operators at Cape Town Radio, and they said they couldn't be sure, but it seemed the yacht was the *Gulliver*, en route from Port Owen on the West Coast to St Francis Bay.

'They had been contacted by the skipper's wife after she got worried because of no cellphone contact since lunchtime, and they had been alerted to, and picked up, an unidentified EPIRB [Emergency Position Indicating Radio Beacon] signal about 12 nautical miles off Cape Infanta.'

On board the *Gulliver* were skipper and owner Greg West, 60,

Franz Sprung, 76, and Shaun Kennedy, 34, all from St Francis Bay, and Mike Morck, 64, from Knysna.

When Greg's wife, Marcelle, couldn't make cellphone contact, she started to make calls. She got hold of an NSRI volunteer friend in Knysna and then Cape Town Radio. She persevered, insisting that the EPIRB signal picked up by an international maritime rescue agency, and relayed to Cape Town Radio, was from *Gulliver*. The Maritime Rescue Coordination Centre (MRCC) in Cape Town called out the NSRI, and the rescue bases at Agulhas (Station 30), Still Bay (Station 31) and Witsand (Station 33) were put on standby.

Attie says, 'After a long period of following the coordinates – and by then it was far out to sea, or seemed to be – we realised the coords had been transposed and were wrong. So we recalculated, and realised the yacht was about 15 nautical miles from the base.

'We launched at 9.10 pm in the 5.5-m rigid inflatable boat [RIB], *Queenie Paine*, with two powerful 60-hp engines.

'The wind was relatively still, blowing northwest, as I set out with Quentin Diener and the late Leon Pretorius, and the bay was lovely. But it was the night of the total eclipse of the moon, so it was very dark, *pik swart donker*, plus the Breede River had just come down in flood so we didn't know where the sandbanks across the mouth were. We hit a sandbank, then crossed the bar, hit one wave, and thought that's it, no problem, easy sailing.'

The moon was blood red.

Just before the total lunar eclipse shut down the night completely, they fired their first illuminating flare to try and find a way through the outer line of breaking surf. The flare started to drop and they fired the next. And another. And another. In this way, as Attie chose his moments, there was enough time to get through the back line 500 m out to sea before darkness swallowed them again. They got through.

The eclipse was at its peak, and clouds closed in. Visibility was down to nearly nothing. The wind was strong, but it was manageable. The little rescue boat was cracking along at a good speed on course to the last position of the EPIRB.

'About five miles out, we hit a lot of phosphorescence; it almost looked as if it was the yacht under water with its running lights on. And then in the last five miles, the wind came up and it started to get very rough. On the way there, I saw a light, but it was a star, and the crew laughed at me. But it happened to all three of us; the visibility was bad.

'We had asked our base to keep an eye on the weather, and Cape Town Radio had told them that there was some very heavy, very bad weather coming.

'We left the shelter of Cape Infanta, and all hell broke loose.

'It was as if someone had pushed a button, thrown a switch. From a nice, even five-metre swell, the wind just slammed into us at gale-force strength, and it just turned into chaos.'

The waves were huge. They were breaking in all directions, and running with the wind behind them, the rescue boat smashed into breaking wave after breaking wave. The spray was blowing from behind straight past them.

'It was crazy,' Leon Pretorius told Andrew not long after the rescue. He was the radio operator on the call. 'We were doing around 35 km/h so the wind must have been at least 60 km/h.' Leon got hold of Cape Town Radio and found out that the weather was deteriorating fast. The swell had gone from five to eight metres.

As Attie opened the throttles again, the rescue crew struggled to see through the spray. He turned the nose of the rescue boat on to the new bearing that the MRCC had provided for the latest EPIRB position. The advice that the crew had been given was to get to the position, fire one flare and, if there was no response, turn around and run for home.

It was simply too dangerous for the small rescue boat to hang about alone in those conditions.

By this time Sea Rescue operations manager, Mark Hughes, was in his office watching the rescue boat track on his computer. It had become obvious that this was an extremely dangerous mission. The Altec Netstar tracker device installed in the rescue boat was proving to be invaluable; all the way up the coast senior NSRI crew were holding their collective breath as the rescue boat's 'bread crumb' line tracked towards the position of the beacon.

Queenie Paine reached the point where they hoped to find *Gulliver*. The sea had been whipped into a maelstrom and the crew had to shout to hear each other above the wind.

There was no yacht. Nothing.

Leon reached for an emergency red flare, pulled the trigger, and it exploded 300 m overhead, casting an eerie red glow over the whitecapped waves. And then it was whipped away and extinguished by the wind.

Attie wiped salt out of his eyes. He thought he had seen a light in the distance.

Maybe.

Then the other two saw it.

They had no idea how far it was, but it was the last chance.

At 10.33 pm Leon depressed the microphone on *Queenie Paine*'s VHF radio: 'Cape Town Radio, Cape Town Radio, Cape Town Radio, this is Rescue 33, Rescue 33, Rescue 33. We have the yacht in sight. Over.'

Attie guided the *Queenie Paine* up to the overturned hull of *Gulliver* and saw that all four crew were in the life raft, which was tied to the hull of the 40-ft catamaran.

'Are you guys okay?' he called.

Communications had again been lost with base, and the shore controllers at Witsand – Attie's wife-to-be, Karen Eybers, and volunteer Rob Wilson – watched the track of the rescue boat drifting at 2 km/h for nearly 20 minutes, not knowing if the rescue boat had now also capsized or if they were simply taking a long time to transfer the survivors.

'There were four crew in the yacht and the skipper told me they had been trying to outrun the storm front under engine, but the wind was too strong, and they pitchpoled [overturned end-to-end, with the stern pitching over the bows] at about 1.30 pm,' Attie said. 'We later found out from them that the youngest crew member, Shaun Kennedy, had first swum under the yacht to activate the EPIRB. Then he later repeated the swim to release the life raft.

'And then the bloody raft blew away. Shaun swam after it, managed to grab it and got it safely back.'

At this stage, they told Attie later, they were still full of hope for a rescue. 'Then it got dark and they started to lose hope, it was over. But Shaun Kennedy decided, "Bugger that, I am going to survive."

'When we got alongside them it was almost 11 pm, so they had been in the water for nearly ten hours. The older uncle [Franz Sprung] was in a bad way with hypothermia; he was so cold that he couldn't swim properly, so we really battled to get him on board the *Queenie Paine*. It was a very difficult transfer on to our boat, but we finally got all four of them on board after about 15 to 20 minutes, and there were now seven of us in the 5.5-metre rescue boat. I apologised to the skipper, Greg West, for coming in such a small boat, and he said, "I'll take it!" But during the transfer, waves had been breaking over the pontoons and the now heavily laden rescue boat was itself in grave danger of capsizing. There was no time to try and get the yachtsmen into foul weather gear. Leon had given one man his jacket and Attie stopped Quentin from taking his off.

'The wind was terrifying. I don't think that I will ever be able to explain it to anyone. It's water from all sides. We just told them to hold tight, and I said, "We'll try and get you home."

'I gunned the engines, and tried to pull away – and nothing. *Niks.* The boat was full of water, and we began to panic. After what seemed like ages the engines forced the hull out of the water, and the deck started to drain and we began to make some headway.

'Then, just as we got the boat up and moving, it felt like a train had smashed into us. The water was straight into our faces like needles. I couldn't believe how fast the weather had changed; we knew we were going to battle, but, until that moment, I never ever had any idea that we might not actually make it back alive.

'The waves were bigger than the boat. I switched off all the lights so I could see the GPS properly. On every wave that came, we didn't know if we were going to land bow first or stern first, the chop on top of the swell was shocking. I hit my head three or four times, my helmet was broken. Quentin moved into the bow to try and give us some stability – a very dangerous move, but we had no option, and we moved the yachtsmen as far forward as we could.'

In the meantime, Leon had managed to reestablish contact with Cape Town Radio. Before communications were once again lost, he had given them their position and said they were battling their way back to base.

As the boat crashed over a wave, Leon dropped the radio and Attie's hand was smashed off the throttles.

'I thought, "Oh no, I've broken the throttle levers,"' said Attie, not realising in the chaos that it was only the dropped radio.

'I just tried to keep the revs up. A few times, I thought Quentin had broken his back because we were being slammed back and forth. I couldn't even guess our speed; I just had to keep my revs.'

Leon (who sadly died of a heart attack in December 2014, aged just 37) kept up a running commentary: 'If it wasn't for Leon, I wouldn't have made it. He just kept saying "Go Attie, go Attie, go Attie," and he was handling the radio, trying to get and maintain comms.

'It was a very scary night. I didn't think that we would make it.'

Meanwhile, Leon had done some fuel calculations in his head and realised they couldn't make it back: *'Daar was geen manier'* (there was no way).

Attie: 'We had extra fuel on board, but there was no way we could refuel, we couldn't stop, it would have flipped us immediately. If the GPS had failed, we would have been stuffed. There were no lights on shore for us to get our bearings, our engines could have failed, we were taking such a beating and there was so much water coming over us we just knew the engines could fail at any minute.'

With the GPS showing 25 km to go to safe harbour, Attie throttled back enough for Leon to put a desperate message through: 'Please send assistance. We aren't going to make it.'

Communications were so bad that it wasn't clear why they needed help, but the response was instant. Cape Town Radio repeated the message and the 8.5-m *Vodacom Rescuer VII* was scrambled from Agulhas, as well as a crew from Still Bay who responded by road.

'According to our GPS they were 40 miles from us. In those conditions it would take us more than two hours to get there,' said Agulhas Station Commander Reinard Geldenhuys.

The tension at Witsand rescue base, where Karen and Rob were handling shore control, was unbearable. 'They had no idea what was going on, what had happened, the comms were gone,' recalls Attie. 'We managed to reach Cape Town Radio once, we said they must send people with petrol because we had two spare tanks, but we couldn't use them.

'I remember thinking, I didn't kiss Karen goodbye. We just left in such a hurry, and I was responsible for two crew on board, both with wives and children, and we were going to die. Nobody would have been able to get to us in that kind of weather.'

But gradually, almost imperceptibly, conditions improved for the little rescue boat as the crew worked their way into the lee of Cape Infanta.

In the distance the crew could see the lights of a trawler, and they headed for it. 'It was one of those big trawlers, a ship really, so we couldn't unload the yacht crew to them, and as we went past I heard them on the radio saying, "But they are going past us." And as we got into the bay, it all calmed down.'

'We had hope again,' Leon recalled. 'We could talk again. We could hear each other. And seven kilometres from the base we got comms again. And we were able to refuel.'

'It was fantastic to hear that Agulhas was on the water. That there was someone on the way for us,' said Attie.

Although *Vodacom Rescuer VII* throttled back, they kept on course until they had confirmation that *Queenie Paine* was safely through the bar.

And then they turned around.

The adrenaline-filled trip that had taken the big 8.5-m rescue boat an hour took two and a half hours on the return trip.

As the *Queenie Paine*'s nose touched the slipway at 1.30 am, Attie started crying: 'Leon and Quentin and I were so relieved, we gave the yacht crew our jackets, we were joking and laughing and crying, and later, the older uncle said he thought we were all going to die, but here we were cracking jokes.

'I think that we were very lucky. I still don't know how we got back. But ja, it was just luck. If anything else had happened it would have been over. I don't know how many angels we had on that boat, but they had their hands full.'

Postscript

At the NSRI's 44th AGM on 18 August 2011, Attie Gunter, Leon Pretorius and Quentin Diener were honoured with Sea Rescue's Gallantry Award Silver class. This is the highest award issued by the NSRI since the award system was introduced in 1998. The award citation read: 'Acting without thought for their own safety and concerned only for the welfare of the four persons in distress, the [Witsand] crew's gallantry, skill and perseverance in the face of daunting odds that night was in the very best traditions of the National Sea Rescue Institute.'

On 28 October 2015 the little 5.5-m *Queenie Paine* was officially replaced by the 8.5-m *Breede Rescuer*, which had been in service since November 2014. The official NSRI media statement at the time read in part that 'after the successful rescue of four sailors from the capsized yacht *Gulliver* in 2011, when three Witsand NSRI volunteers risked their lives by going far out to sea in a terrible storm to go to the aid of the men who had abandoned ship, it was evident that Witsand needed a larger Sea Rescue vessel.

'The new Sea Rescue shed ... purpose built to house her, will allow the crew to launch much faster than they have previously. The large Rigid Inflatable Boat gives the crew greatly improved safety and endurance for the rescue work in the area that they cover, from Cape Infanta to the Gouritz River.'

Lightning Source UK Ltd.
Milton Keynes UK
UKOW05f0851041216
289159UK00012B/197/P